Feud in Medieval
and Early Modern Europe

Feud in Medieval and Early Modern Europe

Edited by *Jeppe Büchert Netterstrøm & Bjørn Poulsen*

Aarhus University Press |

Feud in Medieval and Early Modern Europe
© The authors and Aarhus University Press, 2007
Design and cover: Jørgen Sparre
Front illustration: Ørbæk, Funen, c. 1500, © Axel Bolvig
Typeset and printed by Narayana Press, Gylling
Printed in Denmark 2007

ISBN 978 87 7934 158 6

Published with the financial support of
The Research Network 'War Experiences' (University of Copenhagen)
The Lillian and Dan Fink Foundation
The Danish Research Council for the Humanities
Aarhus University Research Foundation

Aarhus University Press
Langelandsgade 177
DK-8200 Aarhus N
www.unipress.dk

INTERNATIONAL DISTRIBUTORS
Gazelle Book Services Ltd.
White Cross Mills
Hightown, Lancaster, LA1 4XS
United Kingdom
www.gazellebookservices.co.uk

The David Brown Book Company
Box 511
Oakville, CT 06779
USA
www.oxbowbooks.com

Contents

Preface

It is evident that the phenomenon of feud is of broad interest because it is so intimately connected with the developments in society and state. Studies of feud throughout history throw light on some of the most central concepts of all times such as peace, war, and state building. The modern state's monopoly on violence and war should always be understood in relation to the possible common right to possess weapons and to use them, which is the precondition for violent feud. In many societies with weaker state structures, feud constituted right and justice: the element which gave security.

With this publication it is the intention of the editors to underline the importance of the concept of feud, and here we are able to rely on solid research. Interestingly, research on the topic of feud has flourished during recent years and the aim of this book is to present some of the principal positions of this new research. The subject is vast and significant of course, and while it has not been possible to present research that covers all areas and periods, we are fortunate to have a number of the most important scholars in this field as contributors.

Among the contributors are scholars who specialise in geographically and chronologically dispersed areas, and it will become apparent that we are dealing with a complicated concept. While it is not easy to define feud, most of the authors try to pin down definitions of it working from its richly faceted forms.

There is a certain focus in the book which has grown out of an interest in late medieval feud. The late medieval period seems to us to be an interesting example of older structures meeting more modern ones. However, we recognise the evident fact that in order to understand this specific period we should seek broad contexts. We have therefore tried to cover a large span of years that include not only the classic Icelandic feuds of the sagas, but also more recent early-modern incidents. One contribution even takes the reader back to the roots of mankind.

The publication is the result of a symposium held at the University of Aarhus in 2003, which involved cooperation between the Department of History and the Centre of Viking and Medieval Studies at the University Aarhus. To the editors the venue seemed quite natural because it was at the University of Aarhus that the late legal historian Professor Ole Fenger had worked. Here, in 1971, he defended his dissertation *Fejde og mandebod* (Feud and Blood-money) which set a Danish standard in the research of medieval feud.

Unfortunately, because his work is written in Danish it is almost unknown outside Scandinavian circles. With this publication, therefore, we intend to follow his interest by confronting general theories and knowledge of feuds with detailed work on specific cases. While the papers presented at the Aarhus symposium provide the basis of our book, other papers are also included, and one of the editors presents an introductory essay that makes it possible to see the connection between the various contributions.

Some of the speakers at the symposium were, unfortunately, not able to deliver articles for the present book, but we would like to thank them very much indeed for contributing with papers, comments, and discussions at the symposium. They have greatly benefited the making of this publication: Professor Keith Mark Brown (University of St. Andrews), Dr. Klaus Graf (University of Freiburg), Professor Guy Halsall (University of York), Editor-in-Chief Dr. Anne Knudsen (Weekendavisen), and Professor Edward Muir (Northwestern University).

In connection with the symposium, we also thank Professor Sally N. Vaughn (University of Houston) for reading the paper of Christopher Boehm who was, unfortunately, unable to attend personally. The session leaders, Assistant Professor Agnes S. Arnorsdottir, Assistant Professor Anders Bøgh, Professor Per Ingesman (University of Aarhus), and Professor Gunner Lind (University of Copenhagen) we thank for scrupulously sticking to the schedule and promoting stimulating discussions. To Anders Bøgh, former head of The Institute of History and Area Studies (University of Aarhus), whose flexible leadership facilitated the symposium in 2003, we are doubly indebted. Also thanks to PhD Pernille Hermann (University of Aarhus) for assisting us in planning the symposium, PhD Scholar Mikkel Leth Jespersen (The Danish Central Library of Flensborg) for helping out during the symposium, and PhD Scholar Helle I.R. Møller (University of Aarhus) for efficient editorial assistance.

The editors wish to thank The Aarhus University Research Foundation, The Danish Research Council for the Humanities, The Research Network 'War Experiences' (University of Copenhagen), and The Lillian and Dan Fink Foundation for generously supporting this publication financially.

Jeppe Büchert Netterstrøm & Bjørn Poulsen
Aarhus, May 2007

Introduction

The Study of Feud in Medieval and Early Modern History

JEPPE BÜCHERT NETTERSTRØM

Anthropological beginnings

In 1955 the anthropologist Max Gluckman published an essay that was to become very influential on the study of feud in history. "The Peace in the Feud", it was called. At a first glance, the title might appear to be paradoxical or even contradictory. How can there be peace in feuds? Is feud not the direct opposite of peace? Not necessarily, Gluckman asserted. Not denying (although perhaps understating) the violent elements in feuding, Gluckman emphasised the tendency towards peacemaking in feud processes. Basing his claim partly on Evans-Pritchard's study of the Nuer people of southern Sudan, Gluckman pointed out that feuds have a peacemaking effect in two ways. Firstly, the threat or possibility of feud functions as a social control mechanism that limits breaches of norms in much the same way as state prosecution has a preventative function in modern societies. The fear of revenge and retaliation will often enough prevent the conflicting groups from attacking each other. Feud or threat thereof also informs social control within groups, as individual group members depend on the consent and assistance of their fellows when engaging in conflicts. As group liability is normal in societies that have feuds, each group will estimate whether or not the benefits of supporting a group member's feud against outsiders match the liability it incurs by doing so. This tends to limit external violent actions deemed unacceptable or unfavourable by the group. Secondly, when feuds eventually do break out and escalate, they tend to involve an increasing number of persons. Sooner or later the feud will engage or affect persons with ties (of kinship, friendship, residence vicinity or production cooperation) to both the parties. These will then put pressure on the parties to cease feuding and they will act as mediators in the peacemaking process. In societies where feuds function in this way, peacemaking becomes an expected and integrated part of the feud process. Thus, peace and feud are inseparable; there is 'peace in the feud'.[1]

Gluckman's thesis was part of an anti-colonial, anti-eurocentristic tendency in anthropology during the decolonisation era. Indigenous people of the colonies were not to be seen as primitives incapable of organising peacefully functioning societies in the absence of a colonial state carrying the white man's burden. Feud violence was not the outcome of anarchy but rather a structuring, ordering principle in 'stateless' tribal societies. Gluckman's rendering of feud and peace was, therefore, mainly concerned with anthropological studies of contemporary societies. Within anthropology, his work has had a large influence and many anthropologists have followed in his path in studying tribal feud and warfare. Especially in the 1960s and 70s, a substantial number of monographs on feuding were published, and in many studies on third world communities that do not place feud in the centre of focus, it has become common to include the functionality of revenge and feud violence or at least give attention to that subject.[2] But Gluckman actually anticipated the impact that his essay would have also on historians studying pre-modern European societies. He thus suggested that the peacemaking mechanisms detected in primitive tribal feuding also applied in Anglo-Saxon kindred feuds of the Middle Ages which had previously been seen as 'incessant warfare' between clearly divided kin groups.[3]

---

1   Max Gluckman, "The Peace in the Feud", *Custom and Conflict in Africa*, Oxford 1955, pp. 1-26. The essay was based on a BBC radio lecture given in the spring of 1955. Also published in *Past and Present*, 8, 1955, pp. 1-14.

2   Keith F. Otterbein and Charlotte S. Otterbein, "An Eye for an Eye, A Tooth for a Tooth: A Cross-Cultural Study of Feuding", *American Anthropologist*, 67, 1965, pp. 1470-1482. Emrys L. Peters, "Some Structural Aspects of the Feud among the Camel-Herding Bedouin of Cyrenaica", *Africa*, 37, 1967, pp. 261-282. Margaret Hasluck, "The Albanian Blood Feud", Paul Bohannan (ed.), *Law and Warfare. Studies in the Anthropology of Conflict*, New York 1967, pp. 381-408. E. Adamson Hoebel, "Feud: Concept, Reality and Method in the Study of Primitive Law", A.R. Desai (ed.), *Essays on Modernization of Underdeveloped Societies*, 1, New York 1972, pp. 500-513. Jacob Black-Michaud, *Cohesive Force. Feud in the Mediterranean and the Middle East*, Oxford 1975. Christopher Boehm, *Blood Revenge. The Anthropology of Feuding in Montenegro and Other Tribal Societies*, Kansas 1984. Keith F. Otterbein, *Feuding and Warfare. Selected Works*, 1994. Rolf Kuschel, "Killing Begets Killing: Homicides and Blood Feuds on a Polynesian Outlier", *Bijdragen tot de Taal-, Land- en Volkenkunde*, 149, 1993, pp. 690-717. Tor Aase, "The Prototypical Blood Feud. Tangir in the Hindu Kush Mountains", Tor Aase (ed.), *Tournaments of Power. Honor and revenge in the contemporary world*, Aldershot 2002, pp. 79-100.

3   Gluckman 1955, pp. 21-22.

The functionalist paradigm in historical feud studies

Medieval historians were not slow to pick up. In a 1959 article on "The Bloodfeud of the Franks", Wallace-Hadrill was clearly inspired by Gluckman's approach in his re-evaluation of the significance of feuding in Merovingian society. Where Gluckman implicitly directed his criticism against ethno-centrism, Wallace-Hadrill formulated his thesis explicitly in opposition to legal historians. The existence of feud and vengeance in early medieval society had far from been ignored by legal history, but within a positivist, evolutionist paradigm they had been judged as irrational, dysfunctional obstacles on a pre-determined road to rational modern justice. 'To legal historians feud dies a slow, inevitable death, yielding to the superior equity of royal justice; chaos and bloodshed give place to good order because they must'. Wallace-Hadrill claimed that in the early medieval period, settlement by violence and composition existed side by side, and stressed that feud was the sanction that made peaceful settlement possible. Composition and peace was not forced through by an embryonic state but by the kin groups and families engaged in conflicts, who often sought for 'reasons and excuses to look for composition first, whether of their own making or under the protection of the courts'. Wallace-Hadrill admitted to the feud regulations of royal legislation and to the effects of the peace ideology of the church, but he found no 'strong and continuous royal pressure against the principle of feud', and even the church took an ambiguous position towards vengeance and private violence. In Merovingian society, 'royal justice and the local courts are still far too unsettled in function and fluid in procedure to offer a clear alternative to feud'.[4]

The approach of anthropologists such as Gluckman, E.L. Peters, Black-Michaud and Christopher Boehm has continued to appeal to social historians seeking functionalist and structuralist explanations for the cohesion of past societies, while at the same time favouring anti-anachronism and disregarding determinism and evolutionism. Since Wallace-Hadrill's seminal work, the tendency has been to 'discover' the existence or 'survival', the functionality and legal or quasi-legal, legitimate character of feuding in more and more historical societies where previous historians had either ignored or denied it or where it was not regarded as having had any significance. This 'discovery trend' combined with the tendency to functionalise, rationalise, legalise/legitimise feuding is still today a major drive in feud research. Following the

---

4   J.M. Wallace-Hadrill, "The Bloodfeud of the Franks", *Bulletin of the John Rylands Library*, 41, 1959, pp. 459-487. Reprinted in (and here quoted from) idem, *The Long-Haired Kings and Other Studies in Frankish History*, London 1962, pp. 121-147.

collected scholarship of the past half century, feud seems to be common in many pre-modern societies and it seems to be a very durable phenomenon, often manifesting itself at surprisingly late dates where private self-help and revenge are supposed to have been wiped out long ago by kings or states claiming monopolies of violence and jurisdiction.

England, Wales, France, and Scotland

In English historiography, the role of feud in the Anglo-Saxon period has long been recognised, and historians are continuing to discuss its significance during that period.[5] It has traditionally been held that the Norman Conquest put an end to feuding in England. In 1969, R.R. Davies contrasted the situation in thirteenth-century England with that of Wales where the institution of *galanas*, meaning both bloodfeud and the blood money that settled it, survived into the sixteenth century due to strong ties of kinship and a proportionately weak force of public authority. In 1280-81, an English clerk was apparently puzzled by the phenomenon, and in a marginal note to the report of a royal commission into the use of Welsh law he reminded himself to 'find out what the law of galanas is'. However, already in the fourteenth century the ancient Welsh custom of feuding was decaying and giving way to the procedures of English criminal law.[6]

Recently, Paul R. Hyams has contested the assumption lying behind this contrasting of England and Wales, namely that the Norman and Angevin rulers of England were entirely successful in outlawing revenge killings and feuding during the High Middle Ages. Regarding the century after the Conquest, Hyams states that:

we possess anecdotes and enough other evidence to argue that full feud action persisted as a possible option for some and to suggest that it was not so rare that prudent men could afford to omit it from their calculations. This is not to say that it was a normal occurrence. Once men have ridden off in hot blood to seek vengeance, matters have gone to extremes. These are the exceptional cases. But they buttress a more far-reaching

---

5   Paul R. Hyams, *Rancor and Reconciliation in Medieval England*, Ithaca 2003. Idem, "Feud in Medieval England", *Haskins Society Journal*, 3, 1992, pp. 1-21. Idem, "Nastiness and Wrong, Rancor and Reconciliation", Warren C. Brown and Piotr Górecki (eds.), *Conflict in Medieval Europe. Changing Perspectives on Society and Culture*, Aldershot 2003, pp. 195-218.
6   R.R. Davies, "The Survival of the Bloodfeud in Medieval Wales", *History*, 54, 1969, pp. 338-357.

contention that the everyday world of twelfth-century England was one in which men were on the alert for wrongs done them and ready to seek their redress as and where they best could.

Hyams is thus able to establish 'the continuing existence in the twelfth century of both a vengeance culture and its occasional employment in direct action to redress wrong'. Not denying the pacifying effects of the expansion of the king's peace and the development of the common law, Hyams goes on to detect an 'enmity culture', a feud mentality, in the thirteenth century that concretely led to 'feud-like' behaviour and mortal enmities at all social levels.[7] In dealing with the Late Middle Ages, Howard Kaminsky has recently pointed out a number of similarities between armed conflicts among the English nobility and noble feuds of late medieval Germany. Although private feud was always technically illegal outside the Marches, noble feuding seems to have been so frequent that it was effectively accepted as a sort of legal right belonging to aristocrats who used it to defend their lordships.[8]

French historiography has had the same leaning as the English to portray feuding as an occurrence that was alien to the medieval monarchy and thus abandoned at an early stage. The apparent increase of violence in the period after Charlemagne and before the growth of the French nation state in the twelfth-thirteenth centuries was seen as part of the 'feudal anarchy' during that intermezzo in the evolution of State. In the 1980s, the American scholar Stephen D. White reassessed the violence of that period within the framework of feuding societies known from historical anthropology. Rather than expressing anarchy, feuds were an ordering principle in society around the year 1100.

During the later eleventh and earlier twelfth century, the feud, far from constituting an aberrant form of political behaviour, was an integral part of European noble life. For the period was one in which no single power monopolized the legitimate use of force and no well-developed state existed. Thus, people often used force to avenge injuries they had sustained, not only because they were not legally barred from doing so, but also because there was no one else to do so regularly.

Feuds, however, were not only waged to avenge wrongs and assert strictly legal claims but also to acquire property, prestige and political power. Initial-

---

7   Hyams, *Rancor*, 2003. Quotes from pp. 137 and 153.
8   Howard Kaminsky, "The Noble Feud in the Later Middle Ages", *Past and Present*, 177, 2002, pp. 55-83.

ly inspired by the feud studies of social and historical anthropology, White pointed to a number of factors that made European feuding around the year 1100 different from that of egalitarian tribal communities studied by Gluckman and his followers. 'Highly stratified and probably becoming more so and endowed with a military technology that could only have accentuated class differences with respect to the ability to use force, the society in which the Noyers[9] feuds broke out differed markedly from the egalitarian tribes for which anthropological theories about feuding have usually been developed'. Because of social stratification, the main victims of the feuds that were waged between noblemen were peasants who had no chance of defending themselves. This made the peasants 'more vulnerable to seigneurial exploitation'. Although the society studied by White also differed from tribal feuding societies in that the inherent peace-in-the-feud-mechanisms were supplemented by the efforts of 'external' peacemakers such as monasteries, feuding was frequent enough to reinforce feudal lordship.

If the enterprises customarily identified as feuds were often linked with the dynamic processes by which local lords and/or their followers fought their equals and struggled to extend their dominance over peasants, then the claim that there was a 'peace' in the medieval French feud, achieved through monastic mediation or by other means, needs to be counterbalanced by the claim that there was often a feud in the medieval peace as well.[10]

That neither the Angevin state did succeed in establishing a monopoly of violence is demonstrated in Daniel Lord Smail's work on feuds between urban factions in fourteenth-century Marseille.[11] Howard Kaminsky, uncovering private wars over disputed rights waged by the French aristocracy in the Later Middle Ages, notes that 'the remarkable thing is not the ubiquity of the noble

---

9 White's study focuses on seven feuds from the region of Touraine that are described in documents deriving from the peacemaking process in which the abbey of Saint Mary of Noyers acted as mediators.

10 Stephen D. White, "Feuding and Peace-Making in the Touraine around the Year 1100", *Traditio*, 42, 1986, pp. 195-263. On French historiography, see Stephen D. White, "From Peace to Power: The Study of Disputes in Medieval France", Esther Cohen and Mayke B. Jong (eds.), *Medieval Transformations. Texts, Power and Gifts in Context*, Leiden 2001, pp. 203-218.

11 Daniel Lord Smail, "Common Violence: Vengeance and Inquisition in Fourteenth-Century Marseille", *Past and Present*, 151, 1996, pp. 28-59. Idem, "Telling Tales in Angevin Courts", *French Historical Studies*, 20, 1997, pp. 183-215. Idem, *The Consumption of Justice. Emotions, Publicity, and Legal Culture in Marseille, 1264-1423*, Ithaca 2003. See also Smail's contribution to the present volume.

feud but the failure of French historians to come to grips with it'.[12] Stuart Carroll has recently shown that feuding played a role as late as the end of the sixteenth century, when especially the Wars of Religion gave opportunity to pursue private grievances violently; which, however, was a practice not confined to times of civil war.[13] A common finding of Smail and Carroll is the intertwining of court actions and violent actions used in feuds, which seems to challenge the strictly phased history of centralised law courts taking over from feuding and the private settlement of disputes. Similarly, Carroll shows that the classic genealogy of group feuding being replaced by individual duelling obscures a much more complex transition as duels could arise from or cause feuds between kin groups.

Scottish bloodfeud has been interpreted in light of social anthropology. Jenny Wormald has made a point of discarding the dualist view of early modern state justice versus private justice in bloodfeuds waged and settled between agnatic kin groups or clans. Kin based procedures were integrated into new legal practices, for instance by private settlements being supplemented by royal pardon or ancient rules pertaining to bloodfeud being worked into legal scholarship and day-to-day procedures at the law courts. Together with factors such as strong agnatic kinship and localism, this interaction is the most important explanation for the survival of bloodfeud in Scotland until the middle of the seventeenth century.[14] Keith Mark Brown has presented an extensive study of a large number of feuds in early modern Scotland 1573-1625 and has provided one of the most elaborate accounts of the disappearance of a feuding society available in international research. The Scottish feud system did not simply disappear as a result of a steadily growing central state implementing criminal justice and sanctioning the verdicts of its law courts. Due to religious strife and political crisis, Scottish society actually experienced an upsurge in feuding during the sixteenth century, which can be taken as a

---

12   Kaminsky, 2002, p. 66. According to Kaminsky, the reason for this failure of French scholars 'is that historians who identify the interest of the nation with the rise of the state are not moved to focus on mentalities and practices whose prima facie import was to interfere with that rise, as well as to destroy the civil peace whose enforcement would be the main business of the post-medieval state'.

13   Stuart Carroll, "The Peace in the Feud in Sixteenth- and Seventeenth-Century France", *Past and Present*, 178, 2003, pp. 74-115. Idem, *Blood and Violence in Early Modern France*, Oxford 2006.

14   Jenny Wormald, "Bloodfeud, Kindred and Government in Early Modern Scotland", *Past and Present*, 87, 1980, pp. 54-97. Reprinted, in a slightly shortened version, as "The Blood Feud in Early Modern Scotland", John Bossy (ed.), *Disputes and Settlements. Law and Human Relations in the West*, Cambridge 1983, pp. 101-144.

general warning against presupposing a steady decline in feud and violence over the centuries. From around 1600 it was the classically belligerent nobility, rather than a strong monarchy, that became the vanguard of the abandonment of feuding. This happened as the need for political stability (that followed upon the unstable period that had caused the increase in feuding) coincided with the Calvinist Reformation that changed the attitude towards private violence, making it a crime against God that required punishment instead of settlement between the parties.[15]

Iceland and Scandinavia

Feuding was so abundant in early modern Scotland and is so conspicuously present in the extant source material that there has been little need for the historians to 'discover' or 'reveal' its 'survival' in the same way as with feuding in perhaps less obvious cases such as fourteenth-century Wales or sixteenth-century France. The same might be said about bloodfeuds in Saga Iceland. The famous family sagas written in the thirteenth century, which protagonise the authors' ancestors of the ninth-twelfth centuries, centre revenge killing and feuding as the most important literary motifs. No one who reads the sagas doubts that they are all about feud. But for long, Icelandic historians were generally reluctant to accept the sagas as reliable sources and therefore distrusted or simply ignored the revenge narratives in them as valid evidence of the social behaviour of the Icelanders of the Land-Taking and Free State period (870-1262). In the 1980s this changed as two American scholars, Jesse Byock and William Ian Miller, combined the insights of anthropological feud research with a new appreciation of the sagas as products of a feuding society displaying a fairly correct picture of the mentalities and social mechanisms governing it, if not presenting entirely accurate accounts of historical events uninfluenced by literary forms and ideological biases of the time when they were put into writing.[16]

---

15   Keith Mark Brown, *Bloodfeud in Scotland 1573-1625. Violence, Justice and Politics in an Early Modern Society*, Edinburgh 1986.

16   Jesse L. Byock, *Feud in the Icelandic Saga*, Berkeley 1982. Idem, *Medieval Iceland. Society, Sagas and Power*, Berkeley 1988. William Ian Miller, "Choosing the Avenger: Some Aspects of the Bloodfeud in Medieval Iceland and England", *Law and History Review*, 1, 1983, pp. 159-204. Idem, "Justifying Skarphedinn: Of Pretext and Politics in the Icelandic Bloodfeud", *Scandinavian Studies*, 55, 1983, pp. 316-344. Idem, *Bloodtaking and Peacemaking. Feud, Law, and Society in Saga Iceland*, Chicago 1990.

Byock and Miller have differing opinions regarding the role of feud in Icelandic society, in part according to different receptions of the anthropological literature they both operationalise for purposes of illuminating Icelandic feud by comparing it with feud in other stateless societies. Miller tends to interpret the Icelandic feud system within the classical peace-in-the-feud model of Gluckman as developed by later anthropologists. Miller perceives blood vengeance or the threat hereof as an important source of social control. Peacemaking is identified as an integrated part of the feud process, much as Boehm has demonstrated was the case in the Montenegrin bloodfeud. The peacemaking mechanisms and the remarkable interest in and ability of lawmaking in stateless Iceland could not, however, prevent a widespread use of violence that was sometimes out of control. On this point, Miller criticises Gluckman's optimistic and over-rationalistic peace-in-the-feud. Rules of feuding were frequently broken. Settlement by arbitration did not always ensure eternal peace and offered no absolute guarantee against new revenge killings. Although Miller points to differences as well as similarities between Icelandic feud and feud in the 'primitive' societies studied by anthropologists, he places more emphasis on the similarities than Byock does.

Byock stresses more the restraint in Icelandic feuds and attributes much autonomous significance to the institutions of arbitration and settlement that made the use of feud violence purportedly more limited in Iceland than in the tribal societies of the Mediterranean and the Middle East, which Byock finds less capable of peaceful dispute resolution. In some of these cultures, feuds are perceived as interminable. This was not the case in Iceland, and according to Byock this was because of the legitimacy and respect enjoyed by the peacemaking institutions and because of the fact that Iceland was not a tribal society with agnatic kinship. The latter mode of organising kin groups universally seems to enhance the chances of prolonged feuding because the kin groups are closed and friendly relations between individual members of the conflicting entities are fewer. In Iceland, kinship was cognatic, and cross-cutting ties furthered the chances of negotiations and restraint. Inspired by E.L. Peters, Byock makes a distinction between vendetta killings within villages and feuds between larger tribes. In this context, vendetta killings are regarded as limited acts of revenge between groups that exert restraint because their members have to live in the same community. Tribal feuds are more uncontrolled because the parties are not inhibited by common interests or by proximity of kin or place of residence. Byock finds that although the Icelanders did not live in villages but in single great households widely dispersed over the sparsely inhabited island, they all belonged to the same intimate community. Byock envisions this structure as 'the great village' of Viking Age Iceland.

The Icelandic bloodfeuds thus resembled limited village vendettas more than tribal feuds.[17]

A final point of discrepancy to be mentioned here concerns the impact of social stratification on the peacemaking process and *vice versa*. In Byock's view, the institution of advocacy, where strong chieftains (godar) assisted or advocated for more average farmers (thingmen) in feud and litigation, contributed significantly to the settling of conflicts and to the cohesion of Icelandic society and thereby, in a sense, also to its relatively egalitarian and power-balanced structure. Miller sees in advocacy a source of power for chieftains over their clients. By taking over law suits and feuds the chieftains could add to their honour and, since advocacy entailed transfer of property from the client as payment of the support received, also to their material power resources. These stratifying mechanisms are described by Jesse Byock as well. Both scholars agree on relativising them by pointing to the fundamental difference between the chieftain-thingman bond of Iceland and the lord-vassal/villein bond of contemporaneous continental Europe. Both note that the Icelandic thingman was free to choose his chieftain. There seems to be consent that the Icelandic feud system – due to this flexibility of its adjacent protection system – could not work to consolidate or expand social stratification or create territorial or feudal lordship in the same way as in the feuding society of Touraine studied by Stephen D. White, at least not until the end of the Free State period. On the whole, however, in spite of many convergent observations and views, Miller stands for a more conflict-and-power oriented view of the feuding society of Iceland, while Byock stands for a more consensus/cohesion-and-balanced-power oriented view.

Icelandic feuding was a Viking Age phenomenon but probably somewhat distinguished itself from feuding in the other Viking societies of Scandinavia that were influenced by a higher degree of political centralisation and social stratification. The graveness of the violent behaviour of Vikings is currently debated.[18] Although the Vikings' infamous atrocities on raids abroad hardly reflect their everyday behaviour at home and in times of 'peace', many would probably take for granted that the heathens of Norway, Denmark and Sweden lived in feuding societies. This is, however, hard to qualify in the absence of

---

17   Jesse L. Byock, "Feuding in Viking-Age Iceland's Great Village", Warren C. Brown and Piotr Górecki (eds.), *Conflict in Medieval Europe. Changing Perspectives on Society and Culture*, Aldershot 2003, pp. 229-241. E.L. Peters, "Foreword", Black-Michaud 1975, pp. ix-xxvii, at p. xiii.

18   Guy Halsall, "Playing by whose rules? A further look at Viking atrocity in the ninth century", *Medieval History*, 2, 1992, pp. 3-12.

source material comparable to the Icelandic sagas. Analysis of Norse mythology suggests that actual feuding experience so permeated the world view of the Scandinavians that feud was fundamental to their beliefs about the creation of the world by the god-king Odin's slaying of the giant Ymir, about the ensuing mythological battle between gods (æsir) and giants (jotnar), and about the end of the world in Ragnarok.[19]

The process of Christianisation in the nineth-eleventh centuries entailed the creation of an ecclesiastical peace ideology that, from the twelfth-thirteenth centuries, combined forces with kingship to produce legislation that tended to limit and regulate feud violence. However, private feud and self-help persevered well into the High and Late Middle Ages. The Danish legal historian Ole Fenger investigated feud and kin liability in homicide legislation in medieval and early modern Denmark and stressed the notable endurance of these legal institutions. Inspired by anthropological and historical feud research, Fenger described feud and vengeance as legal means of protecting the kin group in a society that had limited possibilities of official crime prosecution.[20] In Norway and Sweden, historians have not obtained the feud theories of international anthropology and historiography to any important degree. However, Norway is depicted as a society in which feuds existed until the thirteenth century and perhaps beyond,[21] and in Sweden, sustained peace legislation during the thirteenth-fifteenth centuries implies a pervasiveness of revenge killings and feuding.[22] Historians are currently working to interpret evidence of feuding in late medieval Denmark, Norway, Sweden and Iceland.[23]

---

19 John Lindow, "Bloodfeud and Scandinavian Mythology", *alvíssmál*, 4, 1994, pp. 51-68.

20 Ole Fenger, *Fejde og mandebod. Studier over slægtsansvaret i germansk og gammeldansk ret*, Copenhagen 1971.

21 Sverre Bagge, "Ideologies and mentalities", Knut Helle (ed.), *The Cambridge History of Scandinavia*, 1, Cambridge 2003, pp. 465-486, esp. pp. 468 and 470-471. Bagge seems to distinguish between rational, political violence and emotion- and honour-based revenge and feuding. According to Bagge, the Norwegian monarchy succeeded in banning feuds in the national Landlaw of 1274 but sees the Later Middle Ages as a period of transition: "The state now intervened in the conflicts between people and prevented them from developing into feuds, but there still existed an honour-based society demanding strong and often violent reaction to insults". Bagge then contrasts the Norwegian ban on feuds to the situation in Denmark as described by Ole Fenger.

22 Mia Korpiola, "'The People of Sweden shall have Peace': Peace Legislation and Royal Power in Later Medieval Sweden", Anthony Musson (ed.), *Expectations of the Law in the Middle Ages*, Rochester 2001, pp. 35-51. On feuds in Sweden, see also below n. 81.

23 See Erik Opsahl (ed.), *Feider og fred i nordisk middelalder*, Oslo 2007. Bloodfeud seems to have continued to exist in Finland at least until the 16th century, but Finnish research appears to be reluctant to use international feud theories or make comparisons with other feuding societies. See Heikki Ylikangas, "What Happened to Violence? An Analysis of the

The *Sonderweg* of German feud research

In Germany, advanced research on feuding was initiated, in fact, earlier than the Gluckman School that has dominated research outside of Germany. In 1939 Otto Brunner published his seminal book *Land and Lordship* which placed a comprehensive description of feud narratively at first place and thematically in the centre of focus.[24] The book was primarily about late medieval Austria (called South East Germany in the first edition of the book) but it also displayed evidence from other parts of the Empire and appeared to claim representativity for the whole Germanic area if not the entire medieval culture. Brunner argued that feuds carried out by noblemen were not illegal or non-legitimate in the way that the positivist legal historians of the nineteenth century had described them, basing their claims on biased sources produced by ecclesiastics and burghers that were notoriously hostile towards the nobility. The projection of modern views on violence and state justice onto medieval society represented one of many anachronisms confronted by Brunner. The distinction between public and private was another one which Brunner could refute by showing that no clear distinctions were made between public and private warfare in the terminology used by medieval people themselves – both phenomena were labelled 'feud' (*Fehde*). Brunner generally demanded that historians investigate the 'basic concepts' (*Grundbegriffe*) of past society in order to establish the nature of its 'constitution' (*Verfassung*, meaning both the political constitution and the societal, legal and normative order). Among the central basic concepts of late medieval Germany was the feud (*Fehde*).

Development of Violence from Medieval Times to the Early Modern Era Based on Finnish Source Material", Heikki Ylikangas, Petri Karonen and Martti Lehti (eds.), *Five Centuries of Violence in Finland and the Baltic Area*, Columbus, OH 2001, pp. 1-83. Research (which is much more advanced in Sweden, Norway and Finland than Denmark) into the use of violence during the early modern period recognises a culture of honour and shame closely associated with private violence and dispute settlement, and a Norwegian historian has explicitly asserted a continuity of violent behaviour from the Viking ages until the 16th century. See Eva Österberg and Sølvi Sogner (eds.), *People Meet the Law. Control and conflict-handling in the courts. The Nordic countries in the post-Reformation and pre-industrial period*, Oslo 2000.

24   Otto Brunner, *Land und Herrschaft. Grundfragen der territorialen Verfassungsgeschichte Südostdeutschlands im Mittelalter*, (1939), 4th Revised Edition 1959. English translation by Howard Kaminsky and James Van Horn Melton, *'Land' and Lordship. Structures of Governance in Medieval Austria*, Philadelphia 1992. Brunner already investigated feuding in an earlier article but in more limited scope and without integrating it into a synthesis of the medieval order in the same way as in the book from 1939. Idem, "Beiträge zur Geschichte des Fehdewesens im spätmittelalterlichen Oesterreich", *Jahrbuch für Landeskunde von Niederösterreich*, 22, 1929, pp. 431-507.

Feuds were carried out by noblemen to defend their lordships and peasants. Feud was a means of enforcing legal claims concerning land titles, rights *over* and *of* peasants, pledges, monetary debts and so forth. The lords feuded according to a set of rules that made it possible to differentiate rightful, honourable feud from unlawful robbery. A feud had to be based on a legal encroachment and the feuder was required to attempt a legal claim in a court of law or in some other judicial way before resorting to violence. Notions of self-defence against contumacy and other injustice in the litigation process often motivated feuds. Before commencing a feud it was obligatory to declare the opening of hostilities by a letter of defiance (*Absage, diffidatio*). Only noble lords and other lordships such as abbeys and cities were entitled to wage feuds. Peasants did not enjoy the full right to feud since they were subject to a lord within an unequal reciprocal relationship in which the peasant owed rents and services in return for protection. Neither were individual non-noble burghers fully allowed to feud because they were subordinate to the protection of the feud-entitled city in which they lived. In this way, feud was closely associated with lordly protection (*Schutz und Schirm*), another basic concept of medieval society that formed the nucleus of all kinds of lordship and governance (*Herrschaft*) in the medieval 'constitution'. Peasants and burghers were partially entitled to feud in that they maintained the right of bloodfeud (*Totschlagsfehde, Blutrache*), i.e. vengeance allowed in response to homicide, which was, however, strictly limited by criminal law in the Late Middle Ages. Although Brunner admitted that the legal distinction between these two types of feuding (noble feud and bloodfeud) would seem somewhat blurred by incidents of peasants stubbornly re-enacting their probably ancient practice of feuding, he insisted that commoners' feuds were entirely outlawed. Feuders of non-noble status were stigmatised as criminals by the word 'defyer' (*Absager*) that referred to precisely the same act of defiance that was the legal prerequisite of honourable noble feuding.

Brunner's work was clearly influenced by the period in which it was written, the author himself being a member of the National Socialist party. His critique of the backwards projection of modern legal dogmatic was embedded in a general right-wing conservative opposition to the liberal-democratic ideology of the nineteenth century and the Weimar Republic. His favouring of 'basic concepts' in historiography emanated from a political wish for 'concrete order' to substitute the abstract legal concepts and rights of democratic jurisprudence.[25]

---

25 Brunner became candidate member of the party shortly after *Anschluss* in 1938 and was accepted as member in 1943. On this, and generally on Brunner as historian, see Howard Kaminsky and James Van Horn Melton, "Translators' Introduction", in Brunner 1992.

Gadi Algazi has recently asserted that Brunner's reassessment of medieval feuds must be understood in the context of the National Socialist rehabilitation of violence and war as political instruments.[26] Whereas Gluckman's re-evaluation of tribal feud was part of an anti-colonial, anti-racist and anti-eurocentristic agenda, Brunner's analogously positive view on noble feud was part of a program that tended towards fascism and nationalism. Despite similarities, Brunner's methodology was not functionalist in the anthropological or social historian sense. It was more constitutional, legal, and philological. However, after the War, Brunner's synthesis was revised politically and his approach transformed methodologically to fit a new materialist, structuralist social history of which Brunner himself became a prominent figure. The Brunnerian critique of positivism was shared by many social historians just as focus on the historicity of concepts and norms could be assimilated by a historiography that increasingly became interested in mentalities and cultural history. *Land and Lordship* has inspired many detailed studies of feud (often in limited regional settings) and today German historiography exceeds by far any other national historiography as to the quantity of feud studies produced.[27] This

---

26 Gadi Algazi, "The Social Use of Private War: Some Late Medieval Views Reviewed", *Tel Aviver Jahrbuch für deutsche Geschichte*, 22, 1993, pp. 253-273. Cf. idem, *Herrengewalt und Gewalt der Herren im späten Mittelalter. Herrschaft, Gegenseitigkeit und Sprachgebrauch*, Frankfurt a.M. 1996. Idem, "Otto Brunner – 'Konkrete Ordnung' und Sprache der Zeit", Peter Schöttler (ed.), *Geschichtsschreibung als Legitimationswissenschaft 1918-1945*, Frankfurt a.M. 1999, pp. 166-203. See also Hans-Henning Kortüm, "'Wissenschaft im Doppelpass'? Carl Schmitt, Otto Brunner und die Konstruktion der Fehde", *Historische Zeitschrift*, 282, 2006, pp. 585-617.

27 In addition to the literature quoted elsewhere in this essay, German feud historiography includes: Herbert Asmus, *Rechtsprobleme des mittelalterlichen Fehdewesens*, Göttingen 1951. Udo Tewes, "Zum Fehdewesen zwischen Weser und Elbe. Fehde – Sühne – Urfehde", *Lüneburger Blätter*, 21-22, 1970-1971, pp. 121-200. Elsbet Orth, *Die Fehden der Reichsstadt Frankfurt am Main im Spätmittelalter. Fehderecht und Fehdepraxis im 14. und 15. Jahrhundert*, Wiesbaden 1973. Dieter Neitzert, *Die Stadt Göttingen führt eine Fehde. 1485/86. Untersuchung zu einer Sozial- und Wirtschaftsgeschichte von Stadt und Umland*, Hildesheim 1992. Manfred Kaufmann, *Fehde und Rechtshilfe. Die Verträge brandenburgischer Landesfürsten zur Bekämpfung des Raubrittertums im 15. und 16. Jahrhundert*, Pfaffenweiler 1993. Gerhard Dilcher, "Friede durch Recht", Johannes Fried (ed.), *Träger und Instrumentarien des Friedens im hohen und späten Mittelalter*, Sigmaringen 1996, pp. 203-227. Gerd Althoff, *Spielregeln der Politik im Mittelalter: Kommunikation in Frieden und Fehde*, Darmstadt 1997. Alexander Patschovsky, "Fehde im Recht. Eine Problemskizze", Christine Roll (ed.), *Recht und Reich im Zeitalter der Reformation. Festschrift für Horst Rabe*, Frankfurt a.M. 1997, pp. 145-178. Thomas Vogel, *Fehderecht und Fehdepraxis im Spätmittelalter am Beispiel der Reichsstadt Nürnberg (1404-1438)*, Frankfurt a.M. 1998. Janine Fehn-Claus, "Erste Ansätze einer Typologie der Fehdegründe", Horst Brunner (ed.), *Der Krieg im Mittelalter und in der Frühen Neuzeit: Gründe, Begründung, Bilder, Bräuche, Recht*, Wiesbaden 1999, pp. 93-138. Volker Honemann, "Gründe und Begründungen für den Ausbruch der Soester Fehde in den zeitgenössischen Quellen", Horst Brunner (ed.), *Der Krieg im Mittelalter und in der Frühen*

self-sufficiency of feud studies probably explains why German feud research has neither significantly obtained the foreign anthropological and historical literature on feud nor compared the German feud system (*Fehdewesen*) to the feuding societies of, say, Icelandic peasants or Scottish aristocrats.[28] Conversely, German research has not been justifiably noticed by students of other feud cultures, but this is perhaps more than anything else due to language barriers between the scholarly traditions.

German historians have corrected and elaborated on many details of Brunner's picture of feud but its argument for the legality of lords' feuds was not fundamentally contested until the 1980s when the social historian Werner Rösener reinvigorated the romantic notion of the 'robber knight' that Brunner had seen as a typical product of outdated anti-aristocratic historiography. Rösener formulates his so-called 'robber knight thesis' within the framework of recent findings on the social consequences of the late medieval agrarian crisis: The crisis led to the impoverishment of the low nobility which in turn attempted to compensate by raiding and plundering each other's peasants under the veil of a legal right to wage feud that was, however, more challenged by contemporaries than Brunner had thought.[29] Gadi Algazi, in his recent

---

Neuzeit: Gründe, Begründung, Bilder, Bräuche, Recht, Wiesbaden 1999, pp. 217-227. Oliver Volckart, "The Economics of Feuding in Late Medieval Germany", *Explorations in Economic History*, 41, 2004, pp. 282-299. Alexander Jendorff and Steffen Krieb, "Adel im Konflikt. Beobachtungen zu den Austragungsformen der Fehde im Spätmittelalter", *Zeitschrift für Historische Forschung*, 30, 2003, pp. 179-206. Christine Reinle, "Fehden und Fehdebekämpfung am Ende des Mittelalters. Überlegungen zum Auseinandertreten von 'Frieden' und 'Recht' in der politischen Praxis zu Beginn des 16. Jahrhunderts am Beispiel der Absberg-Fehde", *Zeitschrift für Historische Forschung*, 30, 2003, pp. 355-388. See also Reinle's contribution to the present volume. Christoph Meyer, "Freunde, Feinde, Fehde: Funktionen kollektiver Gewalt im Frühmittelalter", Jürgen Weitzel (ed.), *Hoheitliches Strafen in der Spätantike und im Frühen Mittelalter*, Köln 2002, pp. 211-266. On Switzerland, see Hans Georg Wackernagel, "Fehdewesen, Volksjustiz und staatlicher Zusammenhalt in der alten Eidgenossenschaft", *Schweizerische Zeitschrift für Geschichte*, 15, 1965, pp. 289-313.

28 However, recent German feud research has experienced a reception of models and conceptions of 'dispute processing', 'conflict management' and the like, but this seems to be inspired by general anthropological models on conflict resolution and by the history of crime that broke through in Germany in the 1990s, more than a direct reception of feud scholarship in anthropology or other historiographies.

29 Werner Rösener, "Zur Problematik des spätmittelalterlichen Raubrittertums", Wilhelm Maurer and Hans Patze (eds.), *Festschrift für Berent Schwineköper zum 70. Geburtstag*, Sigmaringen 1982, pp. 469-488. On one of the most famous German robber knights, see Frank Göttmann, "Götz von Berlichingen – überlebter Strauchritter oder moderner Raubunternehmer?", *Jahrbuch für fränkische Landesforschung*, 46, 1986, pp. 83-98. Volker Press, "Götz von Berlichingen (ca. 1480-1562). Vom 'Raubritter' zum Reichsritter", *Zeitschrift für württembergische Landesgeschichte*, 40, 1981, pp. 305-326.

criticism of Brunner's view on feud and lordship, has picked up on the theme of noble feuds being waged by attacks on the peasants belonging to the opposing nobleman. Echoing Stephen D. White's results regarding the social effects of noble feuding in France around 1100, Algazi asserts that the feud practice of the German nobility in the Late Middle Ages contributed to the solidification of social stratification and to the reproduction of the feudal organisation of society in an age of otherwise growing peasant self-confidence and communal autonomy. The aristocracy in effect waged an incessant, albeit uncoordinated and unintended, class war on the peasants. The noble feuds created a need for protection among the peasants, a protection which was in turn provided by the feuding aristocrats that demanded obedience and services in return. Feud and protection were thus instruments of exploitation, domination and class control rather than Brunnerian 'basic concepts' of governance widely accepted by members of the German 'constitution'.[30]

Algazi's criticism of Brunner and the alternative feud model that he offers (which may in fact be seen partly as a reallocation of elements already present in Brunner's work[31]) has been accepted by some[32] and rejected by

---

[30] In addition to the literature quoted above n. 26, see Gadi Algazi, "'Sie würden hinten nach so gail.' Vom sozialen Gebrauch der Fehde im 15. Jahrhundert", Thomas Lindenberger and Alf Lüdtke (eds.), *Physische Gewalt. Studien zur Geschichte der Neuzeit*, Frankfurt a.M. 1995, pp. 39-77. Cf. idem, "'Sich selbst vergessen' im späten Mittelalter: Denkfiguren und soziale Konfigurationen", Otto Gerhard Oexle (ed.), *Memoria als Kultur*, Göttingen 1995, pp. 387-327. Idem, "Lords Ask, Peasants Answer: Making Traditions in Late-Medieval Village Assemblies", Gerald Sider and Gavin Smith (eds.), *Between History and Histories: The Making of Silences and Commemorations*, Toronto 1997, pp. 199-229. Idem, "Pruning Peasants: Private War and Maintaining the Lords' Peace in Late Medieval Germany", Esther Cohen and Mayke B. de Jong (eds.), *Medieval Transformations. Texts, Power, and Gifts in Context*, Leiden 2001, pp. 245-274.

[31] This claim only extends to the parts of Algazis thesis referred to above. Another part of his criticism is directed against the reciprocal protection relationship (*Schutz und Schirm*) as described by Brunner. Here, Algazi argues that the 'protection' consisted of guarantees that the lord would not attack his own peasants, much like a mafia protection racket. Since this part of his thesis logically contradicts the part on feud as producer of protection against *outsiders* it is ignored in the present context. Algazi has been convincingly refuted regarding this inconsistency as well as the empirical foundations of his claim for a 'protection racket' by Sigrid Schmitt, "Schutz und Schirm oder Gewalt und Unterdrückung? Überlegungen zu Gadi Algazis Dissertation 'Herrengewalt und Gewalt der Herren im späten Mittelalter'", *Vierteljahrschrift für Sozial- und Wirtschaftsgeschichte*, 89, 2002, pp. 72-78.

[32] Joseph Morsel, "'Das sy sich mitt der besstenn gewarsamig schicken, das sy durch die widerwertigenn Franckenn nitt nidergeworffen werdenn'. Überlegungen zum sozialen Sinn der Fehdepraxis am Beispiel des spätmittelalterlichen Franken", Dieter Rödel and Joachim Schneider (eds.), *Strukturen der Gesellschaft im Mittelalter. Interdisziplinäre Mediävistik in Würzburg*, Wiesbaden 1996, pp. 140-167. Also Hillay Zmora, see references below n. 36.

others.[33] Christine Reinle has challenged Algazi's assumption that feud was a strictly aristocratic practice.[34] She has revealed a large number of feuds waged by peasants in late medieval Bavaria and points to evidence of non-noble feuding from other parts of Germany as well. She questions the real extent of prohibitions against non-noble feuding in a society characterised by legal pluralism and ambiguous implementation of the laws that Brunner as well as Algazi and many others take as solid evidence of a noble monopoly of violence. Peasant feuds, sometimes waged against the peasants' own lords in response to breaches of traditional rights, were a widespread phenomenon which often seems to have enjoyed what Reinle describes as 'social acceptance'. If peasants were not submissive victims of noble violence, Algazi's model needs to be modified profoundly. Furthermore, Reinle criticises Algazi, an active member of the Israeli peace movement, of being just as biased by the political environment of his time as he alleges Brunner to have been by the political situation in the 1930s. Reinle's findings also undermine Brunner's view on class differences regarding feud prerogatives which is basic to his 'constitutional' synthesis of medieval lordship. But in many ways, Reinle is closer to Brunner since she agrees with him that feuds (i.e. including peasant feuds) were legitimate and that feud was in fact preservation of honour and enforcement of legal claims and not just a bad excuse for robbery.

33 Klaus Graf, "Gewalt und Adel in Südwestdeutschland. Überlegungen zur spätmittelalterlichen Fehde", on-line (http://www.histsem.uni-freiburg.de/mertens/graf/gewalt.htm), 2000.

34 Christine Reinle, *Bauernfehden. Studien zur Fehdeführung Nichtadliger im spätmittelalterlichen römisch-deutschen Reich, besonders in den bayerischen Herzogtümern*, Stuttgart 2003. Idem, "Fehden im Spannungsfeld von Landesherrschaft, Adel und bäuerlicher Bevölkerung", Werner Rösener (ed.), *Tradition und Erinnerung in Adelsherrschaft und bäuerlicher Gesellschaft*, Göttingen 2003, pp. 173-194. Idem, "Von Austreten, Landzwang und mutwilliger Fehde: Zur bäuerlichen Fehdeführung in Altbayern im Spätmittelalter", *Zeitschrift für Geschichtswissenschaft*, 52, 2004, pp. 109-131. On non-noble feuding in Germany, see also: Monika Mommertz, "Von Besen und Bündelchen, Brandmahlen und Befehdungsschreiben. Semantiken der Gewalt und die historiographische Entzifferung von 'Fehde'-Praktiken in einer ländlichen Gesellschaft", Magnus Eriksson and Barbara Krug-Richter (eds.), *Streitkulturen. Gewalt, Konflikt und Kommunikation in der ländlichen Gesellschaft (16.-19. Jahrhundert)*, Köln 2003, pp. 197-248. Jan Peters, "Leute-Fehde. Ein ritualisiertes Konfliktmuster des 16. Jahrhunderts", *Historische Anthropologie*, 2000, pp. 62-97. Ekkehard Kaufmann, "Michael Kohlhaas=Hans Kohlhase. Fehde und Recht im 16. Jahrhundert – ein Forschungsprogramm", Gerhard Dilcher and Bernhard Diestelkamp (eds.), *Recht, Gericht, Genossenschaft und Policey. Studien zu Grundbegriffen der germanistischen Rechtshistorie. Symposion für Adalbert Erler*, Berlin 1986, pp. 65-83. Christoph Müller-Tragin, *Die Fehde des Hans Kolhase. Fehderecht und Fehdepraxis zu Beginn der frühen Neuzeit in den Kurfürstentümern Sachsen und Brandenburg*, Zürich 1997. Arne Dirck Duncker and Malte Diesselhorst, *Hans Kohlhase. Die Geschichte einer Fehde in Sachsen und Brandenburg zur Zeit der Reformation*, Frankfurt a.M. 1999.

Werner Rösener's 'robber knight thesis' has been firmly rejected by, among others,[35] Hillay Zmora.[36] His study of fifteenth-sixteenth-century Franconia shows that the feuding noblemen did not belong to the lower strata of the aristocracy. Quite to the contrary, they formed the elite of the noble estate. Their feuding activities could hardly have been caused by any general late medieval 'crisis of the aristocracy'. They frequently figure among the princes' officers and pledge-holders, which also demonstrates that they were intimately tied to the princely state. Zmora understands noble feuding as a component of the state-building process of the German principalities. In the fierce contest between those expanding states, aristocrats waged by proxy feuds against the enemies of their own prince to achieve 'proximity to rule'. In addition they feuded to expand their own lordships which contributed to the territorialisation process because private lordship merged with the official powers that were increasingly distributed by the state. It furthermore entailed a process of social stratification within the nobility and augmented noblemen's control of peasants (cf. Algazi). Princes not only tolerated noble feuds because they depended on the aristocracy for political and military support and financing. They actively used noble feuding to build states.

Princely territorialisation put an immense strain on the nobility. Being able to mesh one's own interests with those of a prince promised economic and social success … The result was a fierce struggle for access to resources. Feuds functioned to effect the proximity to a prince which was the necessary condition for having this access. By expanding their lordships, partly through feuds, noblemen obtained the resources which could then be placed at a prince's disposal. Concurrently, they were able to spearhead the consolidation of the realm of the prince whose favor they either already enjoyed

---

35 Hans Patze, "Grundherrschaft und Fehde", Hans Patze (ed.), *Die Grundherrschaft im späten Mittelalter*, 1, Sigmaringen 1983, pp. 263-292. Regina Görner, *Raubritter. Untersuchungen zur Lage des spätmittelalterlichen Niederadels, besonders im südlichen Westfalen*, Münster in Westfalen 1987. Klaus Graf, "Feindbild und Vorbild. Bemerkungen zur städtischen Wahrnehmung des Adels", *Zeitschrift für die Geschichte des Oberrheins*, 141, 1993, pp. 121-154. Kurt Andermann, "Raubritter – Raubfürsten – Raubbürger? Zur Kritik eines untauglichen Begriffs", Kurt Andermann (ed.), *'Raubritter' oder 'Rechtschaffene vom Adel'? Aspekte von Politik, Friede und Recht im späten Mittelalter*, Sigmaringen 1997, pp. 9-29. This collection of essays is dedicated to disproving the robber knight thesis.

36 Hillay Zmora, *State and nobility in early modern Germany. The knightly feud in Franconia, 1440-1567*, Cambridge 1997. Idem, "Adelige Ehre und ritterliche Fehde: Franken im Spätmittelalter", Klaus Schreiner and Gerd Schwerhoff (eds.), *Verletzte Ehre. Ehrkonflikte in Gesellschaften des Mittelalters und der Frühen Neuzeit*, Köln 1995, pp. 92-109. Idem, "Princely State-Making and the 'Crisis of the Aristocracy' in Late Medieval Germany", *Past and Present*, 153, 1996, pp. 37-63.

or sought. These services were often enough offered to the highest bidder among the princes. Reward came in the form of coercive powers, mainly district governorships. These were then turned to good account, put to use against both rival noblemen and subject commoners.[37] ... Lordship was the cogwheel connecting two contests: one between princes over territorial lordship, the other between noblemen over land-lordship. The feud assumed here a decisive function. For it was very much the generator of lordship. It had the capacity, inherent in the uses of 'protection', to bring about an accumulation and concentration of lordship. Therefore feuds readily lent themselves to an application by princes to territorial consolidation. Princely state-making had – in Charles Tilly's formulation – the character of organized crime. This paradoxical nature of the gestation of the state, the violent establishment of a violence-controlling agency, explains the preponderance of eminent noblemen, especially high office-holders, among feuders. It was the result of a dialectic relationship between state formation and social stratification. The demands made on the nobility by the developing 'finance state' led to the creation of an élite of office-holding families. These owed their success to their ability to make themselves useful to the princes. Instrumental in this achievement was their persistent prosecution of feuds. It facilitated the amalgamation of their interests with those of princes. In the process they enhanced their control over commoners and marginalised other noblemen. ... By the late fifteenth century the competition among the nobility was largely restricted to a relatively small circle of participants struggling for a share in state power.[38]

But if noble feuding was part of early modern state-building in Franconia then why did it decline during the first half of the sixteenth century? The answer, according to Zmora, is that at some point the princely states of Franconia became too strong for the nobility to keep at arm's length. This happened toward the end of the fifteenth century. In 1495 the princes supported the Imperial Common Penny tax that was to be levied (by agency of the princes) from all inhabitants including the nobility. At the same Imperial Diet an eternal proscription of noble feuds was issued. It was not, however, this imperial ban on feuds that directly ended noble feuding in Franconia. The nobility reacted to the 1495 Diet by organising itself in the Franconian Knighthood, the purpose of which was to resist the princes and preserve the traditional liberties of the nobility such as the exemption from taxes and the right to feud. Paradoxically, the consequence of this was not an increase in noble feuds but rather a decrease as the collective aristocratic movement required that its

---

37   Zmora 1997, p. 117.
38   *Ibid.*, p. 118.

members abstained from feuding each other. One side-effect of this process was the disappearance of the connection between noble lordship-making and princely state-making that had been one of the deep causes of noble feuds. In the 1520s the vulnerability of the Knighthood was exposed through wars and peasant revolts. The nobles now allied themselves with the emperor to avoid the grasp of the princes but in this process they 'had to go out of their way to collaborate in a project of conscious self-disciplining' and definitively give up feuding.[39] Zmora thus rejects simplistic explanations of the decline of feud as the result of a straightforward state-building process carried through by a progressive central power in opposition to an intransigent aristocracy.

New trends

Over the last two decades, feud studies have moved in new directions as historiography in general has distanced itself from traditional sociological approaches. Feud and vendetta have shown to be model themes of a new cultural history inspired theoretically and methodologically by narratology, social constructionism and micro-history. Feud is no longer merely perceived as a structuring principle in societies with weak or no state organisation. People living and dying in feuding societies are seen as more than instruments of an established institution that compels them to act automatically within a preset scheme of social behaviour. They make choices and strategies. They construct the disorderly, the uncontrollable and the meaningless as order, control and meaning. They create feud narratives to explain their history and society. They have feelings. They sometimes take revenge when they should not and make peace when they, according to the expectations of modern observers, ought to exact vengeance. The prominence of functionalism and rationalism in anthropological and social historian feud studies gives way to emphasis on dysfunctional and irrational behaviour (without reversion to condemning descriptions of a primitive, anarchic society). Investigations of major patterns of feud are succeeded by studies of unique events in feuds. Focus is shifting from the effects of feud on the fundamental structures of society (cohesion, social stratification and distribution of political power) to cultural and micro-social phenomena activated by concrete feud practice. The role of gender in – and the construction of gender through – feuds is given much more attention

---

39 *Ibid.*, p. 146.

than earlier.[40] Feud actions are increasingly perceived as communication, representation, symbols and signs.[41] Feud and vendetta are revealed to have been ambiguous to contemporaries; not all agreed on the interpretation of concrete feud actions; not all saw feuding as such as legitimate or lawful. The perception of feud as a uniformly accepted and obligating legal institution is contested. Not only were there conflicts in feuds, there was also conflict about feud. Of course, these new trends in feud studies epitomise no consensual or concerted effort. But there is a common tendency to attach significance to aspects that structuralism neglected and to approach the past by using innovative methods that may be subsumed as deriving from a post-structuralist or post-modernist paradigm. It does not, however, abandon earlier approaches to the extent of justifying talk of a paradigmatic revolution.

Narratives and micro-histories: Italian vendetta studies

Two recent studies of Italian vendetta in the Middle Ages and Renaissance may serve as examples of these new trends. Suspicious of the Florentine experience as typical of Italian vendetta as an institution condoned by law and demanded by tradition, Trevor Dean sets out to investigate evidence from other Italian city states of the Late Middle Ages. In showing that vendetta was not accepted to the same degree in the law codes of Northern Italian despotic cities, Dean is firmly within the boundaries of comparative legal history. But from there, he moves on to investigate revenge stories in chronicles from a narratological point of view. Dean shows how chroniclers made sense of past violent events and political processes by shaping them into 'revenge narratives' that were easily comprehended by the audience. They were often constructed

---

40 Stephen Wilson, *Feuding, Conflict and Banditry in Nineteenth-Century Corsica*, Cambridge 1988, pp. 211-223. Edward Muir, "The Double Binds of Manly Revenge in Renaissance Italy", Richard C. Trexler (ed.), *Gender Rhetorics: Postures of Dominance and Submission in History*, Binghampton 1994, pp. 65-82. See also Jesse Byock's contribution to the present volume.

41 In addition to the literature quoted in the following chapters, see: Claudia Garnier, "Symbole der Konfliktführung im 14. Jahrhundert: die Dortmunder Fehde von 1388/89", *Westfälische Zeitschrift*, 152, 2002, pp. 23-46. Mommertz 2003. On signs and symbols of peacemaking in feuds, see: Klaus Schreiner, "'Gerechtigkeit und Frieden haben sich geküsst' (Ps. 84, 11). Friedensstiftung durch symbolisches Handeln", Johannes Fried (ed.), *Träger und Instrumentarien des Friedens im hohen und späten Mittelalter*, Sigmaringen 1996, pp. 37-86. Gerd Althoff, "Amicitiae (Friendships) as Relationships Between States and People", Lester K. Little and Barbara H. Rosenwein (eds.), *Debating the Middle Ages: Issues and Readings*, Oxford 1998, pp. 191-210.

as beginning with a broken marriage promise followed by vendetta ending in mutilation. 'Vendetta stories ... were purposeful means of remembering and explaining disputes, not objective descriptions'. They were stories about how not to behave rather than stories about how people behaved.

Vendetta narratives placed in chronicles carried implicit moral lessons, in the fashion of the best medieval history. They served as exemplary tales ... Histories of quarrels over trifles or gambling that led to violent slaughter taught men not to covet their neighbour's goods. The more general and simple warning message of all such tales was that boys, servants and women had to be disciplined and kept under firm parental, magisterial or marital control, lest their errors and disorders cause slaughter among menfolk ... The way in which vendettas were remembered thus had significant Christian and moral connotations. It was also heavily gendered.[42]

The ambition of Trevor Dean's deconstruction of vendetta narratives is not to refute the existence or import of vendetta in late medieval and renaissance Italy. The point is that chronicles and other revenge narratives are not precise accounts of why and how feuds were performed. Tales of the mutilation of bodies of revenge victims may be exaggerated or simply invented. The causes of conflicts may be misinterpreted or misrepresented. Instances of revenge not taken may be omitted. Dean's analysis of the chronicles furthermore elucidates the specific way people selectively remembered injury and constructed vendetta stories to justify here-and-now actions. Just as a chronicle could explain a conflict as the outcome of a long-standing vendetta, people currently involved in violent conflicts could explain their actions as vengeance of some past injury and as the continuation of the vendetta ensuing from it. Dispute participants could choose to forget such injuries, feuds were not interminable, and there was no universal obligation of revenge. They could then recall the injury if this was demanded by political expediency. 'In such cases, vendettas were constructed in hindsight when such memories were reactivated. This is not to deny, of course, that many feuds (*inimicizie, guerre*) were waged consciously by their participants, but it stresses that it was conditions of political and territorial competition that allowed past injuries to be remembered and avenged'.[43] By

---

42 Trevor Dean, "Marriage and Mutilation: Vendetta in Late Medieval Italy", *Past and Present*, 157, 1997, pp. 3-36, quotation pp. 31-32. Note a similar observation in Gluckman 1955, pp. 22-23, that 'we must not take sagas and tales of feuding as evidence, for they may ... stand as warnings. Or even as historical records they may have been better warnings'. See also Trevor Dean's contribution to the present volume.

43 Dean 1997, p. 36.

'conditions of political and territorial competition' Dean is referring to the fact that this competition was fiercer in republics than in despotic city states. This difference of conditions for political conflict explains why the republic of Florence according to the legislation investigated by Dean was softer on feud than cities with despotic rule – and why people living in republics were better at 'remembering' feuds.

The narratological approach is also present in Edward Muir's thorough examination of a more than two centuries long vendetta waged between two noble clans, the Savorgnan and the Della Torre, and their respective factions in the Venetian backland province Friuli.

Although the Savorgnan and Della Torre vendetta evolved from the feudal wars of the late patriarchate and revealed deep structural contradictions in Friulan society, contemporaries saw the struggle as an intensely personal affair among people with identifiable names and faces, with known histories, and with acknowledged friends. Vendetta was not just a social phenomenon for resolving group conflict or a form of primitive justice but a medium of collective memory, a way of structuring clan history around deeds of infamy and of valor. Vendettas were stories.[44]

In Muir's view the vendetta was, however, far from solely a literary construct, a device of collective memory or a mental mechanism for contemporaries of understanding the society they lived in. The vendetta was very real as were the political conflicts and the 'deep structural contradictions' that caused it and were shaped by it.

Muir approaches these conflicts and contradictions by a detailed examination of Friuli's economic, social and political conditions: Production and trade, fiefs and estates, jurisdictions and legal systems, peasant communities, townships, factions, as well as the relationship between Venice, the castellans of its subject territory of Friuli, and its external foes. Muir shows that there was a fundamental conflict in Friulan society between, on the one hand, noble castellans that formed the Strumiero faction led by the Della Torre clan which tried to maintain autonomy from Venice by forging alliances with the Habsburg Empire and, on the other hand, the masses of discontent peasants and citizens that assembled around the populist Savorgnans in the Zambarlano

---

44 Edward Muir, *Mad Blood Stirring. Vendetta and Factions in Friuli during the Renaissance*, Baltimore 1993, p. 90. See also pp. 208-214. For a review of this and other recent work on Italian vendetta, see Daniel Lord Smail, "Factions and Vengeance in Renaissance Italy", *Comparative Studies in Society and History*, 38, 1996, pp. 781-789.

faction, which capitalised politically on staying loyal to Venice. Much of Muir's description of Friuli is far from alien to structural history but it is a departure from this tradition in focusing on a peripheral region of limited extent and importance rather than on an economically and politically important region or international system. It is also post-structuralist in accentuating single, unique events of the vendetta between the agents of those contradicting economic, social and political forces. The most spectacular of these single events being the culmination (but not the ending) of the vendetta in Udine on Fat Thursday 1511 when the Zambarlani led by Antonio Savorgnan massacred between twenty-five and fifty members of the Della Torre and other nobles of the Strumiero faction in a combination of private vendetta and popular revolt.

The close scrutiny of a limited and peripheral geographical area and of the deep cultural meaning of single events represents a methodology characteristic of Italian micro-history. This direction in historiography, in which Muir explicitly inscribes his work, favours study of the 'normal exception' over study of the average and typical because 'exceptional events such as riots, uprisings, and crimes reveal vast areas of behavior which may usually be hidden by the social and cultural distance of the participants from the institutions of the state which produced the records'.[45] The massacre of 1511 (and each of the micro-histories of it told in rare, idiosyncratic records) represents one such 'normal exception'. This 'vendetta-revolt' was carried out during the carnival and Muir shows how carnivalistic mentalities informed the actions of the avengers:

The carnival killers revealed a particular *modus operandi*: they murdered, mutilated or dismembered, prevented the burial of their victims, and fed the remains to street scavengers. More than just cruel brutality, this pattern evolved out of carnival itself and reveals the peculiar bond between the body-centered nature of carnival imagery and the style of vendetta murder. In revenge as in carnival, the human body and its parts produced the vocabulary and syntax for symbolic communications.[46]

The message of carnivalistic revenge was made especially clear in the killing of Federico Colloredo, a noble member of the Strumiero faction, during the 'Cruel Carnival' of 1511. According to an eyewitness, Federico was killed and slashed 'with so many wounds that one could see all of his insides, which were eaten by dogs; the remains were not allowed to be buried'. Muir comments:

---

45 Muir 1993, p. xxii.
46 *Ibid.*, pp. 169-170.

In murdering Federico Colloredo, the Zambarlani degraded him on many levels: by hacking at the corpse, they inflicted additional agony on him; by making him the meat of beasts, they transgressed his status as a man and likened his fate to that of executed criminals; by shaming him in the public streets, they humiliated his surviving relatives; and by disfiguring his body, they destroyed the collective body of castellans he represented. In his death the methods of carnival and vendetta merged completely.[47]

The employment of such methods of vendetta communication was not restricted to seasons of riot and carnival. This is demonstrated by the murder of Antonio Savorgnan in revenge of his role in the Cruel Carnival. In 1512 he was ambushed by a group of Strumiero lords and wounded in the head, 'but before he died a giant dog came there and ate all his brains' as one participant of the avenging faction later recounted.[48] The incidents of dogs eating the corpses of vendetta victims lead Muir to investigate the cultural meanings and implications of such habits. Muir shows that the ritual of factional vendetta killing borrowed heavily from hunting practices.

Nourished in innumerable expeditions when lords and their retainers rode out together into the forests in search of game and sport, the hunting ethic with its emphasis on comradeship, cooperation, the acceptance of authority, and the proper forms of killing was easily transferred to the hunting of men. In particular, avengers relied on two practices derived from hunting: the butchering of the victim according to a hierarchy of body parts and the incorporation of dogs into the act of killing.[49]

The manhunting avengers not only used dogs to degrade the victim but also imitated its rabid madness to justify their own outbursts of primitive behaviour when killing in revenge. The killers were taken over by their animal instincts; they were beside themselves and did not know what they were doing. By becoming dogs they transformed themselves into wild creatures living outside the boundaries of civilisation and were thus not responsible for their own actions. By commanding or allowing their dogs to eat the vendetta victim they may even have projected a desire of their own for satisfying the hunger for revenge by taking it to its extreme conclusion of symbolic cannibalism.

While he finds that such 'wild' practices and mentalities reveal a seemingly incomprehensible cultural gap between the civility of modern man and the

---

47   *Ibid.*, p. 199.
48   *Ibid.*, p. 220.
49   *Ibid.*, p. 278.

primitive otherness of his ancestors, Muir also points out that the use of animal metaphors to excuse vendetta cruelty exposes a deep ambivalence about revenge killing. Vendetta was in fact, to a large degree, regarded as an uncivilised phenomenon. On the other hand, animalistic behaviour was not unequivocally perceived as malicious and alien to being human. As shown, for instance, by Carlo Ginzburg, whose famous micro-histories take place exactly in Friuli, there was a widespread belief that men could metamorphose into animals, typically wolfmen or dogmen, and fight night battles against the forces of evil to protect the crops. Vendetta killing and the feelings motivating it could, at one and the same time, be regarded with disgust and understanding and in both cases the reference to animal wildness, which was equally engulfed by ambivalence, provided the mental context. Muir uses these insights to criticise traditional feud research:

Because much modern scholarly work on feuding has emphasized the structural elements of vendetta which make it appear to be a reasonable form of conflict resolution, it might be useful to note the ambivalence that Friulans felt about their own desires for revenge, an ambivalence deriving not only from their mixed legal and ethical traditions but from their very understanding of the nature of humanity and wildness.[50]

The irrational wildness of Friulan vendetta may in itself serve as a correction to rationalistic understandings of feuding societies and at the same time the ambiguities vis-à-vis this vendetta wildness may serve as a correction to assumptions of uniform behaviour and homogenous thinking in such societies.

The combination of material and mental explanatory factors is carried through, with emphasis on the latter, in Muir's interpretation of the decline of the vendetta in sixteenth-century Friuli. Muir describes how the Friulan factions were dissolved due to Venetian pressure after the Cruel Carnival whereby the feuding clans were deprived of their retinue of clients. When the Savorgnan-Della Torre vendetta flared up in mid-century after having lain dormant for decades, it was no longer coupled with the interests and conflicts of large social groups. It now had the character of a truly 'private' vendetta but was still carried out in much the same way as earlier. This, however, soon changed as the vendetta became a matter of individual duelling. In 1568 the vendetta was actually ended by a duel between two members of the feuding clans in which both duellists died. Muir explains that this change from vendetta to duelling was

---

50 Ibid., p. 229.

not the consequence of the Venetian state becoming tougher on violent crimes, since the general level of private violence in Friuli continued to be high and even rose toward the end of the century. Although the waning of the factions was an important political and social factor, the transition from vendetta to duelling was mostly the result of a change of mentality and ideology. This change came about as the Friulan aristocrats adopted the refined manners of princely courts which they visited (often exiled due to crimes committed in the vendetta) or read about in fashionable books. The imitation of courtly etiquette demanded the nobleman to deny his impulses, control his feelings, sublimate his sexual appetites and channel his anger into the duel. It furthermore compelled him to consciously abandon all animal-like behaviour, not just when observing sophisticated table manners but also when defending his still important honour. In this process he deserted the traditional representation of revenge which had relied on a blurring of the boundaries between humans and animals.

The traditional mores of vendetta fighting acknowledged the reality and legitimacy of anger, managing it through carnival and hunting motifs that focused on human and animal bodies. The eclipse of a culture that had accepted the naturalness of the human body, its processes, and its emotions was the necessary prerequisite for delegitimizing revenge, a change that eliminated some of the ambivalence about vendetta but created new problems, the modern problems that come from the repression of emotions.[51]

The 'civilising process', emotions, representations and discourses

Edward Muir's account of the termination of vendetta practices in renaissance Friuli closely resembles and explicitly indebts itself to Norbert Elias' 'civilising process' theory. According to this theory, the repression of violent instincts was part of a broader psycho- and socio-genetic process which took place during the Early Modern Era as political centralisation demanded the restraint of emotions from noblemen attracted to the courts of kings and princes that claimed a monopoly of violence. The new values of self-restraint and the abjuration of violent urges subsequently diffused, by means of imitation and

---

51 *Ibid.*, pp. 278-279.

governmental repression, downwards in society and outwards from center to periphery.[52]

The premises of this theory – that medieval man was unable to curb his passions and thus acted out of lack of self-control when using violence – seem generally to be challenged by the functionalist view on medieval feud violence. More directly and explicitly, the premises of the civilising process theory are contested by recent studies that deal specifically with the representation of aggressive emotions, such as anger and hatred, in medieval feuding societies.[53] Stephen D. White has investigated such public displays of anger by kings and aristocrats that Marc Bloch saw as reflecting the emotional instability and political unpredictability that he thought characteristic of the Middle Ages. White finds that lordly anger was much more than impulsive outbursts of feelings. It was rather a communicative device which could be consciously and controllably deployed for specific political purposes. In connection with political competition and legal disputing, the publicising of anger signalled that an injury suffered had created a shift of social relations between the contestants which would soon lead to revenge. Anger was thus 'not a physiologically generated response to external stimuli that medieval culture did not adequately repress'. Nor did it stimulate political irrationality or generate rampant violence.

When public displays of anger are located in eleventh- and twelfth-century political narratives, they do not provide evidence of emotional instability; instead they reveal the position occupied by displays of anger in a relatively stable, enduring discourse of disputing, feuding and political competition ... Anger was incorporated into political postures and processes; it was part of an entire discourse of feuding or retaliatory disputing which provided scripts or schemas for representing, interpreting, and experiencing competition for honor and other kinds of conflict ... Whether or not displays of lordly anger express what we would recognize as anger, they were gestures of a feuding culture.[54]

---

52   The civilising process theory is predominant in much history of crime as an explanation of the decline of interpersonal violence during the early modern period. Peter Spierenburg, "Violence and the Civilizing Process. Does it work?", *Crime, History and Societies*, 5, 2001, pp. 87-105. Criticism in Gerd Schwerhoff, "Criminalized Violence and the Process of Civilization: A Reappraisal", *Crime, History and Societies*, 6, 2002, pp. 103-126.

53   See also Thomas L. Wymer and Erin F. Labbie, "Civilized Rage in 'Beowulf'", *The Heroic Age*, 7, 2004. Gerd Althoff, "Schranken der Gewalt. Wie gewalttätig war das 'finstere Mittelalter'?", Horst Brunner (ed.), *Der Krieg im Mittelalter und in der Frühen Neuzeit: Gründe, Begründung, Bilder, Bräuche, Recht*, Wiesbaden 1999, pp. 1-24.

54   Stephen D. White, "The Politics of Anger", Barbara H. Rosenwein (ed.), *Anger's Past. The Social Use of an Emotion in the Middle Ages*, Ithaca 1998, pp. 127-152.

Daniel Lord Smail reaches similar conclusions in his study of hatred in thirteenth-fifteenth-century Marseille. Smail shows that the 'hatred' spoken about in notarised peace acts, court records and fiscal records 'did not necessarily describe an inner experience of hatred'. Hatred in some contexts tended to be synonymous with enmity and as such possessed a jural quality. Hatred against an enemy was a formal right belonging to an injured party which could cede or remit its 'hatred' in connection with peacemaking. Hatred was demonstrated publicly in formulaic and conventional ways through insults or posturing of coldness. 'It was posturing that effectively activated the legal claims that accompanied hatred. Without posturing, hatred was merely an internal emotional state and therefore invalid'. Hatred was an 'idiom' or a 'script' of hostile behaviour; it was more a legal or political stance than a pathological state. Thus, the feud violence that occasionally emanated from this discursive hatred was not an outlet of uncontrolled emotions. As Smail's investigation focuses on hatred among the lower social classes of an urban society, it demonstrates that this civility of emotions in medieval feuding societies was not restricted to the royal and aristocratic spheres studied by Stephen D. White.[55]

It should be noted that Edward Muir points out that vendetta violence in renaissance Friuli was restrained and targeted and thus far from out of control. In exposing the ambivalence about revenge, Muir shows that emotions were not allowed to be acted out uninhibitedly. Thus, Muir partly regards emotions such as anger and vengefulness as phenomena that were 'represented' and 'managed' through rituals and other conventionalised modes of behaviour. But Muir's emphasis on carnivalistic and cannibalistic vendetta wildness and his adherence to Elias' civilising process theory nonetheless differs markedly from the viewpoint of White and Smail, although it can also be added that White and Smail do not entirely ignore the existence of genuine feelings behind the discursive manifestations of anger and hatred – or behind the materialisations of feud violence.

Definitions and concepts: Feud and vendetta

The preceding chapters attempted to give a rough sketch of the study of feud in primarily Western European medieval and early modern historiography over

---

55 Daniel Lord Smail, "Hatred as a Social Institution in Late-Medieval Society", *Speculum*, 76, 2001, pp. 90-126.

the last half-century. It also pointed out some of the debates that have taken place within and between the paradigms of that field of research. If there is indeed such a thing as an international field of feud scholarship, it is a more or less fragmented field, consisting of research that is often set within the frameworks of present day nation state historiographies and their respective traditions, problems and debates. However, theories about feud originating from anthropological models seem to facilitate transgression of these historiographic barriers, perhaps due to anthropology's special capability of claiming general validity. What these disjointed research efforts do have in common; what makes this transgression of spatial, temporal and topical confines possible; and what thus justifies talk of an international field of feud research that shares roughly the same interests and investigates apparently similar phenomena while using comparable theories, is the utilisation of the two key concepts, 'feud' and 'vendetta'. Of these two, the concept of feud is more widely applied than the concept of vendetta which seems to be more specific to Mediterranean, Southern European and Middle Eastern contexts. Thus, feud is often used synonymously with vendetta in studies of such southern surroundings, while vendetta is rarely used as another word for feud in Northern and Western European perspectives. Feud and vendetta, then, are the central words of what may appear to be a relatively coherent historical specialty. But does this imply that all scholars studying those ostensibly analogous themes mean the same when they use the central concepts, feud and vendetta? The answer to that rhetorical question is definitely negative. Like many other central historiographic concepts, feud and vendetta take on a variety of meanings and can be defined in many different, even mutually contradicting, ways. In the following, some of the definitions and conceptions of feud and vendetta that are available in the existing scholarly literature will be presented and discussed. Emphasis will be on feud more than on vendetta.

First a brief look at the etymology of the modern scholarly concepts in question. The modern English word *feud* and its cognates in German and in the Scandinavian languages is derived from the Germanic words *faehde*, *faithu*, *faida* and the like, which in the Early Middle Ages could mean both enmity and legal vengeance. Its original meaning seems to be 'enmity', etymologically related to words for enemy (cf. modern German *Feind*, *Feindschaft*; English *foe*, *fiend*). This meaning was retained in the translation of *faida* into the Latin *inimicitia*.[56] In the Old English heroic poem Beowulf, *fæhd* describes an ongoing

---

56 *Deutsches Rechtswörterbuch*, on-line (http://drw-www.adw.uni-heidelberg.de/drw/), 2004.

relationship of retaliatory violence between two groups.[57] Modern philologists translate Anglo-Saxon *fæhde* into the modern English *feud*, but the modern word actually seems to be of post-medieval origin, directly imported from the German area.[58] In high and late medieval Germany, *Fehde* meant an on-going reciprocal enmity as well as a unilaterally declared hostility.[59] *Vendetta* is Italian for vengeance, revenge. It is derived from Latin *vindicta*. In medieval Italy, *vendetta* seems to have been used in a wide variety of contexts and meanings, much as 'revenge' and 'vengeance' in modern usage, and not necessarily in any specific 'feud'-sense.[60]

The original core meanings of 'feud' and 'vendetta' are preserved to some degree in their modern uses, in everyday as in scholarly discourse. Both words still today carry connotations of enmity, violent conflict, retaliation and revenge. Despite the obvious parallels between the meanings of 'feud' and 'vendetta', however, their central meanings partly diverge. The word *vendetta* tends to have a more singular meaning of vengeance. In comparison, it is possible to interpret the word feud, on the one hand, as a broader category (enmity, contention, quarrel) than vendetta and, on the other hand, as an even more specific (but sequentially more prolonged) form of vengeance than vendetta, namely as an extended chain of revenge actions, when 'vendetta' is taken to signify either a single act of revenge or revenge as a more abstract concept.

This difference in core meanings probably helps account for the fact that some modern scholars make a distinction between 'feud' and 'vendetta'. As mentioned earlier, such a distinction is made by E.L. Peters (followed by Jesse Byock). In that instance, the distinction relates to conflicts on different levels of group organisation in placing vendetta at 'village level' and feud at 'tribal level'. Conflict between higher forms of social organisation, thus, is 'war'. As we shall see, this socio-hierarchic differentiation of violent conflicts is very common in anthropological and sociological definitions. Here, the more restricted central meaning of 'vendetta' as limited revenge is set in opposition to an interpretation of 'feud' that favours its more wide-ranging and protractive meaning.[61]

---

57 David Day, "Hwanan sio fæhd aras: Defining the Feud in Beowulf", *Philological Quarterly*, 78, 1999, pp. 77-95.
58 Hyams, *Rancor*, 2003, pp. 57, 66 and 73-74.
59 Brunner 1959, *passim*.
60 Dean 1997, *passim*.
61 Cf. above n. 17.

In other research, a distinction between vendetta and feud is made somewhat differently. Trevor Dean notes that Italian late medieval chronicles often embedded vendetta in warfare. War often 'started in retaliation for some injury or loss, consisted of a series of revenge attacks, and could generate further vendetta after victory'. This observation 'creates difficulties for anthropological analysis of feuding based on clear theoretical definitions of separate categories of dispute (revenge, feud, war)'. What nonetheless distinguished 'vendetta' from 'feud' was, according to Dean, that 'vendetta' was vengeance of limited extent for specific injury whereas 'feud' was a state of continuous animosity in which the violent actions taken might be retaliation of a more generalised injury.[62] Other scholars that distinguish vendetta from feud place emphasis on the kind of injury that leads to retaliation and on the means of that retaliation, especially whether or not the conflict is homicidal. In this view, vendetta is homicidal (i.e. consists of a chain of revenge killings), whereas feud is not necessarily so. Vendetta, in this sense, equates 'bloodfeud' as set apart from 'feud'.[63] Finally, as already observed, some scholars prefer to use feud and vendetta synonymously.[64] Edward Muir may be mentioned as an example of this and it may be noted that the vendetta studied by him was mainly a bloodfeud.[65]

We now leave aside 'vendetta' and turn to some hard definitions of 'feud' as they appear in dictionaries and encyclopaedia. This is how the *Shorter Oxford English Dictionary* defines feud:

---

62 Dean 1997, p. 15. Cf. Trevor Dean, *Crime in Medieval Europe 1200-1550*, 2001, p. 99.

63 Boehm 1984, p. 218: "To most people … 'vendetta' signifies a protracted conflict involving multiple killings and is best reserved as a synonym for 'feuding'", which distinguishes vendetta from single revenge killing. Kaminsky and Van Horn Melton (cf. above n. 24) translate Otto Brunner's words for blood revenge (*Blutrache*) and homicide-feud (*Totschlagsfehde*) into 'vendetta'. Also Kaminsky 2002, pp. 55-56.

64 For instance, Wilson 1988 labels as 'feud' what other scholars as well as contemporary Corsicans called 'vendetta', see Anne Knudsen, "Internal Unrest: Corsican Vendetta – A Structured Catastrophe", *Folk*, 27, 1985, pp. 65-87, who also uses 'vendetta' and 'feud' synonymously. For criticism hereof, see Kuschel 1993, p. 691. Christian Lauranson-Rosaz, "Feud", *Encyclopedia of the Middle Ages*, 1, 2000, pp. 538-539, equates 'interminable vendettas' with *faida* which was purportedly 'vengeance, or rather the right and especially the sacred duty of vengeance, which was passed on from generation to generation, decimating kinship groups'. White 1986, p. 195, does not distinguish between 'feuds, private wars (*guerres privées*), or vendettas', cf. below n. 98.

65 Muir 1993, p. xxiii. Muir believes that the usual modern distinction (which he refuses to use himself) between the two concepts is between vendetta, seen as a finite conflict between individuals, and feud, seen as an interminable one between groups.

Feud: A state of bitter and lasting mutual hostility; especially such a state existing between two families, tribes or individuals, marked by murderous assaults in revenge for some dreadful insult or wrong.[66]

This definition emphasises the long lasting character of feud, the reciprocity between the feuding parties and the mutuality of their violent actions; it furthermore emphasises the homicidal aspect and the revenge element; it does not distinguish between feud and other forms of violence on the basis of a hierarchy of social organisation, since both families, tribes and individuals may be in a state of feud; but it makes feuding the business of small social entities, not of states.

The *Encyclopedia of the Social Sciences* defines feud as 'relations of mutual animosity among intimate groups in which a resort to violence is anticipated on both sides'.[67] Starting from this definition, the *International Encyclopedia of the Social Sciences* states that there are two major criteria of feud: Violence and intimate (or related) groups. Concerning feud violence it summarises as follows:

(1) The violence of a feud ranges in intensity from injury to killing; (2) It is initiated on behalf of a particular individual or family that is a member of the more inclusive 'injured group'; and (3) it is of long duration, involving at least three instances of violence – injury, revenge, and counterrevenge. Hostile acts consisting of an injury and of an equivalent revenge that is accepted as final by both parties do not merit the term feud and should more properly be called self-redress. The nature of self-redress is, in most cases, basically different from the prolonged violence called feud.

Feud violence need not be 'murderous' but may consist of non-lethal physical harm. Feud is of long duration, and this definition is more precise and exclusive than many others in requiring a minimum of three instances of violence. Concerning the second criterion of feud, it is stated that the parties of a feud must be members of the same society; otherwise the conflict should be labelled 'war' or 'external self-redress'. It is concluded that:

---

66 *Shorter Oxford English Dictionary*, 1986, p. 744. Quoted from Matthew Bennett, "Violence in eleventh-century Normandy: feud, warfare and politics", Guy Halsall (ed.), *Violence and Society in the Early Medieval West*, Woodbridge 1998, pp. 126-140, at p. 126.

67 Harold D. Laswell, "Feuds", *Encyclopedia of the Social Sciences*, 6, New York, 1931, pp. 220-221.

the essence of feud has been found to be a series (at least three instances) of acts of violence, usually involving killings, committed by members of two groups related to each other by superimposed political-structural features (often involving the existence of an over-all political authority) and acting on the basis of group solidarity (a common duty to avenge and a common liability).

This article also sets feud apart from law ('feud is an internal affair, conducted by members of the subgroups of an over-all political organisation who ignore or even defy its political authority'), a distinction which explicitly runs counter to some of the anthropological literature that the definition is based on (e.g. Max Gluckman) and which is not concurring with much research on historical European feuding. According to this definition, the first instance of revenge of the original injury (which is not feud but (internal) 'self-redress') may be accepted as a just punishment by the over-all political authority and by the kin group of the original killer, and in that case 'the sanctioned reprisal constitutes a case of legal self-redress that is true law'.[68]

The *International Encyclopedia of the Social & Behavioral Sciences* offers no stringent definition of feud but instead analyses definitions of earlier anthropological research.

Scholars use two strategies to define the terms 'feud' and 'internal war,' strategies that might be labeled qualitative and quantitative, respectively. The qualitative strategy treats feud and war as distinct subtypes of violence; the quantitative strategy locates feud and war at different points on the same continuum of violence.

This encyclopaedia rejects the so-called qualitative strategy in favour of the quantitative strategy for defining feuds. The claim is that:

feud and war (as well as other forms of self-help, such as assault, homicide, and retaliatory killing) differ not in kind but in degree: war is more violent... In practice, there is often an additional contrast: the parties to war are usually large groups, such as societies (external war) or tribes (internal war) while feuds are contested by smaller groups, such as families. In the quintessential war, then, armies trade multiple rounds of lethal violence, seek to slaughter as many of the enemy as possible, and exempt nobody from attack. In the quintessential feud, antagonistic families kill at least once, abide by the principle of 'a life for a life,' and avoid targeting women, children, and non-kin.

---

68 Leopold Pospisil, "Feud", *International Encyclopedia of the Social Sciences*, 5, 1968, pp. 389-393.

War and feud are thus not fundamentally different; they are two subtypes of violent 'conflict management', just of different scale. Perhaps this view, that feud belongs to the same continuum of violence as war, explains the definitions' great emphasis on homicidal violence. War and feud, however, are (perhaps confusingly) said 'in practice' and 'usually' to be *quintessentially* different regarding the modes and rules of combat. This definition of feud, by the way, appears to require only two acts of violence (i.e. killings), one by each family (which is asserted to be the typical feuding entity), which would make it different from definitions that require three acts of violence. As homicide and retaliatory killing, however, are both seen as something different than feud, the meaning may be that an imagined 'chain' of retaliatory killings does not become a true feud before a third killing (the counterrevenge killing) occurs, whereby the feud (more than) fulfils a minimum requirement of one killing per family (plus one more by one of the families).[69]

The last-mentioned definition equates 'feud' with what others, more particularly, label as 'bloodfeud'. This likening of 'feud' and 'bloodfeud' is not uncommon in anthropological research. Keith F. Otterbein defines feuding as a 'type of armed combat occurring within a political community in which, if a homicide occurs, the kin of the deceased take revenge through killing the offender or any member of his kin group'.[70] In a cross-cultural study of feuding, Keith F. Otterbein and Charlotte S. Otterbein worked from the premises that:

---

69 M. Cooney, "Feud and Internal War: Legal Aspects", *International Encyclopedia of the Social & Behavioral Sciences*, 8, 2001, pp. 5605-5608. The quoted passage seems to contain a misunderstanding of *lex talionis* ('a life for a life'). What characterises the *lex talionis* ('an eye for an eye, a tooth for a tooth') is that an accurately measured act of retribution (or revenge) ends the conflict which, then, never becomes what Cooney defines as feud (i.e. a protracted conflict consisting of at least three incidents of violence). For correct interpretations of the principle of *lex talionis* in contrast to feud, see Guy Halsall, "Violence and society in the early medieval west: an introductory survey", Guy Halsall (ed.), *Violence and Society in the Early Medieval West*, Woodbridge 1998, pp. 1-45, p. 22, and Hyams, *Rancor*, 2003, p. 3. The association of *lex talionis* and feud is very widespread, see e.g. Lauranson-Rosaz 2000. It seems to be an erroneous association when feud is defined as a long lasting chain of revenge actions which may, furthermore, be exacted on other persons (e.g. relatives of) the one who committed the injury avenged. *Lex talionis* may, of course, be applied to a situation where a homicide is retributed by a homicide targeted at the original killer (but the purpose of this particular type of vengeance is precisely to prevent further revenge taking). It may also be applied in a more generalised sense as an expression of vengeance as abstract principle. *Lex talionis* may, then, be correctly associated with feud if feud is defined either as an accurately measured revenge action (that is specifically *not* followed by another act of vengeance) or (vaguely) as 'vengeance'.

70 Otterbein 1994, p. 100.

feuding ... was defined as blood revenge following a homicide ... Ethnographic materials ... were coded on a three-point scale; frequent, infrequent or absent. A society was considered to have frequent feuding if, after a homicide, the kin of the deceased was expected to take revenge through killing the offender or any member of his kin group. If the kin of the deceased sometimes would accept compensation in lieu of such revenge, the society was coded as having infrequent feuding. Feuding was considered to be absent in those societies which had formal judicial procedures for punishing the offender, which always settled such matters through compensation, or which were reported to rarely have homicide.[71]

Here, feuding is plainly homicide in revenge of homicide. No other kinds of violence or armed combat would count as feuding. There is no demand as to any specific number of revenge actions required to constitute a feud. One instance of homicide in revenge of an original killing would thus constitute a feud. But societies in which the feud sometimes does not continue after the first revenge killing is not regarded as having frequent feuding. Only societies where compensation is never accepted and feuding thus goes on eternally are regarded as having frequent feuding. The consequence of Otterbein and Otterbein's evaluation of the overall frequency of feud therefore is that proper feuds are theoretically interminable processes of revenge-counter-revenge killings.

Other anthropologists distinguish between such homicidal feuds and other forms of feud and call the former 'bloodfeud'. Such a distinction was, for instance, made by Evans-Pritchard.[72]

A similar distinction between feud and bloodfeud is, as already noted, predominant in German feud research. In German historiography there has been a long standing discussion about the origins and development of feud: Was bloodfeud (*Totschlagsfehde*, *Blutrache*) the original form of feud (*Fehde*) and the lordly feud (*Ritterfehde*) thus a later development, an 'offspring' or

---

71   Otterbein and Otterbein 1965, p. 1470. Severe criticism of their definition as well as their results in Adamson Hoebel 1972, who offers the following 'working formulation of feud' at p. 506: 'Feud is a state of conflict between two kinship groups within a society, manifest by a series of unprivileged killings and counter-killings between kinship groups, usually initiated in response to an original homicide or other grievous injury'.

72   Boehm 1984, p. 196 and 218 with reference to Evans-Pritchard. Also Lindow 1994, p. 51, who comments: 'This distinction no longer seems tenable, given the recognition that homicide is only one possible strategy in the larger process of dispute resolution encompassed by feuding, but it is helpful in pointing up the recognition that feud societies themselves seem to make of the qualitative as well as quantitative distinction that homicide possesses over compensation and other forms of redress'.

restricted form, of the 'authentic' feud (i.e. bloodfeud)? Was noble feud perhaps something completely different, emanating from high medieval feudal law, than bloodfeud which had its offspring in an ancient Germanic legal institute? Or was 'feud' originally a broader category of enmity which could be initiated in response to a whole range of injuries and which could take the form both of homicidal revenge and of non-lethal combat such as burning, plundering and assaulting – a broader category of 'enmity' which later due to legalistic redefinitions divided into what in the high and late middle ages stand out as relatively sharply separated forms of feud?[73] Brunner, commenting on the Later Middle Ages, regarded bloodfeud and lordly feud as subdivisions or differently legalised forms of a broader concept of feud which he occasionally called 'enmity' (*Feindschaft*).[74]

What is special about the distinction between feud and bloodfeud in German research on the Late Middle Ages, compared to similar distinctions in other historiographies and in anthropology, is that 'feud' (*Fehde*) is identified as a prerogative of a distinct social class (i.e. the aristocracy). What sets 'feud' (*Fehde*) and 'bloodfeud' (*Totschlagsfehde, Blutrache*) apart from each other is thus not only the causes and means of violence, but also a difference of legal entitlement based on social criteria. It is furthermore characteristic of late medieval German feud research that it primarily studies 'feud', not 'bloodfeud'. This seems to be, quite simply, due to the fact that the bloodfeud was strictly limited (both regarding its legality and its actual use) in that period, whereas lordly feud was condoned by law (within limits described above) and very widely practiced. In German research, then, the prefix *Totschlags-* in *Totschlagsfehde* (homicide-feud) (or *Blut-* in *Blutrache* (blood revenge)) marks off that type of feud as subordinate to a wider concept of enmity or as a type of feud that is regarded as less important than (lordly) feud. When in the German context no prefix, either 'homicide-' or 'lordly', is added to 'feud', what is implied is either 'lordly feud' specifically or 'enmity' in a wider sense, and normally not 'bloodfeud'. In anthropological study, the prefix 'blood' is often a precising addition signalling what is taken to be essential to 'feud', namely its homicidal quality. When the prefix 'blood' is not present, what is meant is either 'bloodfeud' or feud in a broader sense.

The correlation of 'feud' and non-bloodfeud in German research also applies in recent criticism of the assumption that 'feud' was restricted to a

---

73 Asmus 1951, pp. 8-10. Andrea Boockmann, "Fehde, Fehdewesen", *Lexicon des Mittelalters*, 4, 1989, column 331-334.

74 Brunner 1959, *passim*.

social elite. In her work on peasant feuds, Christine Reinle states that 'feud' stands in sharp contrast to 'acts of violence that are characterised by the direct application of violence against the person (of the opponent) such as brawls, duels, knife fighting and assaults, because the feud is targeted primarily against the economic basis of the opponent'.[75] True feud, in this context, is qualitatively different from bloodfeud and not necessarily congruent with any form of interpersonal violence. Feud is not aiming at physically harming the opponent but at subduing him into accepting the feuder's legal claim. Feuds may involve interpersonal violence, and often do, but then violence is an indirect consequence of attacks on the opponent's economic basis. What makes Reinle able to assert that non-nobles had a 'socially accepted' right to feud, and made use of it, is thus not a redefinition of the concept 'feud' through the dissolution of the distinction between the socially discriminate 'feud' and the socially indiscriminate 'bloodfeud'; it is the documentation that non-nobles were quasi-entitled to feud, and in fact did practice feuding, for the same purposes and in (qualitatively) much the same ways as lords were and did.

Feud, war, and rebellion

Common of many definitions of 'feud' is, obviously, the attempt to distinguish between feud and other forms of violence. It is almost universal in such efforts that feud is differentiated from both such forms of violence that are believed to be less grave, less organised, on a smaller scale, and more crude than feud; and forms of violence that are deemed as more serious, more organised, more 'public', and on a greater scale than feud. In anthropological definitions, the main concern is often to make a distinction, on the one hand, between feud and simple revenge killing and, on the other hand, between feud and war. Some anthropological definitions furthermore operate from a distinction between internal and external warfare. In such distinctions, of course, what is most contiguous to feud is internal warfare.[76]

Distinctions based on quite similar lines of thought are found in much historical scholarship. Historians, however, generally seem to have a harder time arriving at clear cut divisions between feud and other types of violence. In German research, a precise distinction between feud and war is hard to make as contemporary sources use the word 'feud' (*Fehde*) (and its related

---

75 Reinle, *Bauernfehden*, 2003, p. 61. Translated from German by the present author.
76 E.g. Otterbein 1994, pp. 97-117.

semantic field of enmity, defiance, peace) both for private feud and (what we would almost instinctively call) public or state war. As mentioned above, this terminological imprecision was taken by Otto Brunner to be characteristic of a society that generally lacked clear distinctions between 'private' and 'public' and, thus, between private feud and public war. Feud and war were also identical concerning the rules governing the initiation, conduct and termination of armed conflict. As noted by Hillay Zmora, Brunner actually did recognise that contemporaries were able to see the difference between noblemen's feuds and large scale warfare waged by kings and princes.[77] However, if one applied the analysis of the *International Encyclopedia of the Social & Behavioral Sciences*, this definitional distinction between feud and war would seem to be more quantitative than qualitative.

Defining feud in contrast to rebellion proves to be as difficult a task. Here, anthropological definitions that differentiate feud from other types of violence seem insufficient since such definitions are shaped primarily to analyse primitive societies that lack political authorities to rebel against and have no social stratification that is important enough to create any class based discontent in the first place. The anthropological concept of 'internal war' is coined to describe conflicts between groups of at least roughly equal social status, not civil wars characterised by the inequality of the social status of the opposing parties. Anthropologists who work from a very stringent definition of feud (i.e. bloodfeud, blood revenge) as something essentially different from warfare would probably not see any problem at all in differentiating between feud and rebellion.

Historians who use a broader (or variant) definition of 'feud' and study societies with relatively solid socio-economic hierarchies and advanced political centralisation often feel a more urgent need of a definition that disentangles noble feuds from aristocratic rebellions and peasant feuds from peasant revolts. It has been proposed that what characterises rebellion is that it builds on collective grievances and that it attacks the prevailing societal order whereby it is by all measures unlawful; whereas feud aims at the solution of an individual conflict in which the basic order is not doubted whereby it may be lawful. Still, as individual peasant's feuds against the authorities could escalate into full scale peasant revolts and as such revolts could employ the traditional forms and semantics of lawful feud, the demarcation between feud and revolt might

---

77 See Hillay Zmora's contribution to the present volume. Day 1999, pp. 85-86, surprisingly claims that already in "Beowulf", feud is set off from other types of warfare.

not be so easily drawn up.[78] This is even less so in the case of aristocratic rebellion.[79] In medieval Germany, noblemen's rebellion against their prince, or princes' rebellion against the king or emperor, could be regarded simply as lawful feud like any other lordly feud, although there were often differences of opinion about that.[80] When private and public interests and actions of both aristocrats and commoners are observed to have merged in rebellions, the divide between rebellion and feud may be especially difficult to establish. It has been suggested that late medieval Scandinavian risings, which often combined aristocratic and peasant discontent and activism, were indeed feuds in the Brunnerian sense of the word.[81] In Friuli on Fat Thursday 1511, the aristocratic feud between the Savorgnans and the Della Torre fused completely with the riot of the commoners against the Della Torre in what Edward Muir describes as a 'vendetta-revolt'.[82]

Definitional incoherence

To sum up: The meanings of the scholarly concept 'feud' are manifold. And not just that: These meanings may contradict each other in very fundamental ways. In many contexts, 'feud' equals 'bloodfeud'. Within such contexts, the margins of 'feud' and 'revenge', and of 'feud' and (internal) 'warfare', may vary significantly. But, what seems even more problematical, this whole definitional branch uses the word 'feud' to describe violent conflicts that are not directly compatible with what others associate with the same word. As a particularly striking example of this, one can take the definition of (lordly) 'feud' in research on late medieval Germany and confront it with the cited encyclopedic definitions. The former describes feud as a type of violence which is primarily

---

78 Reinle, *Bauernfehden*, 2003, p. 62. Mommertz 2003 sees criminal peasant feuds in the early modern period as including an element of peasant resistance against the authorities.

79 Kaminsky 2002, pp. 67-68.

80 The aristocrat's right to feud against his own ruler was embodied in the so-called right of resistance. Brunner 1959, pp. 48, 140 and *passim*. Reinle, *Bauernfehden*, 2003, p. 63. Timothy Reuter, "Unruhestiftung, Fehde, Rebellion, Widerstand: Gewalt und Frieden in der Politik der Salierzeit", S. Weinfurter and H. Seibert (eds.), *Die Salier und das Reich*, 3, Sigmaringen 1992, pp. 297-325.

81 Peter Reinholdsson, *Uppror eller resningar? Samhällsorganisation och konflikt i senmedeltidens Sverige*, Uppsala 1998, which also offers examples of noble feuding in late medieval Sweden.

82 Muir 1993, p. 153. The Fat Thursday massacre in Udine quickly spread to the countryside and became, according to Muir 1993, p. 152, 'the largest and most destructive peasant uprising in Renaissance Italy'.

directed at the economic basis of the opponent and explicitly contrasts it to bloodfeud; the latter only accept long-lasting bloodfeuds as proper feud, and contrast it more or less sharply to other forms of 'self-redress'. Many German (lordly) feuds would simply not accomplish the criteria demanded by most anthropological definitions. Conversely, many bloodfeuds of primitive societies would not match the criteria of the German definition.

This problem of definitional incoherence may be solved in more than one way. Scholars of medieval and early modern Europe have applied differing strategies in trying to arrive at a solution to this problem. One solution is to formulate a tentative *description* of feud rather than attempting to arrive at a stringent and universally encompassing *definition* which claims to be able to set off feud clearly from all other forms of conflict and violence. A second solution is to use the concept but consciously refrain from defining it with any rigour. A third solution is to dismiss the concept entirely and stop using it. In the following chapters, these three possible solutions will be presented through examples of strategies employed by historians in connection with concrete research on feud in medieval and early modern Europe.

Description over definition: 'Distinctive features' of feud

William Ian Miller, in his work on Icelandic saga bloodfeud, states that no universally accepted definition of feud has emerged from medieval and early modern historiography. The hard definitions developed by anthropologists do much better 'describing the particular culture with which the anthropologist is most familiar than describing a cross-cultural phenomenon'. Miller pleads in favour of avoiding ethno-centricity by 'abandoning conventions of terseness traditionally associated with the definitional style'. He instead suggests a more comprehensive and less categorical description of 'distinctive features' of feuding. Miller then lists 'certain features and impressionistic observations' that to him 'seem to characterize feud in a way that distinguishes it from other types of violence such as war, duels, or simple revenge killings that involve no one beyond the killer and his victim'. Miller's list consists of the following nine items:

1. Feud is a relationship (hostile) between two groups.
2. Unlike ad hoc revenge killing that can be an individual matter, feuding involves groups that can be recruited by any number of principles, among which kinship, vicinage, household, or clientage are most usual.

3. Unlike war, feud does not involve relatively large mobilizations, but only occasional musterings for limited purposes. Violence is controlled; casualties rarely reach double digits in any single encounter.

4. Feud involves collective liability. The target need not be the actual wrongdoer, nor, for that matter, need the vengeance-taker be the person most wronged.

5. A notion of exchange governs the process, a kind of my-turn/your-turn rhythm, with offensive and defensive positions alternating after each confrontation.

6. As a corollary to the preceding item, people keep score.

7. People who feud tend to believe that honor and affronts to it are the prime motivators of hostilities. Cross-culturally, there appears to be a correlation between the existence of feud and a culture of honor.

8. Feud is governed by norms that limit the class of possible expiators and the appropriateness of responses. For instance, most feuding cultures recognize a rough rule of equivalence in riposte, the *lex talionis* being but one example.

9. There are culturally acceptable means for making temporary or permanent settlements of hostility.[83]

Many of these features are drawn from anthropological definitions such as those discussed above. What makes Miller's list of distinctive features different is that it follows an explicit denunciation of the terseness of the 'definitional style' and that it formulates several of the single items more flexibly, thus transforming obligatory 'criteria' of feud into less-mandatory 'distinctive features': Feuding groups can be recruited by *any number of* principles, of which certain principles are *most usual*; feuds involve *relatively* small groups of combatants; the body count in any single fight *rarely* exceeds a one digit number; the revenge-counter revenge process is a *notion of* exchange, a *kind of* my-turn/your-turn rhythm; feuders *tend to* think that they act primarily in defence of their honour, and there *appears* to be a cross-cultural connection between feud and honour; rules of equivalence are *rough* and exist in *most* feuding cultures.

This definitional elasticity implicitly estimates some of the distinctive features to be less imperative than others. It consequently has a potential of allowing a wider range of violence and conflict types to be included in the concept of feud. Miller sees group activity as typical of feuding; but apart from many anthropologists, he judges no specific group organisation or recruitment, such as family or kin, to be *the* standard feuding entity. Miller believes that feud is small-scale; but even as he quite precisely enumerates a maximum death toll in any single clash, he is reluctant to dismiss the possibility of larger battles in

---

83   Miller 1990, pp. 179-181.

feuds. Miller places emphasis on feud being a reciprocally alternating revenge-counter revenge process; but a feud needs not follow this pattern stringently: What is important is that there is a notion of exchange which, sometimes only approximately, makes the process resemble game-like turn-taking. Miller regards honour to be an important motivation for feuders but would not disregard that violence committed on the basis of other types of motivation may be identical to feuding. Finally, Miller sees norms of appropriate violence as typical of feud; but he is aware that such norms are sometimes vague, that they might be broken and that this should not necessarily lead the historian to typify such cases as something completely alien to feuding.

According to Miller, his list of distinctive features is better suited than concise definitions for avoiding ethno-centricity and, thus, for approximating cross-cultural relevance. At the same time, however, he says that the prime purpose of the list is to guide the reader through the ensuing description of Icelandic feud. Miller intends the list to 'serve as an orientation to the reader, nothing more', and one might agree that it seems especially apt to fit the Icelandic experience. Most notably in the present context, Miller's list of distinctive features is about bloodfeud, not other forms of feud. Even though he sees any Icelandic feud as a broader process which included 'the relationship between the groups, the state of the participants' minds, the postures of defiance, antagonism, and coldness filling the intervals of time between hostile confrontations', Miller stresses that, 'the overarching image, the nonreducible core of what it meant to be in a state of feud or to have feuding relations, was ultimately the obligation to have to kill and in turn to suffer the possibility of being killed'.[84] However, as this emphasis on killing is implied, and therefore not spelled out, in the nine items on Miller's list of distinctive features as quoted above, the list may – also due to its flexibility – show to be more cross-culturally applicable than Miller imagines.

If one uses Miller's list to test such feuds that were not primarily bloodfeuds, for instance medieval German, English, French or Danish noble feuds, *many* of these would match *most* of Miller's distinctive features: (1) All noble feuds are hostile relationships, most of them between two groups, especially if a group can be defined as consisting of a lord and his retinue. (2) Noble feuding may theoretically be an individual matter but rarely is in practice; it most often involves groups that may be recruited by any of the principles mentioned by Miller (kinship, vicinage, household, and clientage) and often by a mixture of those. (3) Noble feuds usually involve relatively small mobilisations which,

---

EDINBURGH UNIVERSITY LIBRARY
WITHDRAWN

however, may in some cases consist primarily of permanent miniature armies (the lords' retinues) that are not only mustered for the limited purposes of one specific feud action. The same, parenthetically, could probably also be said about household recruitments in Icelandic bloodfeuds. In noble feuds, violence is controlled and casualties are usually low. (4) Noble feuds involve collective liability. The target is very often someone else than the wrongdoer, frequently his dependants, and the vengeance-taker is not always the person most wronged. (5) A notion of exchange often governs the process of noble feuding, especially if one sees litigation and disputing as part of the feud process (as does Miller[85]). However, the my-turn/your-turn rhythm is not always discernable, and in many cases the feud is unilateral with an active feuder attacking a passive opponent. Such feuds are not reciprocal or alternating at all. This makes many, but not all, noble feuds different from the typical bloodfeud.[86] (6) In noble feuds, people keep score; but if a noble feud is one-sided and does not alternate, the passive part's scorekeeping takes a different form and is intended for litigation and complaints over the feuder to a higher authority rather than for purposes of measured revenge or calculations of the economy of honour. (7) Noblemen who feud tend to believe that affronts to their honour motivates the feuding. This does not preclude that they often act from political incentives as well, or in some cases use honour as pure pretext,[87] but the same thing may often be said about people who engage in bloodfeuds.[88] (8) Noble feuds are governed by norms regarding legitimate expiators (women, children and ecclesiastics are usually spared) and rough rules regarding the

85   Miller agrees with Andreas Heusler who considered feud in the Icelandic context to be characterised as much by lawsuits and arbitration as by vengeance. *Ibid.*, p. 180.

86   It might, however, be open for discussion if all 'anthropological' bloodfeuds abide by the exchange model as meticulously as sometimes portrayed in the literature. Miller's flexible formulation concerning this point may be due to doubts about that. Seen from a different angle, it might also be asserted that an alternating bloodfeud at any point of the process is in fact unilateral with nobody knowing for sure whether the feud will continue, whether it will be ended by permanent settlement before the 'next' revenge action, or whether it will simply be 'forgotten'. This argument could also be used to question the stringency of divisions between bloodfeud and 'simple' (i.e. unilateral) revenge killing. It should be noted, furthermore, that unilateral noble feuds often have an inbuilt potential of escalation and thus of becoming bilateral.

87   Zmora 1995.

88   There can also be observed a significant difference of honour and its connection to feuding between societies that have noble feuds and more egalitarian ones that have bloodfeuds, a difference which pertains to a social differentiation of honour in the former. In late medieval Germany, a specific kind of honour was attached to each societal estate, and some scholars believe that feuding was a constituent part of the code of honour that was special to the aristocracy, e.g. Morsel 1996.

appropriateness of responses. (9) Noble feuds are purposeful means to an end which entails that there are always culturally and legally acceptable means for making both temporary and permanent settlements.

The point of making such a test and, in that process, of underlining the similarities of bloodfeud and other types of feud, is not to harmonise phenomena that are clearly not similar by making them fit into the same slack model under the heading of an easily comprehensible, but also very vague and multi-facetted, concept. The dissimilarities between, on the one hand, Icelandic peasants or Bedouin camel-herders killing each other in protracted revenge chains and, on the other hand, a German nobleman plundering a village in order to damage his adversary's source of revenue are all too obvious. The point is neither to duplicate the statement that 'feud can have various forms in various times and places'.[89] Such a hypostatisation, which turns 'feud' into an abstract essence that exists autonomously, outside of time and space where it occasionally 'manifests' itself in different 'forms', is ontologically highly problematical. The point is to initiate a cross-cultural comparison of different types of (what modern scholars and, in some historical contexts, contemporaries call) 'feud' which comprehends the similarities as something more than products of sheer coincidence (or analytical imprecision) and which attempts to explain the differences as variations on a common theme – and then, exactly by making that comparison, try to find out what this common theme consists of and what factors are most basic to it. This is not the place to make such an effort at any greater length. But it can be cursorily sketched out that the most apparent similarities between (blood)feud, as described by Miller, and the type of feud which in this essay has been chosen to represent an especially deviant meaning of that concept, the noble feud, seem to be features such as: Mutual hostility with resort to violence; self-help that aims at forcing the opponent to give in to a political, moral or legal demand; retribution, retaliation, revenge; legality, legitimacy; limited mobilisation, controlled violence; potential for continuance and escalation; notions of honour as motivation; conflict management including settlement. The major differences are: The absence of mutuality in many noble feuds; a significant difference in the degree of restraint of homicidal violence with noble feuding having, relatively speaking, lower casualties; a somewhat different organisation of noble feud groups (in which a large proportion of the group is subordinate to the principal aristocratic feuder); a different configuration of collective liability with more emphasis on socially inferior dependants as

---

89   Miller 1990, p. 180. This conception seems fairly widespread in feud research.

expiators in noble feuds and more emphasis of kinship in bloodfeuds. The explanation for these differences may be boiled down to differences in degree of social stratification and political centralisation of the societies that stage the feuds. The absence of mutuality in some noble feuds my be due to very substantial dissimilarities of power between the conflicting entities which make retaliation impossible for the weaker part; it may also be due to the existence of relatively well-functioning courts (resulting from some degree of political centralisation) which give choices to victims of encroachment other than direct violent retribution, and sometimes succeed in resolving potentially protractive conflicts at an early stage. Even in late medieval Germany, which was very much politically fragmented and decentralised in comparison with other pre-modern monarchies such as England or France, each of the political entities, into which the Empire was split up, possessed judicial institutions and coercive powers that by far outranked the institutions of stateless societies (such as Free State Iceland), however telling it may be that stateless societies have such institutions at all. Such factors probably also account for the relatively low frequency of killing in noble feuds and the fact that hostile actions are directed at other targets than the opponent's life and limbs. Differences pertaining to the degree of social stratification and political centralisation also seem be the main explanation of the differences regarding group organisation, recruitment, expiators and notions of honour in feuds. Bloodfeud and noble feud may then be variations on a common theme with socio-structural factors such as social stratification and political centralisation (there may be other equally important factors[90]) determining the nature of these variations. The common theme that lies at the base of feuding may be reduced to: A competition for survival and power which implies attacks on or retaliation against competing individuals or groups, but also includes intra-group cohesion and an ability to manage and terminate conflicts within and between groups for the sake

---

90 The availability of resources is another factor which seems to be important in condition-
    ing the frequency and intensity of conflicts and thus for the potential of such conflicts esca-
    lating into feuds. This factor was given prominence by Jacob Black-Michaud 1975, p. 160,
    in his thesis of 'total scarcity' of resources as a prerequisite of feuding, and the same line of
    thought can be detected in European feud research as well, e.g. in Werner Rösener's (1982)
    robber knight thesis. See also below, item 12 on Christopher Boehm's list of distinctive fea-
    tures. Muir 1993, p. 17, evokes Black-Michaud but sees Friulan feuding not so much as a re-
    sult of 'total' scarcity but more of 'the habitually unequal distribution of scarce resources'.
    Generally, it seems problematical to apply Black-Michaud's radical thesis on European feud-
    ing societies without modifications. For example, late medieval peasant feuds may, in fact,
    have resulted, at least in part, from the improvement of the peasants' economic and social
    status during that period.

of optimising peaceful cohabitation and production. These competitions and conflicts are often structured as feuds in ways that vary according to differences of the structure of the given society in which they occur. Insofar as feuding is universal, then, it is not as an abstract essence, but as a combination of universally manifest properties of individual psychology and human group behaviour.[91]

Miller's solution to the conceptual problem is inspired by Christopher Boehm's list of 'distinctive features' of (blood)feud which is presented in his historical-anthropological study on Montenegrin feuding. The list is based on that study as well as on an elaborate discussion of anthropological definitions.

1. Feuding involves the indigenous assumption that retaliatory homicide is a righteous act and that one homicide legitimately deserves another.

2. Regulation of feuding comes through established rules, which are understood by both sides. This implies a mutual relationship between the feuding parties.

3. Feuding involves the idea of scorekeeping.

4. Feuding most often is alternating, in that the two sides take turns at offense and defense. This alternating status is determined by a score that is known by both sides.

5. Some means is available for permanently or temporarily stopping the conflict. This is done either automatically, by reaching parity, by truce, or by payment of material wealth for blood, and is based on precise scorekeeping.

6. Feuding is motivated and rationalized in terms of need for manly esteem or "honor," but more fundamentally it has to do with dominance relations.

7. Feuding involves notions of dominance between groups as well as between individuals: a homicide that is accepted passively invites further aggression toward both the person and the group that fails to retaliate. This is the practical disadvantage that accompanies "dishonor."

8. Feuding, in essence, involves the notion of controlled retaliation, which is directed at an aggressor and/or his close associates. The degree of control is determined by how much the particular groups stand to lose by being at feud.

    a. Within a very closely cooperating group, feuding is generally outlawed by definition: the group cannot exact blood from itself; therefore, potential feuds are precluded.

    b. With groups that are separate but cooperate usefully, a potential feud is tightly controlled and is resolved with dispatch because of practical concern for loss

---

91   See Christopher Boehm's contribution to the present volume.

of benefits. In such cases, strong community pressure helps to outweigh the demands of honor.

c. When feuding groups do not ordinarily cooperate and are not part of the same cohesive community, then termination of feuding becomes problematical, although conformity to the general pattern of feuding does limit escalation of the conflict.

9. Feuding is retarded to the degree that the hostile groups are connected by cross-cutting social ties such as marriage alliances or economic relationships.

10. Feuding can be used as a means of avoiding warfare, because feuding allows people to retaliate for homicide in a controlled way such that the conflict is not likely to escalate into warfare.

11. Feuds tend to be very difficult to resolve, because the game tends to be one with a less-than-zero sum insofar as honor is concerned. Thus, feuds, in fact, can be long-lasting or all but "interminable" unless some strong force militates for pacification.

12. From an evolutionary standpoint, feuding seems to correlate with a high-enough population density relative to natural resources so that avoidance mechanisms become politically unfeasible or economically too costly as a means of controlling serious conflicts.[92]

Boehm's list is somewhat more categorically formulated than Miller's (note however the elasticity in items 4, 10, 11 and 12), but it is less terse. It includes more features than Miller's that specify the social mechanisms of feuding and the factors that limit or amplify it. One could perhaps expect that this inclusion of features would make the list harder to appropriate for types of feud other than strict bloodfeud (which the list intends to describe). But it seems that several of the extra features of Boehm's list would fit such other types of feuding as accurately as the features in Miller's list. For example, the view that dominance relations is such a central motivation of feuding that it needs to be included among feud's 'distinctive features' (items 6-7) would probably make sense to many students of feuding (in the broader sense) in medieval and early modern Europe.

The idea of working from an elaborate and flexibly verbalised list of distinctive features rather than an over-stringent definition is adopted by Paul Hyams in his recent work on feud in medieval England.

1. Feud starts as an effort to avenge injury, generally violent injury, and often a killing.

---

92   Boehm 1984, pp. 218-219.

2. It represents the injury as the act of an enemy and signals a lasting enmity between the man (or men) who inflicted it and the "victim."

3. The wrong that provokes and justifies feud is understood to affect a larger group that included the original victim but was in part known and even recruited in advance of trouble. Its solidarity has been set in doubt and may need reassertion.

4. Given a similar sense of the vicarious liability of the injuring party's associates, they were sometimes targeted for vengeance in the principal's stead.

5. The level of response is constrained by a notion of rough equivalence, requiring the keeping of "score."

6. Emotions both fuel the response and determine its quantum and nature.

7. The response is ritualized in various ways to proclaim the acts to all as legitimate vengeance.

8. Action from the side of the "victim" nevertheless raises the high probability of further tit-for-tat from their enemies.

9. To dispel this and offer hopes of an end to the violence, something much more than the punishment of individual offenders is necessary, amounting to a veritable peace settlement between the wider groups involved.[93]

First of all, one notices that Hyams' list is not only about bloodfeuds. It is more generally about 'injury' and responses to 'injury' within the context of lasting enmity. However, violence is prominent among the injuries that might entail feuds and this violence is 'often' homicidal. Hyams' list of distinctive features differs from its precursors also in including emotions and in ascribing more explanatory power to them than Miller's and Boehm's lists do. According to Hyams, emotions determine the quantum and nature of response to injury, whereas according to Boehm, the degree of control in feuding is determined by much more rational, strategic considerations such as the level of inter-group-cooperation and cross-cutting social ties.

Hyams' items 7 and 8 explicate, more than the previous lists do, a paradox of feuding: That it is based on a general norm that violence is a legitimate response to injury (which according to Hyams is in concrete instances ascertained by public communication through ritualisation, which is a feature that is absent from the previous lists) while, nevertheless, any one instance of revenge often generates further 'tit-for-tat' (although it should have been accepted as legitimate and thus should not have allowed further retaliatory actions from the counterpart).

---

93   Hyams, *Rancor*, 2003, pp. 8-9.

This paradox might be resolved by stating that feuding very often includes and in fact bases itself on a discrepancy between, on the one hand, generalised, societal norms about proper responses to injury and, on the other hand, subjective evaluations on the part of actual conflict participants of the properness of actual responses to actual injuries. This discrepancy between objective and divergent subjective interpretations of legitimacy might then be seen as a central feature of feuding[94] which corresponds adequately with the pervasive scholarly position that feuding is most common and uncontrolled in societies that lack a single political authority that exerts a monopoly not just of violence as such but of defining the general societal norms and of evaluating their relevance in actual instances.

This means that a feud, according to Paul Hyams, is not necessarily a perfect tit-for-tat chain reaction. What seems most important to Hyams about feud is that violence is regarded as an acceptable means of legal redress between sworn, public enemies that act out of emotions that compel them to retaliate wrongs done to them; and that those subjective emotions make them refute the counterpart's (publicised) claim to objective 'truth' about the legitimacy of its actions; which often, but not always, generates long lasting series of mutual violent retaliation.

The last item on Paul Hyams' list seems at a first look to mirror the items on Boehm's and Miller's lists that talk about arbitration, peacemaking and settlement as integrated factors in feud processes. Hyams, since he mentions 'punishment of individual offenders', does not seem to necessarily imagine exactly the same process that anthropologists do when they describe dispute resolution in stateless societies. What Hyams' formulation seems to make room for is a feud-and-settlement system in a society that indeed has law courts and some sort of centralised coercive forces that sentence and punish criminals – institutions which are, however, insufficient to stop feud violence in face of the emotional intransigence of the feuding collectives whose acceptance of the settlement is therefore needed. If one translates this feature of feud into

---

94 This would, of course, not make a *distinctive* feature of feud since the same discrepancy lies at the base of many conflicts ranging from minor quarrels to major wars. But this discrepancy may be especially important, perhaps even a basic principle, in feuding and in feuding societies. It can be added that what may be portrayed as 'objective' societal norms, *in casu* toward revenge and feud, might not be all that general in all feuding societies. If there is divergence about the norms regarding revenge and the right to feud it may in fact contribute in itself to the conflict potential in such societies. The existence of different norms toward feuding within a given society may, however, also have the reverse effect of providing legitimacy to conflict participants or intervening parties (such as state or church) seeking peaceful solutions to disputes.

a methodological potential for empirically detecting feuding in such societies that have comparatively centralised judicial institutions, this means that the existence of 'private' peace settlements supplementing law court proceedings and enforcements indicates the presence of what Hyams would call an 'enmity culture' or 'feud-like behaviour'. Such settlements and peace acts are found side by side with relatively well-developed judicial institutions, for instance, in thirteenth-century England, in fourteenth-century Marseille, and in late medieval and early modern Germany, Scotland and Denmark.

Phenomenological and philological solutions to the conceptual problem

One method to solve the problems concerning the conceptual inconsistencies and contradictions surrounding the word 'feud', a method which is quite common, is to use it even more flexibly than the above-mentioned lists of distinctive features. Sometimes, definitional problems are not recognised at all by users of the concept.[95] More often, the historian is aware of such problems but offers arguments in favour of avoiding any clear cut or explicit definition. Hillay Zmora believes that 'a positive definition of the feud is better avoided', the main reason being contemporary terminology's lack of consistency. Zmora instead prefers to let 'the sense of what a feud was like' emerge from examples of typical feuds, of which he then goes on to give detailed descriptions.[96] Christine Reinle has labelled this approach 'phenomenological'. Instead of placing historical events and processes into *a priori* schemes which may serve as catalysts of anachronisms, the historian ought to first examine and describe these phenomena unbiased and in detail and then construct a loose definition based on what has been found to be the typical and most telling features of the investigated phenomena.[97] Stephen D. White, writing about France around the year 1100, states that because of the conceptual irregularity on the part of modern historians as well as contemporaries, 'no rigorous definition of the medieval French feud for our period can now be formulated, or, perhaps, should ever be proposed'. White sees a direct advantage in working from a concept which remains almost undefined because using any stringent definition

---

95   See e.g. criticism of a widespread mistake among English historians 'of seeing simple quarrels as feuds' (which is surprising in light of the tradition within English historiography of regarding feud to be extinct after the Conquest) in Dean 2001, p. 104.

96   Zmora 1997, p. 15.

97   Reinle, *Bauernfehden*, 2003, pp. 44-45.

makes the historian unable to grasp the complexity and richness of medieval disputing and its terminology.[98] When Wallace-Hadrill proposed a very broad definition he made sure to stress that it was to be taken merely as a 'working definition'. He also pointed to the elusiveness of contemporary terminology as one reason for this approach.[99]

Keith Mark Brown questions the relevance of trying to arrive at a common definition of 'feud' that makes it possible to associate e.g. Mediterranean or Middle Eastern feuds with European feud which he sees as a phenomenon that is historically unique. Brown, however, acknowledges similarities between European and non-European feuding. In his own study of Scottish bloodfeuds, Brown, as a starting point, identifies feuds by the use of the word in contemporary sources, since 'the general principle of accepting contemporary perceptions as the basis for identification seems to be the most useful one'. Brown then uses these cases in which the word 'feud' appears as a norm against which he puts other possible feuds and finds a number of conflicts in which the word was not seen put to use but was 'acted out in much the same way ... in their use of violence, their language, and in the observance of ritual behaviour'. Finally, he identifies feuds by sources that bear witness to an effort from its participants or outsiders to bring peace to the dispute (mediation, arbitration, mutual assurances, and acts of caution) but, likewise, without using the word 'feud'.[100]

In Brown's case, the definitional problem is resolved by using contemporary terminology, and the same approach is widespread also among German scholars that work with source material in which the word 'feud' (*Fehde*) is omnipresent.[101] This seems also be the case with students of Italian and Corsican 'vendetta'.[102] It may be that the need for a stringent definition is not so strongly felt when historians work with a historical setting that used the same word as the one that

---

98 White 1986, pp. 195-196.

99 Wallace-Hadrill 1962, p. 123: 'As an institution, feud remains undefined by those who have resort to it". Wallace-Hadrill's working definition is as follows: "We may call it, first, the threat of hostility between kins; then, the state of hostility between them; and finally, the satisfaction of their differences and a settlement on terms acceptable to both. The threat, the state and the settlement of that hostility constitute feud but do not necessarily mean bloodshed', p. 122.

100 Brown 1986, pp. 1-5.

101 Recent German research, however, has attempted to define the concept more ideal-typically, but the tie to contemporary language usage is still strong. See, for example, Reinle, *Bauernfehden*, 2003, pp. 45-46.

102 Muir 1993, p. xxiii, prefers to work from Renaissance rather than modern definitions of vendetta because modern distinctions obscure 'the manifold Renaissance uses of the word *vendetta*'.

has been made into a modern scholarly concept.[103] This probably helps explain the fact that more effort has been put into defining feud in historical contexts, such as high medieval England and Saga Iceland, where 'feud' was not part of the vocabulary. It may be stated that it is somewhat more uncomplicated to adopt a phenomenological approach when the phenomenon studied had a name that is easily recognised by modern observers. On the other hand, as noted, a similarly non-stringent solution to the definitional problem may also be based exactly on the complexity of contemporary word usage and, thus, the absence of one clear feud-word (White; Wallace-Hadrill; partly Zmora).

A revisionist view

It is a well-known fact that central scholarly concepts have a tendency of becoming overused. As is for instance the case with 'feudalism' (with which 'feud' must of course never be confused), such central concepts will, as time proceeds, be utilised in more and more different historical and cultural contexts by a rising number of individual scholars and will consequently accumulate an ever increasing multitude of meanings. It also has a tendency of becoming 'tyrannical' in that it demands the historian to interpret a very wide and complex range of phenomena in certain ways which are tied specifically to the mode of thinking that is, sometimes unconsciously, embedded in the concept; it leaves little room for interpretations or investigation of themes lying outside its reach; it permeates the historian's entire perception of what a given period or culture was like.

It seems to be an in-built component of the concept construction process that these problems will at some point exhaust the once productive concept and that this will lead to heavy criticism or even abandonment of that concept. Abandoning 'feud' as an analytical tool, then, can be seen as a solution – the most drastic one – to what has here been presented as a conceptual problem of 'feud'; a problem which others have consciously attempted to resolve by softening or widening that problematical concept, or by following historical terminology.

---

103 The same could probably be said about Danish research which has hitherto not attempted to present any sort of definition of the concept even though the word 'fejde' is not used in the sources that are extant from the period which is usually taken to be the heyday of feuding, i.e. the early and high middle ages. This is probably because the word was used (being imported from German) during the Later Middle Ages.

A frequent occurrence in connection with criticism or rejection of central historiographic concepts is, furthermore, that the criticism of the concept as such becomes closely associated with a denial of the subject matter that has formerly been thought to lie behind the concept. In connection with the concept 'feudalism', for example, Elizabeth A.R. Brown's conceptual criticism of that 'tyrannical construct' led directly to Susan Reynolds' doubting that concrete elements of what had previously been categorised as 'feudalism' ever really existed.[104] In such cases, criticism of the concept goes from debating whether or not it is a useful analytical tool to hard historical revision of its contents.

The concept 'feud' has, like so many other central scholarly concepts, been subjected to this sort of mixture of conceptual and material revisionism. For unknown reasons, the criticism has come primarily from early medieval historians. In 1987, Peter Sawyer criticised the vagueness of the concept and argued that it is virtually impossible to find the kind of violent relationships in the Early Middle Ages that would fit a more stringent definition of 'feud'.[105] Recently, Guy Halsall has advanced this criticism.[106] Halsall takes his point of departure in the definition of the *Shorter Oxford English Dictionary* (as quoted above). He takes this as representative of what most scholars would believe to be essential to feuding. 'Most would agree that a feud is a relationship of lasting hostility between groups, marked by periodic, cyclical, reciprocal violence'.[107] He then to a large degree follows Sawyer in asserting that it is very difficult (but not wholly impossible) to find this kind of violence in the early medieval West. Halsall briefly criticises the way some scholars are 'bending the general definition' (which according to Halsall materialises in the Oxford dictionary) to make it fit their own case studies, and then states: 'It is time to wrench ourselves free of this construct. Feud, as understood in modern definitions, was not generally practised in the early Middle Ages; what early medieval people called *faehde*, or similar, was something rather different'.[108] In the Early Medieval Period, according to Halsall, the Germanic words for

104 Elizabeth A.R. Brown, "The Tyranny of a Construct: Feudalism and Historians of Medieval Europe", *American Historical Review*, 79, 1974, pp. 1063-1088. Susan Reynolds, *Fiefs and Vassals. The Medieval Evidence Reinterpreted*, Oxford 1994.

105 Peter Sawyer, "The Bloodfeud in Fact and Fiction", Kirsten Hastrup and Preben Meulengracht Sørensen (eds.), *Tradition og historieskrivning*, Århus 1987, pp. 27-38.

106 Halsall 1998. Idem, "Reflections on Early Medieval Violence: The example of the 'Blood Feud'", *Memoria y Civilización*, 2, 1999, pp. 7-29. The term 'feud' is also rejected in Bennett 1998.

107 Halsall 1998, pp. 19-20.

108 *Ibid.*, p. 20.

feud meant legal vengeance. The modern connotation of 'feud' (reciprocal, mutual, on-going hostility) is a later linguistic development. What Halsall finds in the early medieval sources is not feud but legal revenge, or, as he calls it, 'customary vengeance'. That is, one vengeance killing which legally retaliates a first killing and ends the dispute (as in the *lex talionis*). Further revenge taking does not seem to have been legitimate. Halsall recognises the possibility of such single revenge killings entailing counter revenge and, in turn, feuding. But he maintains that such processes are 'difficult to detect' in the early medieval evidence, which is primarily due to 'the existence of many forces (community, 'state' and church) militating against such escalation'.

We thus have a choice. Either we make it clear whether we are using 'feud' in its medieval or its modern sense, or (probably preferably) we should banish the word 'feud' from our discussions of early medieval violence, except in the handful of instances where it is justified, keep it as a separate category of violence, and use 'customary vengeance' instead to describe instances where, after a violent attack the aggrieved party uses, or threatens to use, retaliatory violence to bring about an end to a dispute (through compensation, where violence is not actually employed). If we choose it we do no more than remove a term which has become unhelpful, and unhelpfully value-laden, and replace it with one which fits the data exactly.[109]

Halsall, thus, proposes that 'feud', as a modern scholarly concept, is given up in order to liberate the historian of prejudice about the violent 'Dark Ages'. Enduring feuds almost never occurred during that period because community, state and church curtailed the escalation potential of 'customary vengeance'. Historians unwilling to abandon the concept 'feud' should either use it in its contemporary meaning or in keeping with a tight and narrow modern definition.

Halsall only claims his conceptual revision to be relevant to the study of early medieval Western Europe. However, since it questions the validity of a central anthropological and historiographical concept, it seems to have much broader implications. These implications would of course be hardest felt by European medieval and early modern historians. Although the idea has been abandoned that feud in these periods represented the direct continuance of an ancient Germanic institution many would probably find it hard to make Halsall's claim about the absence of feud in the Early Middle Ages fit their own findings on feuding in later periods. Halsall's thesis seriously challenges the

---

109 *Ibid.*, p. 28.

survival-of-feud tendency which more or less intentionally is part and parcel of much work on European feuding. Although much European feud research has made a point of rejecting straightforward evolutionist explanations of the development and decline of feud, many would probably still imagine the potential of widespread feuding to have been larger in the Early Middle Ages than in the Early Modern Period. And that later feuding in one way or the other had its roots in earlier feuding.

Conclusions

This introductory essay has attempted to approach the study of feud mainly from a historiographic and conceptual angle. Focus has been on how historians of medieval and early modern Europe, and the anthropologists that have inspired some of them, have perceived feud in relation to society: The social causes and consequences of feud and the societal causality of the termination of feud. It has been shown, rather unsurprisingly, that the ways historians think about feud and society result to some extent from contemporary understandings of how societies generally function and develop, and that these understandings may be shaped considerably by political ideas and beliefs on the part of the historian. In most of Western Europe, the kind of feud research which still today seems roughly acceptable to most historians emanated from an anti-eurocentristic direction in anthropology, and in Germany it derived from an anti-modernist direction in legal history. What these politically divergent schools had in common was a profound criticism of the misinterpretations of alien cultures and past societies that had been produced by a positivist paradigm which had seen the liberal-democratic (and colonial) state as the standard against which all such 'primitive' societies should be measured. Within a social historian paradigm dominated by functionalism and structuralism, feud was now perceived as a social and legal institution that was rational insofar as it functioned as a source of social control and societal cohesion. The medieval feud was regarded as an instrument of securing rights and of retributing infringements in the 'absence of' State in the modern sense. Feud also came, variably, to be regarded as an important mechanism of dominance and exploitation as historians diagnosticised major differences between feuding in the highly socially stratified societies of medieval and early modern Europe and the more egalitarian societies studied by the anthropologists. In some cases, this line of thought led to seeing feud as a custom that continuously solidified and reproduced feudal structures. Even as the idea of feud as an 'obstacle' to the evolution of modern nation states was among the most severely criticised, it was, and still is, almost inescapable to the modern observer. In other cases, feud was regarded as a more 'progressive' phenomenon that went hand in hand with the expansion of the medieval and early modern state. Generally, the European experience seems to show that feuding may for a considerable time coexist and cofunction with an 'embryonic' state and its judicial institutions.

The explanatory power of the functionalist-structuralist 'school' of feud studies has appealed to many historians that have produced an ever growing literature on feuding in more and more historical contexts. The survival-of-feud (or discovery-of-feud or rationality-of-feud) tendency, that has motivated much of this research, seems to continue to be able to enrich (i.e. instigate new interpretations, discussions and inquiries within) particular national historiographies such as, for instance, the English, the French, the German and the Scandinavian. At the same time, however, the functionalist-structuralist direction has undergone significant revision – a revision which seems to have come from roughly two sources. Firstly, as research on feud has condensed and elaborated on itself, it has revealed some fundamental problems with the specific theories and models of feud that set it in motion. The rationality of the 'sanitised'[110] feud of Max Gluckman and Otto Brunner has become increasingly difficult to sustain as historians have dug deeper into the subject matter of European feuding societies. Secondly, and probably more importantly than such 'internal' revision within feud research, the functionalist-structuralist paradigm that formed the basis of this view on feud has been contested by more general reorientations in historiography. However, no abrupt break with previous approaches to or interpretations of feud has emerged from this reorientation.[111] Instead, a number of what in this essay have been called 'new trends' has come forward. The proponents of these new trends make no joint effort to supplant earlier perceptions of feuding with any one particular counter-model. To the contrary, it has been shown here that their eclectic uses and allocations of diverse elements inherited from post-modern theory (e.g. focus on narratives, discourses, representations and emotions) make them reach manifestly diverging results regarding feud and its decline. In at least the case of Stephen D. White's recent work on 'anger', the particular way post-structuralist theories on discourses and emotions are being combined even seems to provide verification of the traditional rationality-of-feud view. Much

---

110 Brown 1986, p. 2, commenting on Gluckman. The expression can be reasonably applied to Otto Brunner and much German feud research in general.

111 Apart from Guy Halsall who among his arguments against the prevalence of feuding in early medieval Europe uses a narratological approach to support his claim (i.e. 'true' feuds existed more in tales than in reality).

future work on feud will probably likewise position itself as part of a post-structuralist methodology, but will do so rather by reformulating, elaborating, enhancing or modifying the results achieved by the functionalist-structuralist paradigm than dismissing them completely.

A comprehensive history of European feuding still remains to be written. The problem of writing such a history would not only be a problem of synthesising a large literature on feuding in many different historical contexts over a very long period of time. It would also be a problem of dealing with a historiography which has assigned a great variety of meanings and definitions to what would be the central concepts of such a history. In this essay, an effort has been made to analyse and discuss a selection of the many different definitions and (eventually undefined) uses of 'feud' and 'vendetta' that have accumulated in anthropological as well as historical scholarship. It has been shown that anthropologists and historians have for a long time been aware of the definitional problems involved in the use of those central concepts. What stands out is a variety of strategies to tackle those problems. These strategies can be divided into: 1. Stringent definitions, tersely formulated, as in dictionaries, encyclopaedia, and anthropological cross-cultural studies. 2. Potentially more flexible 'descriptions' of feud through elaborate 'lists of distinctive features'. 3. Conscious avoidance of applying any strict ideal type definition, often coupled with a phenomenological approach and/or a conceptualisation which is based on each feuding society's indigenous vocabulary and norms. 4. A proposal of rejecting feud as modern scholarly concept.

A complete history or theory of feuding, or any other (perhaps slightly less ambitious) endeavour to compare feuding in different past and present societies, would probably do best in basing itself on one of the two first options; in using the third option as a source of native views, norms and laws; and in keeping the fourth in mind for purposes of sustained awareness of the need for definitional stringency – and possibly for the purpose of abandoning any attempt at making such a comparison in case the conceptual inconsistencies prove to be insurmountable. In this essay it has been suggested that a somewhat broader description of feud and its 'distinctive features', like the ones offered by Boehm, Miller and Hyams, might be preferred as a point of departure for comparisons. This should be paired with an attempt at identifying the basic elements of individual and group behaviour that lie at the core of all such conflicts and types of violence that may, if tested positively against these descriptions of distinctive features, be characterised as 'feuds'. Long standing bloodfeuds between Icelandic peasants might then be placed on the same continuum as bloodfeuds between Scottish or Friulan aristocrats as well as the feuds between Franconian noblemen that were not primarily bloodfeuds. It may be found that the extent to which feuds are allowed to escalate in terms of duration and casualties are determined by factors such as, for example, social stratification, political centralisation and availability, and societal distribution of resources. Kinship structures, residence patterns, and culture-specific mental and religious factors may very well be equally important. It should also be kept in mind that there may be historical continuity and even cross-influencing of norms regarding feud, vengeance, and peace between the feuding societies studied.

Edward Muir has tried to place Renaissance Friuli on a spectrum of European feuding societies. At the one end of this spectrum, says Muir, 'might be medieval England, where royal justice stamped out blood feuds earlier than in any other kingdom, and at the other modern Albania, where governments have hardly touched the endemic tribal feuds in the mountains. Although a feudal and not a tribal society, Friuli in the Renaissance came closer to the Albanian than the English end of the spectrum'.[112] It is the opinion of the author of the present essay that an effort to place the feuding societies of medieval and early modern Europe on this sort of spectrum may provide a constructive starting point for further comparison.

---

112 Muir 1993, p. 275. For the idea of a spectrum with England and Albania representing adverse extremes, Muir draws on Wormald 1983, p. 104, who places early modern Scottish bloodfeud (and the rest of the European feud types) somewhere in between without indicating if it was closer to either of the ends of that spectrum.

Feud and Feuding in the Early and High Middle Ages

Working Descriptions and Continuity

Helgi Þorláksson

I

What is feud? The matter is debated, some scholars maintain we mix up many unrelated issues and comprise them under the term feud. They might be right and at least it is common in modern usage to speak of feuds between politicians or companies. By that a serious conflict or a turbulent competition is probably most often suggested. Scholars of course should try to be more precise and discern between the more general conflicts or disputes and the more specific feuds or vendettas.[1]

Did feud exist in Western Europe in medieval times? Most scholars would agree on that, some of them reluctantly. The disagreement manifests itself when we ask questions like: What is it that characterises feud? How are we to know it? Where, when and why did feuds most often occur? Some common generalisations are for instance that feuds occurred where central authority was weak and implied a strong sense of honour and an obligation of revenge. It is debated whether enmity had to be interminable in order to be rightly termed as feud; whether the adversaries could be individuals or had to be groups with common liability; and whether as a part of the feud we should include some peace-process at the end with intermediaries, settlement or arbitration as implicit features.

As far as I know, it is generally accepted among scholars that feud existed in the Icelandic Commonwealth, or what is also called the Free State, prior

---

1   For some critical viewpoints on the concepts feud and bloodfeud, see Peter Sawyer, "The Bloodfeud in Fact and Fiction", Kirsten Hastrup and Preben Meulengracht Sørensen (eds.), *Tradition og historieskrivning*, Århus 1987, pp. 27-38. Guy Halsall, "Violence and society in the early medieval west: an introductory survey", Guy Halsall (ed.), *Violence and Society in the Early Medieval West*, Woodbridge 1998, pp. 1-45, esp. 19-29.

to 1262. Jesse Byock and William Ian Miller have made this well known to medievalists.[2] Miller's description of the Icelandic feud is very well known and often referred to by scholars. Even scholars who consider our usage of the word feud, and what it stands for, to be generally vague and seldom precise, seem to be of the opinion that the Icelandic feud was a real thing and is aptly described by Miller.[3]

What I would like to do here, therefore, is first of all discuss Miller's description, and then give my own description of feud. Having accomplished the aforementioned I would like to try to pinpoint at what stage a feud actually commenced. Do we need a corpse for that or could it even start at the early stage of altercation or discord? In order to do this I would also like to discuss the concepts vendetta, *Blutrache*, customary vengeance and bloodfeud. This further leads me to the early medieval *faida* and how it connects to the feud of the High Middle Ages.

II

Let us turn to Miller's description of feud in Iceland. Miller to a certain extent bases his description on the one by Christopher Boehm for Montenegro, with borrowings from Jacob Black-Michaud's more general discussion. We might call these 'distinctive features', and in my version they are:

1. Two opposing groups are involved.
2. The opposing groups may be formed in a number of different ways.
3. Only a few people are involved in a feud at any one time, violence is limited, there are few casualties.
4. The opposing groups accept collective liability for their actions.
5. The groups take it in turns to carry out acts of violence against one another.

---

2   Jesse L. Byock, *Feud in the Icelandic Saga*, Berkeley 1982. Idem, *Medieval Iceland. Society, Sagas and Power*, Berkeley 1988. *Idem, Viking Age Iceland*, 2001, pp. 77-80, 123-6, 223-5. Idem, "Feuding in Viking-Age Iceland's Great Village", Warren C. Brown and Piotr Górecki (eds.), *Conflict in Medieval Europe. Changing Perspectives on Society and Culture*, Aldershot 2003, pp. 229-241. William Ian Miller, *Bloodtaking and Peacemaking. Feud, Law, and Society in Saga Iceland*, Chicago 1990, pp. 179-220, 349-56.

3   Sawyer 1987, pp. 34-35. Halsall 1998, pp. 21, 26. For other examples from the early medieval times, which Halsall accepts as "true' feud', see *ibid.*, pp. 26-27.

6. Wounds and deaths are tallied precisely, and an equivalent ratio is worked out for the allotment of compensation.
7. The culture of honour is the main motivating factor underlying feud.
8. Customs of propriety pertain; there are limitations on what is considered acceptable in the execution of vengeance.
9. There are culturally accepted procedures for the resolution of feud.[4]

In a more abbreviated version: Feud involves two hostile groups, each with collective liability. They are of mixed origin, not necessarily of kinship. Violence is controlled and casualties are limited. A notion of 'my turn/your turn' rhythm governs the process, and people keep score of wounds and deaths. The participants believe that affronts to honour are the driving force behind hostilities. Feud is governed by norms that limit the class of possible expiators and the appropriateness of response. There are culturally acceptable means for making temporary or permanent settlements of hostility.

This description is most useful, and Miller's chapter on 'Feud, vengeance and the disputing process' in his book *Bloodtaking and Peacemaking* is very important. However there are points that are worth discussing.

Miller considers groups to be the ultimate opponents but there does not seem to have been any impediments to individuals initiating feuds between themselves. Certainly, even if it is accepted that a feud might arise in the first place as an altercation between two individuals, it has nevertheless to be admitted that in most cases groups would sooner or later begin to form on the opposing sides of the dispute. In Iceland this would take place at the very least when the *goðar* or *goðorðsmenn*, meaning the chieftains, who had the individuals in question as followers, decided to take some part in the matter. Yet it must also be accepted that disputes arising between individuals often turned into feuds without any associated groups being formed.[5]

Some scholars who make use of Miller's description take it that the opening move of a feud is the first shedding of human blood, in other words the first killing, and Miller gives reason to think it was so. This would also be much in keeping with what Boehm's and Black-Michaud's explanation. Boehm considers vengeance killing to be one of the most essential prerequisites for

---

4   Miller 1990, pp. 180-181.
5   See for instance the Saga of Egil Skallagrímsson, chap. 80-84.

feud.[6] According to some traditional conceptions of the process, it is generally held that the commencement of a feud between two parties is contingent upon the execution of a killing in retribution for a previous death. In other words the feud starts from the second killing. For me, the first killing would not necessarily mark the beginning either. Of course at the initial stage the opponents in Iceland must have had a row, where some abusive words were uttered, and possessions could have been damaged before any killings took place. However this is usually seen by scholars as some kind of introductory phase, not the real thing. I find it worthwhile trying to make a distinction between a feud and a bloodfeud, the latter beginning as soon as the first human blood is shed: a man wounded, not necessarily killed. The question arises whether it is possible to pin-point exactly when a feud in this sense begins, i.e. not only bloodfeud, and be sure that it has some distinctive features other than human blood which would make it different from disputes generally. I will come to that.

Black-Michaud, it should be noted, places special emphasis on the fact that his account relates only to societies with unilineal kinship structures, in which rights were inherited only through the male line, and where men claimed descent from a common forefather.[7] In such societies, men's duties of revenge were connected with the family and the kinship group alone. Vengeance was only to be directed at men in another family or kinship group, which would usually have been resident in a different district or region. It is easy to understand that for instance North African or Middle East kinship groups (being tribes or clans) could keep on feuding for ever, so to speak, because a resolution was not all that important to them. Each kinship group lived in a territory aside from other groups and interaction was not so common. When clashes between groups occurred they strengthened the ties within the groups and made it clear who 'we' were and who 'the others' were. Should a violent quarrel flare up between men within one group or family, it was not allowed to develop but was suppressed immediately.[8] Records show that this was the

---

6   Christopher Boehm, *Blood Revenge. The Enactment and Management of Conflict in Montenegro and Other Tribal Societies*, Philadelphia 1991, p. 194, cf. pp. 52-53. The emphasis of Boehm and Miller on bloodshed is readily apparent in the titles of their respective works, *Blood Revenge* and *Bloodtaking and Peacemaking*.

7   Jacob Black-Michaud, *Feuding Societies*, Oxford 1975, p. 51, n.

8   *Ibid.*, pp. 51-52, 117-18, 229. Here Black-Michaud is largely in accordance with E.L Peters, cf. Peters' foreword in *Feuding Societies*, pp. xi-xiii. Cf. also M.J.L. Hardy, *Blood-feuds and the Payment of Blood Money in the Middle East*, Leiden 1963.

situation for example among the people of Montenegro in the nineteenth century.[9]

The main observable difference between feuds as they are enacted in societies with unilineal and bilateral kinship structures is that the rules of feud in 'bilateral societies' obtain not only in respect of killing but also in every sort of conflict involving the use of violence. It is in unilineal societies that feud is first and foremost simply a matter of blood vengeance, of slaying.

Iceland was neither tribal nor territorial; it was a 'bilateral society' where followers of different chieftains would live side by side. A friendly neighbourhood was vital for the farmers and peasants but enmity could easily arise and turn into more serious hostility. At the stage of bloodfeud the community would be rather concerned since more and more people were called on to participate. Neighbours would join opposite groups and become adversaries. A solution became imperative, 'men of good will' and intermediaries would turn up and bring about a truce to make it possible to seek a settlement. This would make Gluckman's formulation or thesis on 'the peace in the feud' fit in well for the Icelandic free-state.[10]

Another point is that Miller has been understood as saying that feud in Iceland could be a long-term phenomenon. Miller refers to Black-Michaud who says that feud by nature was interminable, and he also mentions that Boehm does not agree and is of the opinion that feud involves the possibility of resolution. Miller thinks the Icelandic model is distinctly closer to Boehms formulation. He seems to think however that the Icelandic feuds as a rule lasted for a long time, even though they usually were solved in the end.[11]

The only long-lasting feud in Iceland that I know of is the one in the saga of the people in Laxárdal-valley, which went on for some 26 years. I take it that feuds usually only lasted for a few years, some even shorter, which I shall explain further. However what makes things a little complicated is the fact that sooner or later the chieftains in Iceland took the lead in all major feuds and made them their own. Two competing chieftains would keep their hostilities alive by constantly looking for bones of contention, thus making life troublesome for their opponent. But even though they took over feuds from peasants, wishing to keep their contention alive for some time, they

---

9 Boehm 1991, cf. also Keith F. Otterbein, "Feuding - dispute resolution or dispute continuation?", *Reviews in Anthropology*, 12, 1985, pp. 75-83. See p. 75, 'those within the same clan do not feud'.

10 Max Gluckman, "The peace in the feud", *Past and Present*, 8, 1955, pp. 1-14.

11 Miller 1990, pp. 186-187, on reasons for interminability in Iceland. Halsall 1998, p. 20, says that feud was 'a long-term phenomenon'.

were compelled to settle each case, which would be solved by intermediaries or even arbitrators. However, for decades the chieftains might continue taking over new cases of feuds which were settled sooner or later. We could call these long-lasting hostilities of two chieftains a feud, but perhaps this is not helpful. Each individual case between them could develop into a real feud but the hostilities as a whole in the long run are probably better termed 'political strife', or something like that, not a case of feud in the real sense.

So, what is a case of feud? In view of the foregoing observations, and inspired by Black-Michaud, Boehm, Byock and Miller, I shall permit myself to describe a case of feud as follows:

1. Feud is a state existing between two individuals or groups.
2. The initial dispute may arise from insignificant causes but honour compels people to react unrestrainedly, leading to the development of an acrimonious atmosphere between the parties involved.
3. There are clashes between the opposing parties, and the dispute turns into feud when violence is brought into use, with violent acts being perpetrated subsequently by each party in turn.
4. These acts typically involve the damaging of property or livestock, and even personal assaults.
5. The chief characteristic of the feud is that the violence is limited by the fact that the participants repay each other blow for blow, but the level of violence usually escalates gradually.
6. If any individual is killed in the course of these hostilities, leading to the perpetration of a vengeance killing, a bloodfeud may be said to have developed.
7. During the feud the original issue of contention becomes continually less significant as circumstances provide ever more new and pressing matters demanding vengeance.
8. A mutual concern with honour prevents the adversaries from seeking settlement themselves and it is necessary for some third party to intervene in order that the opposing parties may be reconciled.

I would like to point out in the first place that according to this description groups are no prerequisite and, in the second place, that a feud can commence without people being killed or any human blood being shed.

Some students of feud have tried their hand at describing or even defining feud. Hyams, for one, offers what he calls a 'processual definition' according to which he calls 'conflicts between groups of kinsmen and others 'feud' when they are capable of being ended by something that looks like a peace treaty.

They seek redress by way of violent vengeance, often threatened, sometimes actual, but may accept a settlement providing its terms maintain their honour by according with the major norms by which they live'.[12] Hyams obviously leans on Miller's criteria for the feud in Commonwealth Iceland but also, according to his references, other historians of medieval history, foremost Muir for Italy and White for France. In the same article Hyams writes, 'Feud is a continuing conflict over perceived wrong that people need to settle by making peace or the destruction of their enemies ... The peacemaking is at least as important as the acts that start the process, which may not even involve blood'.[13] This seems to be a useful attempt to make a general definition and the mediated settlement is put in its proper place. However one would tend to think that the words on destruction of enemies might be misunderstood. Certainly the meaning must be that such a destruction could turn out to be the last resort; in the beginning it was hardly aimed at, only some redress of perceived wrongs. Hyams does not seem to consider tit-for-tat relations (alternating reactions) and escalation as important components.

Althoff writes on feud in eleventh- and twelfth-century Germany, 'ihr lag vielmehr ein ganzes system von Regeln zu Grunde, das nicht zuletzt darauf ausgerichtet war Gewaltanwendung zu begrenzen, Eskalationen zu erschweren und Bemühungen um die Wiederherstellung des Friedens zu befördern'. He comes to the conclusion that the violence practised in feuds 'nicht auf die Vernichtung des Gegners, sondern auf sein Einlenken zielte'.[14] This is well in keeping with the modern views among scholars of the Icelandic feud, at the outset the aim was to regain one's right and honour, not to destroy one's enemy. But it cannot be denied that medieval feuds could be very violent.

Althoff stresses that the use of violence should be limited, the feud process was subject to norms that had to be heeded. Those norms were intended to compel the enemy to yield and accept claims which were perceived as rightful.

The general opinion among German historians seems to be that feud was all about norms and mediated settlements. I suggest that students of

---

12   Paul R. Hyams, "Nastiness and wrong, rancor and reconciliation", Warren C. Brown and Piotr Górecki (eds.), *Conflict in Medieval Europe. Changing Perspective on Society and Culture*, Aldershot 2003, p. 198. Idem, *Rancor and Reconciliation in Medieval England*, Ithaca 2003, pp. 3-68.

13   Hyams, "Nastiness", 2003, p. 202.

14   Gerd Althoff, "Regeln der Gewaltanwendung im Mittelalter", Rolf Peter Sieferle and Helga Breuninger (eds.), *Kulturen der Gewalt. Ritualisierung und Symbolisierung von Gewalt in der Geschichte*, Frankfurt a.M. 1998, pp. 156, 158.

feud take for instance Althoffs description of feud and add parts of Hyams' description, like honour, and also add components like tit-for-tat or reciprocity and escalation and call this a working description. I think it might benefit further studies.

III

Let's now take two examples of feuds in Iceland. The course of the long lasting feud in the saga of the people of Laxárdal-valley (*Laxdæla saga*) can be set out in a simplified form as follows:

IA.1	Sword stolen from B.		No reaction from B.
IA.2	*Motur* stolen from B.[15]	IB.1	A forcibly locked in for 3 nights
		IB.2	running.
			Land appropriated from A.
IIA	Kjartan killed.	IIB1	Sons of Þórhalla killed.
	Compensation payed.		
		IIB2	Þorkell killed.
		IIB3	Bolli killed
IIIA	Helgi Harðbeinsson killed.	IIIB	Intercession of Snorri goði.
			B pay compensation to A.

So when did the feud start? Did it start when the sons of Þórhalla (Thorhalla) were killed in revenge for Kjartan? Or did it start when Kjartan was killed? Or did it even start earlier?

Here is another example from another saga (Saga of Víga-Glúmr):

A Sigmundr of Þverá and his son Þorkell
B Glúmr and Ástríðr of Þverá

IA	A shift a boundary fence.	IB	A claim B's slaves are guilty of theft.
IIA	Bulls driven onto B's in-field.	IIB	Bulls beaten and driven back onto A's in-field.
IIIA	A insult B openly. Hay mown illicitly on the field *Vitazgjafi*.	IIIB	Glúmr kills Sigmundr.

---

15 The *motur* mentioned was a piece of jewelry.

Glúmr was an aspiring young chieftain and his success in this case made the chieftain family, the Esphælings, rather concerned and they tried to sue Glúmr for the killing of Sigmundr, but to no avail. Finally they were compelled by the friends of both to reconcile with Glúmr. They were displeased of course and sought the first opportunity to make life difficult for Glúmr. For some 42 years Glúmr and the Esphælings went on competing for honour and followers, new cases turned up, some of them typical feuds like this one.

This first feud of Glúmr did not involve many persons. There are some clear examples to be found of only two persons feuding in the sagas, as mentioned above.[16]

IV

As I have shown, in a bilateral society like in Iceland the mechanisms of feud could be at work before any human blood was spilled. Does this mean, for instance, that the feud in the first example had already commenced before Kjartan was killed and in the second before Glúmr killed Sigmundr? This calls for some discussion of the concepts feud, *Blutrache*, customary vengeance and vendetta.

Sawyer describes feud in Western and Northern Europe in terms of revenge and compensation or the archaic system of paying/receiving *wergeld* between kins even though he feels the solidarity of kin-groups has been exaggerated. He writes, 'The truth is that throughout medieval Europe, from the sixth century to the fifteenth, in very different conditions, revenge and compensation were accepted as legitimate'. He warns against using the concept in some extended sense and finds the expression 'feuding-society' misleading.[17]

The constructive criticism of Halsall is also along those lines, he is of the opinion that the early medieval concept of feud should be confined to its legal meaning, and finds the expression 'customary vengeance' most fitting for feud in this sense. He writes, 'Here, compensation is an alternative to vengeance; the threat of vengeance serves to bring about a legal settlement through compensation'. He accepts that customary vengeance could sometimes drag on and turn into a tit-for-tat conflict which could be called 'feud' but he

---

16 Both of the examples above come from the so-called family sagas. The so-called contemporary sagas also are abundant in this respect with corresponding examples of feud, for instance Sturlusaga in the Sturlunga-collection.

17 Sawyer 1987, pp. 27-38, esp. 35-36 and 27.

suggests that the expression 'tactical violence' might be a more appropriate one. And he feels that scholars like Wallace-Hadrill have made up 'feuds' out of cases of vengeance and introduced unfounded attempts at mediation and settlements, outside of courts, as the final aim.[18]

As I see it, Sawyer and Halsall accept feud in its narrower meaning as *Blutrache* but reject the more extensive meaning. German historians sometimes refer to the Italian vendetta which they generally take to be very similar to *Blutrache* (in German literally 'blood revenge'). This is how Brunner understood it and seems still to be the dominant view. In other words *Blutrache* is seen 'als Anschlag auf Leib und Leben von Personen der feindlicher Sippe'.[19] Or put more simply, *Blutrache* means that one person killed another in revenge for manslaughter.[20] It is important to keep in mind the difference between the German *Fehde* and *Blutrache* (Totschlagsfehde). Althoff for instance writes, 'Fehden begannen traditionell damit, daß man Land und Leute des Gegners schädigte, um ihn selbst zum Nachgeben zu zwingen'.[21] Which is not the same as *Blutrache*. *Fehde* or feud is about claiming ones rights, often in a violent manner but without necessarily any spilling of human blood. *Blutrache* is about killing a person in revenge for manslaughter or something equally serious. Such *Blutrache* could turn into repeated killings of people and would in that case probably be more aptly called *Totschlagsfehde* or bloodfeud.

Let us see what Muir and Dean have to say about the medieval Italian vendetta. Muir writes, 'The usual modern distinction between *vendetta*, seen as a finite conflict between individuals, and *feud*, an interminable one between groups, obscures the manifold Renaissance use of the word *vendetta*'.[22] The second part on feud is of course unsuitable for Western and Northern Europe, as I have tried to show above, feud in these regions was not interminable

---

18   Halsall 1998, pp. 22, 28-9.
19   Christine Reinle, "Von Austreten, Landzwang und mutwilliger Fehde: Zur bäuerlichen Fehdeführung in Altbayern im Spätmittelalter", *Zeitschrift für Geschichtswissenschaft*, 52, 2004, pp. 109-131, esp. 110-111.
20   Andreas Widmer, '*daz ein bub die eidgenossen angreif'. Eine Untersuchung zu Fehdewesen und Raubrittertum am Beispiel der Gruber-Fehde (1390-1430)*, Bern 1995, p. 101 however states: 'Blutrache (Totschlagsfehde), die allen Bevölkerungsschichten zugänglich war, aber nur zur Ahndung eines Totschlags und einiger weiterer 'todeswürdiger' Verbrechen geübt werden konnte ... Dazu können etwa schwere Körperverletzungen, tödliche Beleidigungen oder Notzuchtsvergehen zählen'.
21   Gerd Althoff, "Schranken der Gewalt. Wie gewalttätig war das 'finstere Mittelalter'?", Horst Brunner (ed.), *Der Krieg im Mittelalter und in der Frühen Neuzeit: Gründe, Begründung, Bilder, Bräuche, Recht*, Wiesbaden 1999, pp. 1-24, quotation p. 7.
22   Edward Muir, *Mad Blood Stirring. Vendetta and Factions in Friuli during the Renaissance*, Baltimore 1993, p. xxiii.

and not necessarily between groups. Muir tells us that seeing vendetta as 'a finite conflict between individuals' is unsatisfactory and not in keeping with the understanding among contemporaries in late medieval Italy. According to him vendetta concerned both individuals *and* groups. Investigating the people of Friuli, Muir tells us that ties between individuals within the groups (clans) were usually loose, they might call themselves relatives or kin but blood affinities were often faked. The leaders stressed the honour of the group (clan and faction) which had to be defended, and solidarity was appreciated.[23]

The general picture is that during a state of vendetta in an Italian republic, a town or township, where some sort of democracy or oligarchy was prevailing, there might be a conflict with another group and justice was claimed. At a certain point temperance was exhausted, one of the groups was enraged, blood was boiling and they resorted to violence. Someone in the other group was killed in a public place and the executioners declared they were responsible for the homicide. Publicity thus distinguished the vendetta killing. The other group retaliated and men were killed in an alternating way. The common aim of each of the groups was to secure justice for themselves, and the groups replaced social institutions which might have otherwise taken care of these matters. The conflict had to be settled and in this sense the vendettas were finite.

Dean says that historians outline the vendetta as a product of the family, clan or *consorteria* and that an offended family would retaliate, preferably render a corresponding wound in the same place on the same day of the year. Vendetta was seen as 'private justice'. Dean goes on and says that vendetta was found in conflicts between many social groups and between individuals, cities or armies, not just between families. He writes, 'vendetta does clearly stand out in all the sources as vengeance for *specific* injury: vendetta is an event or a response to an event, not a state of continuous animosity'.[24] However, as Dean points out, the groups, with regard to the contentions between them, referred to traditions of old origin, but those stories usually were fabricated or constructed, based on selective memory. He argues there were at least four types of vendettas in late medieval Italian chronicles. One type is often entwined with war and Dean suggests that historians who like to keep war and feud apart should realise this. Another type entwines warfare and outrage of female sexual honour. A third context 'comes with the escalating feud' as he writes, feuds start in a petty exchange and lead to collateral vengeance and

---

23 *Ibid.*, pp. xxiv-xxv.
24 Trevor Dean, "Marriage and Mutilation: Vendetta in Late Medieval Italy", *Past and Present*, 157, 1997, pp. 3-36, quotation p. 15.

even the expulsion of one family. Finally, vendetta is an 'equal and equivalent retaliation against an attacker'. The last type reminds one of *Blutrache* but the rules of *wergeld* are missing. The distinction Dean makes between vendettas and feuds is interesting, he writes for instance, 'vendetta and feuds were part of the aristocratic faction-fighting that flourished in republican cities'.[25] What Muir calls vendetta between two competing groups within towns and townships, Dean would probably in compliance with his sources see as both vendetta, i.e. retaliations in particular cases, and sometimes ongoing feud, but he stresses that the word vendetta was used by contemporaries for all of this.

How would we define medieval Italian vendetta? It seems complicated, one side of it resembles *Blutrache* (as understood by Brunner), another side more the feud of Commonwealth Iceland. Brögger writes for Southern Italy in modern times, 'This process of revenge and counter revenge ... is locally called vendetta even if blood vengeance is not the outcome', which makes vendettas look even more like feuds of Commonwealth Iceland. Brögger writes further, 'Once the vendetta is started, the original issue at stake is almost forgotten and through revenge and counter-revenge an increasing tension is built up between the parties. Unless the conflict is somehow solved, blood vengeance may be triggered off'.[26] According to this, alternation and escalation of violence are implicit features of vendetta which makes it very different from *Blutrache*. On the other hand, Dean has examples from Italy which show how the authorities in the late medieval times were trying through legal means to confine vendetta to one counter-revenge killing, and then only killing the original attacker.[27] This seems to indicate once more that the Italian vendettas could be different, sometimes resembling feuds like in Commonwealth Iceland, in other instances resembling *Blutrache* or customary vengeance.

V

This comparison has shown that in the Italian vendettas we have got feud-like vendettas and *Blutrache*-like vendettas, both of which we could call feuding.

---

25 Dean 1997, pp. 18, 21.

26 Jan Brögger, "Conflict resolution and the role of the bandit in peasant society", *Anthropological Quarterly*, 41, 1968, pp. 228-240, quotation p. 231.

27 Trevor Dean, "Violence, vendetta and peacemaking in Late Medieval Bologna", *Criminal Justice History*, 17, 2002, pp. 1-17.

What is interesting to me is to see the resemblance between feud in Iceland and the feud-like vendettas of Italy and Corsica.

Our example from the island of Corsica dates from the nineteenth century. Traditionally a bilateral system of inheritance obtained on the island. As in Iceland, neighbours were not necessarily related to one another as a result of the fact that families did not dwell within discrete territories. There was no strong central government in Corsica until the French began to tighten their grip on the island at the end of the eighteenth century; at the same time they attempted to put an end to feuding, but for a long time these efforts met with little success. It is often thought that only clans or families took part in feuding in Corsica, but this view is actually incorrect, for once a feud was commenced the parties that became involved formed in an *ad hoc* fashion, just as in Iceland, and they might consist of relatives and unrelated neighbours alike.[28] One example will be cited here, drawn from Stephen Wilson's work on feud in Corsica.[29] The case can be traced right back to its roots:

Feud between family groups X and Y in Arbellara in Corsica:
IA. Y claims X has shown unseemly behaviour in church (grimacing at Y).
IB. March 1826, three bulls owned by X slain (perpetrators unknown).
IIA. X responds (believing Y responsible), killing two bulls and a cow.
IIB. Y responds: three bulls owned by X killed, three seriously injured. Intercession and peace.

Comments: There is an obvious escalation of violence at stage IIB. Mediation is immediately commenced in order to prevent further escalation, implying that society at large considers the matter as a serious dispute, a feud, and not simply a quarrel. Peace is restored, temporarily.

III. May 1827, Y breaks the peace, killing bulls and horses belonging to X; X shoots at a member of Y but misses.
IV. October 1827, Y kills bulls belonging to X; X poisons six of Y's bulls.

---

28 Anne Knudsen, "Internal Unrest: Corsican Vendetta – A Structured Catastrophe", *Folk*, 27, 1985, pp. 65-87, esp. pp. 69-70.
29 Stephen Wilson, *Feuding, Conflict and Banditry in Nineteenth-Century Corsica*, Cambridge 1988.

During November the local mayor tries to make peace; acrimony and hatred prevail, men dare not go out after dark. The mayor plans to bring in soldiers in order to stop the fighting.

V. In 1835 'the feud entered a new phase' (according to Wilson).

Comment: Stephen Wilson refers to this conflict as a 'feud', but he does not indicate at what point he considers a feud to have commenced. It should be noted that at this point there has still been no shedding of human blood.

Y proposes a wedding. X refuses, on account of the attacks on the family's animals, for which Y is held responsible.

The feud continues for a long time.[30]

At this point it seems reasonable to describe the origins and characteristics of feuds in societies with bilateral customs of inheritance as follows:

Feud involves the mutual reciprocation of violence between two parties (whether individuals or groups), which take turns at inflicting violence on each other, or on each other's property. An alternated sequence of at least three acts of violence must have taken place before a state of feud may be said to have developed.[31] The violence escalates as time passes.

According to this description, a state of feud was occasioned in Arbellara with the carrying out of the attack noted at stage IIB.

In her work on feud in Corsica, Anne Knudsen has suggested that such disputes are initiated when people answer some uncustomary act of provocation in a way which is similarly uncustomary, contravening the proprieties of normal life. At this point the rules of feud come into effect. Thus in Knudsen's view feud commences not with the sequence 'provocation-response-provocation (IA-IB-IIA), but with a simple reciprocal exchange, 'provocation-response' (IA-IB).[32] In these instances no killing found place but to be sure killings did often occur in feuds in Corsica.

Similar correspondences with the patterns of feuding apparent in Icelandic sources may also be noted in examples from other areas. Jan Brögger relates an account of an individual in Southern Italy who made charcoal for his

---

30   *Ibid.*, pp. 17-21.
31   Regarding this tripartite sequence see further Leopold Pospisil, "Feud", *International Encyclopedia of the Social Sciences*, 5, 1968, pp. 389-393. Cf. Rolf Kuschel, *Vengeance is Their Reply. Bloodfeuds and Homicides on Bellona Island*, 1, Copenhagen 1988, p. 18.
32   Knudsen 1985, pp. 78-82.

neighbours.[33] On one occasion this man cut down trees right on the boundary of his land, giving rise to a quarrel. The owner of the neighbouring lands demanded that he be given charcoal in compensation for his loss, but the charcoalburner refused. They argued, and the landowner was so offended and enraged that he stole some rabbits belonging to the charcoalburner. The latter retaliated, destroying his opponent's vinyard. Unable to tolerate this act, the landowner killed the charcoalburner. Despite this conclusion to the affair, it should be noted that vendetta in Southern Italy according to Brögger is to be equated with feud, but not necessarily with bloodfeud.[34] Additionally, we may note that familial groups were not necessarily implicated in vendetta. Brögger assumes in his discussion that the alternation and escalation of violence are implicit features of vendetta. Unfortunately he does not identify the point at which the vendetta actually begins, but another of his examples is illuminating in this regard. In this case, a man borrowed money in order to build a house but he never set about the work and nor did he pay back the loan. The money-lender told the debtor's father that if he did not get his money back he would shoot his son, and the father complied accordingly. Although vendetta did not develop here, Brögger implies that one would have commenced had the demands for money been refused.

VI

It has been made clear in the preceding discussion that before a state of feud (feud-like vendetta) may rightly be said to have developed, an alternating sequence of three violent acts must have been carried out, designated here IA, IB, and IIA. This has been referred to as the process of alternation, according to which the opponents in a feud took turns, just as the players in a game of chess would do. The existence of this phenomenon demonstrates that during feud men acted in compliance with certain predetermined rules. At the stage IA, it will usually, but not always, be clear whether or not the conflict was the result of a deliberate act of provocation. This depends upon whether there was already some enmity extant between the parties before the point of violence was reached. In some cases those who suffered some act of provocation had borne no previous grudge against the party responsible, and they were consequently

---

33 Brögger 1968.
34 *Ibid.*, p. 231. Note that 'vendetta' is also often used to refer to feuding in Corsica. Cf. e.g. Anne Knudsen 1985.

uncertain as to the explanation. Three courses of action were open to them: a) they could attempt to settle the dispute by themselves or with the assistance of another party (perhaps in Iceland a *goði* who was prepared to deal with the matter); b) they could retaliate violently; c) they could do nothing. It is likely however that in most circumstances it was necessary to take any act of provocation (IA) seriously and to retaliate unhesitatingly (IB) in order to avoid the appearance of cowardice and a corresponding loss of prestige. Blows and other physical assaults were always to be repaid in kind. In other cases, for instance if possessions had been damaged, or if livestock had been injured or killed, it was possible that the victim of the initial act of provocation (IA) would prefer to receive compensation rather than to respond violently (IB). In this situation there was however a risk of being refused compensation and consequently being publicly shamed.[35] It was also possible to simply be evasive if the nature of the initial provocation (IA) was uncertain. This was the course we find in *Laxdæla saga*, as shown above, Kjartan Ólafsson follows the advice of his father and does nothing in response to the initial provocation of the Laugamenn. In cases where group (or individual) A has serious intent in the initial act of provocation, but group (or individual) B does not react, IA.1 and IA.2 etc. may occur before the enaction of IB (although in the affair between Kjartan and the Laugamenn this repetition elicited a commensurate bipartite response in IB.1 and IB.2). On the other hand, should B respond immediately (IB), it is made clear straight away in the reaction of A whether or not this is to be a matter of feud. If enmity rather than moderation now governs men's actions and the first act of recrimination (IB) is answered with some new provocation (IIA), then an unambiguous state of feud may be said to have arisen. If IB is not answered with a new act of provocation, it may be accepted that IA was unintentional or an unmalicious act not intended to bring about conflict. The opponents are content to remain even, and feud is not incurred.

In accordance with the foregoing outline, feud may be said to have come into being at stage IIA. All things considered it is probably natural to assume, however, that a state of feud exists already after IB if it is apparent in the account that there was some state of enmity (in Icelandic *fæð*, *kali* or *óþykkja*) extant between the adversaries prior to the first occurrence of any serious conflict or violence (IA). As has been seen, this is a common enough situation

---

35   In *Droplaugarsonasaga* (in Jón Jóhannesson (ed.), *Austfirðinga sögur*, Reykjavík 1950), chap. 5, this befell Þorgeirr when he requested compensation from Þórðr of Geirólfseyri. See Byock's discussion of this episode in *Feud in the Icelandic Saga*, pp. 39-40.

and examples are abundant in the sagas. One may refer furthermore to the individual episodes in the ongoing feud identified previously in *Víga-Glúms saga*.[36]

The difference between a feud and a conflict is not always clear. The norms of the feud probably were special and did not apply to all conflicts. People had to know when a conflict had turned into a feud because then the norms of feud would apply. The German Fehde-rules, as known from the High Middle Ages, seem to reveal the necessity to know when the rules of feud were applicable and when they were not. A conflict could turn into a feud but it was only considered to become a feud through a declaration or a formal announcement (*Fehdeabsage, diffidatio*, defiance) and then the parties knew that the rules of feud were applicable. This usually meant, for instance, the upheaval of all social intercourse between the parties involved.

In one interesting case in an Icelandic saga a dispute continues for some time between two poets with an exchange of verses and insults, and finally one of them kills the other. Alison Finlay has termed this dispute a feud.[37] Here we find the mechanisms of feud, the opponents act in turns and an escalation is obvious, the verses get grimmer and the insults gradually more serious, and the opponents keep scores. The case was treated by a law court at this oral stage. Obviously this was a feud, not because one of the opponents killed the other in the end. It was a feud because of the acting in turns, the escalation, and the score-keeping.

I take it for granted that many people find it difficult to imagine feuds without any corpses, or not even shedding of human blood. I have made a distinction above between a feud and a bloodfeud, a bloodfeud beginning when, after some escalation, men are being hurt or killed by their opponents. Feud in the broader sense is about claiming rights and is characterised by action in turns and escalation when claims were rejected. It is not the same as *Blutrache* which usually involves two killings, one in revenge. However, the feud can turn into *Blutrache* and the word 'feuding' can comprise both meanings. Thus *Blutrache*

---

36   Disputes between the Ljósvetningar and the Möðruvellingar also culminated in feud and blood vengeance as did the disputes between Guðmundr the Wealthy and Valla-Ljótr. In both cases this was the consequence of an older enmity existing between the adversaries. Cf. Björn Sigfússon (ed.), *Ljósvetninga saga*, Reykjavík 1940, p. 69, and *Valla-Ljóts saga* (in Jónas Kristjánsson (ed.), *Eyfirðinga saga*, Reykjavík 1956, p. 242 (cf. p. 237). The dispute between Halli and Ljótr was not in itself a feud, but a bloodfeud was initiated when Guðmundr avenged the killing of Halli.

37   Alison Finlay, "Nið adultery and feud in Bjarnar saga Hítdælakappa", *Saga-Book*, 23, 1991, pp. 158-178.

or customary vengeance is feuding in the more narrow sense and often the final stage of a feud. Feud can also continue as bloodfeud with many killings.

VII

In our discussion of feuding so far we have made a distinction between a feud-like vendetta and a *Blutrache*-like vendetta, and take it that such a distinction was made in the High Middle Ages. What about the Early Middle Ages in this respect? *Faida* of early medieval times is the same word as *feud* and seems usually to mean *Blutrache*, which we would then count as feuding in the narrower sense. Is it possible to find a *faida* in the sense of a feud-like vendetta in the Early Middle Ages, in other words feud in the broader sense? The German word *Fehde* has its root in, or is of the same stem as, the Germanic *faida*, which first occurs in 7th century Germanic laws, meaning enmity (hostility).[38] There is no denying that *faida* at this time could mean not only enmity but also the right to retaliate for manslaughter (bloodfeud, *Blutrache*). However it is not at all clear that its legal meaning is also freedom to claim one's rights through the threat and execution of violence. It seems to be in place to ask: Would historians be well advised to refrain from using the word *faida* for the Early Middle Ages except in the narrow meaning of *Blutrache*?

It is difficult to see that *faida* in the Germanic laws means anything more than enmity, generally speaking, and sometimes simple vengeance in a more specific sense. It seems to be generally believed that the aspect of claiming rights through the threat of violence or private execution of it does not occur in the legal texts, let alone the possibility of some mediated settlement as a part of the *faida*.[39] So far the laws. On the other hand a close reading of the classical case of Sichar (in 585-8) as told by Bishop Gregor (Gregory) of Tours († 594) seems to be rewarding.[40] It indicates a feud in this sense at the time,

---

38 According to Elsbeth Orth, *Die Fehden der Reichstadt Frankfurt am Main im Spätmittelalter. Fehderecht und Fehdepraxis im 14. und 15. Jahrhundert*, Wiesbaden 1973, its first known occurrence is in Edictum Rothari in 643. It goes like this, 'faida, hoc est inimicitia'. Cp. Alexander Patschovsky, "Fehde im Recht. Eine Problemskizze", Christine Roll (ed.), *Recht und Reich im Zeitalter der Reformation. Festschrift für Horst Rabe*, Frankfurt a.M. 1997, pp. 145-178, esp. p. 157.

39 See examples of this in Patschovsky 1997.

40 The text is edited with translation in Rudolf Buchner (ed.), *Gregor von Tours. Zehn Bücher Geschichten*, 2, Darmstadt 1974, pp. 153-157, 257-259. A translation is also to be found in Karl Kroeschell, *Deutsche Rechtsgeschichte*, 1, Reinbek 1972, pp. 48-50. A close reading of the text is to be found in Ekkehard Kaufmann, "Die Fehde des Sichar", *Juristische Schulung. Zeitschrift*

i.e. implying freedom to claim ones rights through an act of violence. Would we be reading too much into it by trying to interpret it as a case of feud in this sense? One of the problems with this case is that at the outset there are no claims for the redressing of injustice, a killing is the motivator. Most likely there was some tension in the air. A servant of a priest is killed without any reason given and Sichar as a friend of the priest (ties of *amicitia*) seems to be intending to retaliate for that but has to flee because of a brawl. What might have become simple bloodfeud or *Blutrache* turns into something more. The adversaries of Sichar, under the leadership of Austregisel, kill some of his followers and carry off some goods he had left.

Now an interesting turn of events takes place, a court, *iudicium civium*,[41] finds Austregisel, the leading adversary of Sichar, guilty of homicide and theft and he is sentenced to pay fines. However a few days later a settlement had been reached whereby Sichar is to receive compensation and forgo further vengeance.[42] Wallace-Hadrill does not point out to his readers that this intervention of a legal body of judges and the settlement which followed, probably reached through some intermediaries, did turn this blood-revenge (*Blutrache*), or attempt to take vengeance for manslaughter, into a real feud. Our task as readers of his article is to realise this by keeping in mind the third part of his description of feud, i.e. about the settlement, based on Gluckman's theory on 'peace in the feud'.[43]

Next something unexpected happened, at least unexpected to those who are not familiar with the common procedure of feuds, as in Corsica or Iceland. A few days after the settlement was reached Sichar hears that the goods are in the hands of a certain Auno and others, whom he kills, and takes much property. Wallace-Hadrill does not tell us why he did this. A comparison with other feuding societies suggests that Sichar had to reclaim the goods himself, there were no authorities to do this for him. He was backed up by the *iudicium civium* and by the settlement, and most likely this meant that the community or the general opinion was favourably disposed towards him. It would have been

---

für Studium und Ausbildung, 1, 1961, pp. 85-87, and Patschovsky 1997, pp. 148-151. Gregor's tale is exceptionally detailed since he knew the case very well. He seems to have begun writing about it before it was fully over.

41 In Buchner 1974 translated as 'Gericht der Bürger' with this comment, 'Offenbar das Grafengericht, in dem die Bürger mitwirkten'.

42 In Buchner 1974 this is understood as Sichar fully accepting the fine but it could also mean a new settlement more agreeable to his adversaries.

43 J.M. Wallace-Hadrill, "The Bloodfeud of the Franks", *The Long-Haired Kings and Other Studies in Frankish History*, London 1962, pp. 121-147.

FEUD AND FEUDING IN THE EARLY AND HIGH MIDDLE AGES

generally realised that in spite of the settlement Sichar still had not completed the task he underwent, to retaliate for his friend. There was no way around it, first of all blood had to be replaced by blood, and then and only then a lasting settlement could be reached. In the eyes of the community Sichar's honour had been stained and the stains could only be fully washed off with blood.[44] After Sichar killed Auno and others and took much property, Bishop Gregor stepped in, trying to prevent more bloodshed. However, the adversaries of Sichar under the leadership of Chramnesind, son of Auno, rejected payment in compensation. They burned Sichar's house, killed some slaves and moveable property was seized. Some judges intervened, probably arbitrators, and a solution was found. Later Sichar offended Chramnesind with a remark, following which the latter killed him and finally avenged his father. He felt that otherwise he would be called a 'weak woman'; the debt of blood had to be paid. He hung Sichar's body on his fence to make the killing public and proclaim its legitimacy.

Some scholars feel that the factor deciding whether or not we call this feud hinges on the affinities between Austregisel and Auno.[45] Austregisel disappeared from the story and we do not know if Auno was his kinsman. To me it does not seem to matter, Auno seems to have been of the same group as Austregisel and was keeping the property of Sichar without any right. Therefore he became the target of Sichar's revenge.

When did this case turn into a feud? It seems to have been deemed feud no later than when the court (*iudicium civium*) intervened and the first settlement was brought about. Up to that point, the clash between Sichar and his adversaries was no feud, only a conflict. But now he had some grounds to make a feud of it, by claiming his right through the threat or execution of violence. An individual could hardly decide that a case was a feud and that the rules of it were applicable if it was in opposition to the general opinion and the community did not accept his grounds for it. For his case to become a feud his claims probably had to find some considerable social backing. German historians stress that feud in high and late medieval Germany had to be founded on some accepted grounds on which claims could be based.[46]

---

44 Auer writes about noble values in the Early Middle Ages, 'Kompromißbereitschaft konnte dengegenüber sehr leicht as Feigheit ausgelegt werden'. Leopold Auer, "Krieg und Fehde als Mittel der Konfliktlösung im Mittelalter", *Bericht über den achtzehnten österreichischen Historikertag*, 1991, p. 232.

45 Sawyer 1987, pp. 30-31. Halsall 1998, p. 24.

46 A. Boockmann, "Fehde, Fehdewesen", *Lexikon des Mittelalters*, 4, 1989, pp. 332-333. Christoph Terharn, *Die Herforder Fehden im späten Mittelalter. Ein Beitrag zum Fehderecht*, Berlin 1994, p. 31. Widmer 1995, p. 110.

Physical violence towards people and self-defence (*Notwehr*) did not necessarily lead to feuding in the broader sense, a 'true feud'. Men were entitled to answer a blow immediately with a blow, or a homicide with a revenge killing which we might call *Blutrache* and therefore feuding in the narrow meaning. This would usually lead to a one-time customary vengeance and stop at that. In the case of Sichar, matters developed differently. Feuding in the broader sense, 'true feuds', could also end up as bloodfeuds, men being killed in turn. Feuds which have thus turned into bloodfeuds usually are the most prominent in the sources, feuds that did not reach such an advanced stage most naturally tend to be neglected or forgotten. When it so happens that legal sources and narratives only mention bloodfeuds we should not take it as proof that no other types of feuding did exist. Comparison shows that the norms of feud usually were not written and probably most often 'true feud' was practiced outside of the judiciary system.

We must ask ourselves whether we are reading too much into the Sichar example when we compare it with other communities, especially the Icelandic and the German of the High Middle Ages. Are we only dealing with a case of *Blutrache* which happened to become more complicated than others, dragging on because of attempts to stop it? What seems to support this is that we do not see any claim put forward in the beginning, a claim which became an apple of discord. There also seems to be some inconsistency or discrepancy between the laws and the episode of Sichar with its claims for compensation, leading to settlements and alleged arbitration. Why do we not find anything similar in the Germanic laws, i.e. claims leading to feuds in the broader sense, only *faida* in the meaning *Blutrache*? In fact it is not certain that the laws are void of any indications for feuds originating in claims for rights. Patschovsky writes that Charlemagne in 789 tried to prohibit feud and sees some hints of property claims when the king, 'Totschlag wegen besitzrechtlicher Ansprüche – so sind Ausdrücke wie *avaritia* und *latrocinium* zu deuten – sowie als Rachehandlung zu unterbinden suchte'.[47] We must also consider that *Blutrache* must usually have originated from some disputes, some of which most likely took on the form of feud through public claims being rejected, alternating reactions, violent actions, and the escalation of physical violence, ending in manslaughter. As mentioned, authors would usually be interested only in killings, leaving out their reasons.

White writes about an interesting collection of dispute-cases in eleventh-century France which he understands as feuds and stresses the point that

---

47   Patschovsky 1997, p. 159.

they are all about asserting or claiming rights through violence. He explains that violence was a way 'of symbolically asserting rights, pressuring enemies to settle by distraining property, recovering rights and expressing righteous anger and justifiable enmity'.[48] White finds it most probable that the tenth century was very similar in this respect when disputing parties could easily bypass regal tribunals.[49] This indicates that we might not be reading too much into the Sichar's case, but more investigations are needed.

VIII

One of the creeds of scholarship has been that archaic *Blutrache* or bloodfeud lingered on in the more uncivilised outskirts of Europe, like Scotland and Corsica, until modern times, while it was eradicated in the more civilised areas. This seems to be wrong, the feud-like vendetta in eighteenth-century Corsica and later seems to have been a counter-part to the feud of Commonwealth Iceland with its alternation and escalation of physical violence but without homicides necessarily taking place.[50] It was feud-like even though it is called vendetta and lingered on in that form in Italy, Germany and Denmark until the sixteenth century. We can even add England and France.[51]

When dictators, or so-called tyrants, took over in the Italian cities, as was quite common, they usually prohibited vendetta. This supports the view that under strong governments vendetta or feud was not tolerated. However, even in republics Dean finds the tendency to keep vendettas in check and confine them to one retaliation and not more, in other words make them *Blutrache*-like. This is a trend found in England and Norway of the thirteenth century, the authorities were willing to eradicate feud-like vendettas but tolerate the ones that were *Blutrache*-like. There was a common trend it seems in many countries to restrict feuds and retaliation and it is tempting to relate this not only to the growing power of the secular authorities but also to the peace-movement of the church.

---

48   Stephen D. White, "Debate. The 'feudal revolution'", *Past and Present*, 152, 1996, pp. 205-223, quotation p. 212.
49   *Ibid.*, pp. 219-220.
50   Wilson 1988.
51   Stuart Carroll, "The Peace in the Feud in Sixteenth- and Seventeenth-Century France", *Past and Present*, 178, 2003, pp. 74-115. Howard Kaminsky, "The Noble Feud in the Later Middle Ages", *Past and Present*, 177, 2002, pp. 55-83.

Does a definition or a description of feud-like vendettas, which is applicable for the period 1050-1500, also apply to earlier times? Reuter warns against projecting or extrapolating the almost ritualised German feud of the fourteenth and fifteenth centuries back to the eleventh century. He writes that we should be careful 'bei der Annahme einer allzu formalisierten, regelgebundenen Fehdeführung im 11. Jahrhundert'. However he comes to the conclusion that the word *iniuria* or injustice was in the eleventh century the standard expression for 'eine Beleidigung, die zur Fehdeführung berechtigt'. The conflicts were feud-like with arson and plundering, reminiscent of later periods.[52] I do not know of any account of how the formal feud of the Late Middle Ages came into being or what the feud that became formalised was like. It seems to be the general opinion that this formalising-process took place in the eleventh century under the auspices of the church in some collaboration with the king.

Dilcher has explained how Burchard, bishop of Worms, in the years 1023-5 ardently turned against the feud of some peasants. Two groups, called *familias*, had been killing each other and this conflict is termed *faida* in the sources. A settlement was arranged but the king demanded that *wergeld* should be paid. This *faida* is similar to *Blutrache* and seems to have turned into bloodfeud which the bishop could not tolerate and obviously wanted to eradicate. This episode concerns serfs, but on the other hand it does not tell us what the situation was like in this respect among the free peasants, let alone the knights and the nobles.[53]

Did king and church try to confine the feuding of peasants to *Blutrache* only? Can we take it that peasants in early medieval Western Europe were feuding in the broader sense of the word, claiming their rights through acts of violence? Orth seems to think they did, at least in the German speaking regions, and contends that while the peasants in the 9th century lost their right of feuding and only were allowed the right of *Blutrache*, those who kept the full right of carrying arms could keep on feuding without any restrictions. This is how the *Ritterfehde* came into being, she states, and it came to be concerned with property, not people. She goes on and says that the feud was modified and shaped under the impact of the ideas of Gottesfrieden from the tenth century

---

52 Timothy Reuter, "Unruhestiftung, Fehde, Rebellion, Widerstand: Gewalt und Frieden in der Politik der Salierzeit", S. Weinfurter and H. Seibert (eds.), *Die Salier und das Reich*, 3, Sigmaringen 1992, pp. 297-325, esp. pp. 300, 306, 312-13.

53 Gerhard Dilcher, "Mord und Totschlag im alten Worms. Zu Fehde, Sühne und Strafe im Hofrecht Bischof Burchards (AD 1023/25)", Stephan Buchholz, Paul Mikat and Dieter Werkmüller (eds.), *Überlieferung, Bewahrung und Gestaltung in der rechtsgeschichtlichen Forschung*, Paderborn 1993, pp. 91-104.

on, and those of the *Landesfrieden* from the eleventh century on.[54] On the other hand, Auer does not mention feuding in the broader sense in the early medieval times and traces the origins of high medieval feud back to *Blutrache* which he maintains was aimed at destroying one's enemy. He concludes that the feud became more 'civilised' (my word) in the High Middle Ages under the influence of the church, and writes, 'In der ritterlichen Fehde ging es nicht mehr um die Tötung des Gegners, sondern um verletzte Ehre oder materielle Ansprüche', like this was a novelty.[55]

We can have a closer look at the peace-movement of the church. The letters of peace did allow feuds which were different from *Blutrache*-feuding. In a stipulation of 1103, it was forbidden to break into another ones house or set it on fire. During the time of peace, arresting someone or damaging his belongings because of pecuniary claims was forbidden. In the same year in another stipulation those who happened to meet their enemies when on the road were allowed to damage them despite the peace, and Nitschke sees these stipulations as indicating feud and takes them to allude to the knights.[56] Wadle also sees them as indicating feuds. There is a similar letter of 1179, and in Barbarossa's letter of 1186 where he prohibits arson there is an exception for judges to allow arsons as a punishment in certain cases which Wadle deems as feuds. He feels that the rules of the *Ritterfehde* must have been in existence at this time and sees them fully fledged, so to speak, no later than 1235.[57]

If *faida* in early medieval times only alluded to *Blutrache* but not feud in a broader sense we can ask: Are we to believe that the *Ritterfehde* grew out of the *Blutrache* but developed into something very different? This is a difficult question which needs more investigation.[58] It is difficult to believe that in times of growing power of the church, which fought for peace, the ecclesiastical authorities would allow a novelty like claiming ones rights through violence.

---

54 Orth 1973, pp. 2-3.

55 Auer 1991, p. 232.

56 August Nitschke, "Der Kampf gegen die Fehde und das Recht: Ein Weg zum Frieden", Heinrich von Stietencron and Jörg Rüpke (eds.), *Töten im Krieg*, Freiburg 1995, pp. 324, 328, 331.

57 Elmar Wadle, "Zur Delegitimierung der Fehde durch die mittelalterliche Friedensbewegung", Horst Brunner (ed.), *Der Krieg im Mittelalter und in der Frühen Neuzeit: Gründe, Begründungen, Bilder, Bräuche, Recht*, Wiesbaden 1999, pp. 82-3, 86.

58 Reinle says that Asmus, in opposition to Brunner, was inclined to see the *Ritterfehde* as a part of the feudal development. Brunner assumed a common origin of *Ritterfehde* and the *Blutrache* of the peasants, 'gemeinsame germanische Wurzel der 'Feindschaft''. Christine Reinle, *Bauernfehden. Studien zur Fehdeführung Nichtadliger im spätmittelalterlichen römisch-deutschen Reich, besonders in den bayerischen Herzogtümern*, Stuttgart 2003, pp. 14-15.

We should keep in mind that the peace movement was trying to restrict something that already existed and therefore the *Ritterfehde* most likely grew out of something older, not as formal. It is probably wrong to see the *Blutrache*, as it is usually defined, as the older stage which became transformed into *Ritterfehde*. Usually the *Blutrache* must have been the outcome of some conflicts and all feuds could end up as bloodfeuds, or *Blutrache* in that sense, whether the feuds of knights or peasants. More studies of *Leutefehde* could turn out to prove that feuds among the commoners, the peasants, farmers and burghers, were of the same origins as the *Ritterfehde* and were shaped by the peace movement which aimed at minimising homicides but accepted an old idea of claiming one's rights through the feud. Bishops and kings seem to have resented the *Blutrache* but otherwise tolerated feud with some restrictions. What I am trying to say is that *Ritterfehde* and *Leutefehde* probably should not only be traced back to the eleventh or twelfth centuries, on the contrary the word *faida* and the comparison with other societies suggests that they are of old roots and once again the case of Sichar comes to mind, and also what Patschovsky and White have to say about feud and claiming or asserting one's right in the Carolingian period (see the chapter VII above, closing section). Since feuds were accepted at the times of the peace-movements it is tempting to conclude that feuds in the broader sense were seen as a customary necessity for people to claim their rights. Even though intervention of the authorities was increased in the eleventh century, central power was weak and threats through violence had to be allowed. The outcome was more formalised feuds which were aimed at reducing killings. This leads me to conclude that it could be worth while to try to find a general definition of feud that could be applied for the earlier period also, an open and flexible one.

The matter is not simple; a case has often been built for the word *faida*, also in the early period, to embody the meaning of claiming one's right through the threat and execution of violence. This of course was the meaning in France, Germany, Iceland, and more countries in the High Middle Ages, and to many it seems logical to view the early period in retrospect in this sense. Anthropologists can easily substantiate this appreciation of the early period with vast material from stateless societies in other regions. According to their findings feuds or something corresponding, meaning the procedure of claiming one's right through violence or the threat of it, was common for simple societies with none-existing or weak central power.

IX

It was suggested here that feuds developed differently in bilateral and unilineal societies. In the former they usually were not long-term phenomena because of the pressing need for settlements. To stress the letting of human blood in such societies is wrong; the feud did not necessarily begin with the shedding of human blood. On the contrary the feud could even start before any men were hurt. Only at the stage of the shedding of human blood would the expression bloodfeud be appropriate. There were two types of feuding, one type with alternation (tit-for-tat), escalating violence which could lead to bloodshed, and settlement; this type is called feud-like vendetta. The other type of feuding is *Blutrache*, which occurred when a person was killed in revenge of another. Both types were found in Italy and were called vendetta. Here the *Blutrache*-type has been termed *Blutrache*-like vendetta. The other type is called feud-like vendetta, and it has been explained here at what stage this type commenced and became different from general conflicts. Usually this occurred in cases of provocation-response-provocation. In circumstances of great enmity, it could also start through provocation and response only. It was imperative to know exactly when the norms of feud were applicable, and in Germany this was determined through laws.

The *Blutrache*-like type of feuding is seen here as the more limited type, sometimes – but not necessarily in all instances – the final phase of the feud-like vendettas. Authorities in many regions tried to confine it to provocation (killing) and response (killing in revenge) only.

It is generally accepted that the *Blutrache*-like vendettas were to be found in early medieval Europe, at least in the north, west and south. It has been suggested here that the feud-like vendettas are also tracing their ancestry back to the Early Middle Ages. The idea behind feud-like vendettas was to claim and gain one's rights and restore one's honour. In any event it is difficult to see the feud-like vendetta of eleventh- and twelfth-century Germany and Iceland as a novelty.

Defining Feud: Talking Points and Iceland's Saga Women

Jesse L. Byock

This article concerns two issues. First, we need a working definition of feud, but such a definition has been lacking for years. My solution is to begin with a series of talking points describing aspects of the feuding process in general and then move to a definition of feud in its Icelandic variety. Secondly, although Iceland's sagas are well-known as stories of conflict, their value for the comparative study of feud has not been fully appreciated. This second factor is especially unfortunate, because the sagas are medieval Europe's most extensive portrayal of everyday life – detailing the operation of feud and conflict resolution. Filled with ethnographic documentation and observation, the sagas offer the international study of feud an unusual opportunity for insight. The stories come directly to us from the Middle Ages and capture a wide range of variability. They reveal cultural codes and normative patterns and extend our understanding of feuding back almost a thousand years. In considering case studies from the sagas, the discussion focuses on roles played by women in saga feud, following action and response as conflict escalates and de-escalates.

Written mostly in the thirteenth century about the earlier Viking Age (ca. AD 800 to 1100), the sagas recount disputes and violent exchanges among Icelanders and sometimes Norwegians. In objective sounding prose, they offer detailed descriptions of private and public life, including stories of small-scale chieftains, farmers, labourers, and women, types of individuals usually excluded from medieval narrative writings. At their core, the sagas are stories of disputes involving farmers and local chieftains. In order to employ these stories for our study, we need to learn theoretically and methodologically how to integrate their information into contemporary analysis of feud, violence, and peacemaking.

Comparative Background

By necessity, historical studies of feud rely on written sources, and this reliance causes its own set of problems. Referring to Wallace Hadrill's earlier analysis of feud within the context of Merovingian and Carolingian society,[1] Paul Fouracre noted that the Frankish sources make untenable many overall conclusions about feuding in seventh- and eighth-century Francia. As he states, 'We have so few examples, [and these are] taken from narratives of such variable quality'.[2] Violence is mentioned widely in the Frankish sources, but Fouracre points out that the lack of detail within these narratives limits their usefulness as documentation of feud. More specifically he writes: 'The small quantity and variable quality of the narrative material mean that it is unusual to be able to follow any conflict for more than two rounds'.[3] Fouracre is quite right, two rounds are very little documentation on which to examine feuding. By asking, he brings into question whether the Frankish sources describe feud or simple vengeance taking. Our question is whether the Icelandic sagas fall under the same cloud. As the discussion progresses, I believe we will agree this is not so.

Taking a cue from Fouracre's observation about 'two rounds', we might ask ourselves the larger question of what is meant by feud as opposed to 'simple' vengeance taking. This is a fitting question because many modern scholars refer to death or injury resulting from vengeance or animosity as feud, but if only after one or two rounds; this is not correct. Feud is more long-lived and there are many facets to the phenomenon of feuding. Could we not benefit from assembling the talking points leading to a serviceable definition? As we see, feud has many aspects.

Talking Points: The Seeds for a Definition of Feud

1. Feud is characterised by animosity leading to exchanges of insults and/ or recurrent violent acts against property or persons. Exchanges involve individuals or groups, the latter often families, clans, or tribes, but also

---

1   J.M. Wallace-Hadrill, "The Bloodfeud of the Franks", *Bulletin of the John Rylands Library*, 41, 1959, pp. 459-487. Reprinted in (and here quoted from) idem, *The Long-Haired Kings and Other Studies in Frankish History*, London 1962, pp. 121-147.

2   Paul Fouracre, "Attitudes towards violence in seventh- and eighth-century Francia", Guy Halsall (ed.), *Violence and Society in The Early Medieval West*, Woodbridge 1998, p. 60.

3   *Ibid.*, p. 61, n. 2.

gangs and political and/or religious groups. Feud is both an ancient and modern phenomenon.

2. Animosities, shame, and claims for revenge may be transmitted to subsequent generations. Injurious exchanges continue until the parties wear themselves out, seek settlement, or are forced into settlement by others.

3. Temporary settlements are often enacted, but lasting peace is more difficult. Peace often requires stifling animosities among individuals and groups that hate each other. Hate and acrimony do not easily end. A basic rule of peacemaking is that one does not make peace with one's friends. In other words, one must trust one's enemies in order to terminate a feud. In many cases it is easier to continue feuding than to trust such people.

4. Time works its effect. In many instances commitment to the animosities of the feud dissipate over time or generations, and the feud ends. Marriages between descendants of previously feuding groups are frequently recorded. They do not always work.

5. At its simplest, feud is a contest involving reciprocal giving and receiving of ill-intended actions, escalating at times to injury and in some instances manslaughter. Feud between individuals or groups exists principally where policing or centralising authorities with the coercive power to intervene do not exist, are too weak to control private exchanges, or openly or tacitly allow conflict.

6. Feud's behavioural crucible is that someone, whether through violence, insult, shaming, dishonouring, etc. wants to hurt someone else. The pain that the perpetrator of the last act inflicts (however justified) hurts the psyche and pride of those that have taken the hit, calling for vengeance. Usually there is the choice of stopping when a fresh act avenges a previous 'wrong'. Hence frequent attempts by mediators, peacemakers, and people of goodwill whose services often become temporary and who are pushed aside if the feud continues. Third party interveners, whether successful or not, frequently gain status, honour, respect, power, access, and wealth as part of the process of mediating. Feud can be costly, generating a redistribution of wealth.

7. If a dispute is settled after a few rounds (however violent), it is not a feud, only a dispute that was settled. Feud is distinguished by the sense of longevity.

8. Feud tends to ratchet up rapidly in the early stages. At this time, the subject of the conflict is often understood in quasi-economic terms, especially competition over the access to resources and the gain or loss of something valuable, including intangibles such as reputation. After several rounds of

insult, reprisal, or violence, the feud carries forward almost on its own, and the importance of initial reasons fade into the background.

9. The basis for conflict and animosity is often understood within a context of honour. Feud can occur between individuals, but bloodfeud, by its nature of wounding or killing individuals, removes participants, leaving vengeance to new parties. New action, even when not initially endorsed by one or even both groups, can set in motion reprisals, propelling conflict through numerous additional rounds.

10. Bloodfeud, or vendetta as it is sometimes called, is restricted, managed conflict, undertaken mostly in situations where open warfare is not tolerated. Examples are inter- and intra-tribal reprisals in simple (primitive and egalitarian) societies and gang conflicts within modern, complex communities, such as cities and within small states and regions such as in parts of the Middle East. Modern political and nationalistic struggles, share many of these aspects. In bloodfeud, the group aspect of animosity is decisive, resulting in acts of self sacrifice and destruction that otherwise might not seem rational.

11. Hatred plays a large role, providing identity and cohesion to the opposing sides by distinguishing 'them' from 'us'. Both sides and on lookers keep score of injuries and dishonour. In traditional societies, the tally-keepers and goaders are often women. The accountings, which are mostly public, take the form of lamentations, tallies, and narrative stories which fuel humiliation and long-term animosity.

12. Although subterfuge often occurs during feud or vendetta, rarely is there complete secrecy surrounding the identities of people who are the source of injurious actions or insults. People know or suspect who is responsible and participants think and speak in terms of retribution for wrongs committed; that is, in-kind punishment according to rules of honour: 'an eye for an eye'.

13. Shaming and the removal of shame are fundamental to feud. The terminology surrounding shame often refers to justice, demands of honour, duty of vengeance, and the sweetness of revenge. Feuding societies or social groups can frequently be labelled shame societies.

14. Feud extends time horizons. The importance of the initial offences diminish. Each new offence becomes a fresh affront in the minds of victims even after considerable time has passed since the last exchange.

15. Feud meanders. Along the way, third parties, often women and other tally-keepers in traditional societies, escalate and de-escalate the action. Such individuals retain memory. They remind of honour and dishonour. Animosity and shame can be inherited, lasting for generations.

16. Historically (something that may be changing in the modern world) men have mostly inflicted the violence. As elsewhere in traditional and tribal societies, gender roles are often distinct. The intervention of women is frequently in the background and sometimes private. It occurs mostly within family or clan context, where women influence the flaring up and dying down of the exchanges through their often ritualised roles in mourning and as guardians of the history and the animosity of the conflict. In these contexts, women tend to act as keepers of the group's honour. Functioning both as escalators and de-escalators, they can play either the role of inciters or peacemakers.

17. Vengeance-seeking is not the same as blood-taking. Beyond seeking blood, vengeance-taking has more options. It is action that satisfies the needs of hatred, the calls of duty, and the debts of loss.

18. The end to feud is often marked by compromise, material compensation, banishment, or even limited manslaughter. Arbitration and negotiation enter the picture, and the language of peacemaking frequently focuses on satisfying honour.

The above talking points contain the raw material for defining feud in a wide variety of cultural situations. They account for a key distinction sometimes forgotten, but worth repeating: feuding is not always bloodfeud. Feuding is a pervasive form of human behaviour that can take place between just two people: two neighbours, two school children, two people at the office. Bloodfeud, however, requires groups, since individuals are violently affected or removed.

Feud in Early Iceland

Turning to Iceland, there are initial observations to be made. Overall, I believe that the most difficult part of ending feud is overcoming hatred. The system of dispute settlement that evolved in Iceland got around this central obstacle by decisively splitting vengeance-seeking from blood-taking. Many societies have done this, but in Iceland, because of its extensive medieval lawbooks and the sagas, we have unusually good detail of the systemisation of dispute settlement, including the possibilities for avoiding, in certain instances, blood-taking. In essence, blood vengeance in Iceland became an option rather than a duty. The honour of vengeance, as described in the following examples, could be achieved in many ways. These observations and the above talking points lead to a definition of feud as practiced in early Iceland.⁴ It is a definition that works, in all or part, for many culture groups.

Icelandic Feud: A Definition

Icelandic bloodfeud was a form of vengeance taking. It involved smouldering animosities leading to repeated reprisals. Score was kept of injuries and killings inflicted on enemies. The taking of vengeance was understood as action that satisfied honour, and exchanges of violence could go on for a very long time, frequently over generations. Each vengeful act engendered a response. Although subterfuge often occurred, rarely was there true secrecy surrounding the general source of the action. The exchanges, which frequently escalated rapidly in the early stages, were rooted in competition, not always but often economic, involving access to natural and human resources. The spilling of blood and the attendant animosity resulting from such actions gave both identity and cohesion to the group by openly distinguishing their enemies — 'them' as opposed to 'us'. With time, the initial offence or offences that set the dispute in motion diminished in importance and may even have been forgotten, but the feud could take on a life of its own. Each new offence remained fresh in the minds of the victims even after considerable time and demanded a response, hence the 'duty' of vengeance and the 'sweetness' of revenge. The exchanges continued until the parties either wore themselves out, sought settlement, were forced by others to settle, or procreated new generations who were not committed to the animosities.

Feuding Saga Women

With the talking points, observations about Icelandic feud, and a definition under our belts, let's briefly return to the question of the Frankish sources before moving to the sagas and Iceland's feuding women. Fouracre's earlier

4   The definition stems from a long discussion one night with Helgi Þorláksson in his kitchen in Reykjavík. See Helgi Þorláksson, "Hvað er blóðhefnd?", Gísli Sigurðsson, Guðrún Kvaran, and Sigurgeir Steingrímsson (eds.), *Sagnaþing: Helgað Jónasi Kristjánssyni sjötugum 10. apríl 1994*, Reykjavík 1994, pp. 389-414, and Byock, *Viking Age Iceland*, London and New York 2001, p. 208. For a discussion of the anthropological and ethno-historical nature of the sagas, see *ibid.*, pp. 21-24, and for feud, pp. 207-247. I thank Phelan Hurewitz and Carmina Ocampo for their close reading of a draft of this article and their valuable suggestions.

stated point about the Frankish sources scarcely reaching 'two rounds' concerns us because the Frankish material, has, since at least the mid-twentieth century, served as a core historical example of feud in early Europe.[5] At this point in time, in the twenty-first century, it would be timely to determine if the limitations concerning the Frankish narratives likewise apply to the Icelandic sagas. I hope to show in the remainder of the article that they do not. At the same time, assessing female roles during Icelandic feud provides a fine entry point for exploring the sagas as sources for social and cultural analysis.[6]

Concerning women in feud, the focus tends to be on the inciter, who goads for blood vengeance. In part this focus springs from the narratives themselves. The sagas are undeniably a literature of conflict in a contentious culture and surely saga authors, as storytellers, sought to make their tales more dramatic in portraying women willing to risk the lives of their male relatives and children. Still, there is room for more balance in our picture of gender roles during Icelandic feud, especially concerning women. Not much attention has been directed to women who influenced peace making, and the following pages offer examples both of inciters and peacemakers in feuds that go on for many rounds and sometimes generations.

'Cold are the councils of women' reads a famous line from *Njal's saga* quoted later in this article.[7] The chieftain Flosi uttered these words in one of the most memorable scenes in the saga, and they mean what they say. The background to that statement is this: a young *goði* or chieftain named Hoskuld is killed by his foster brothers, the sons of the wise but now aged Njal. Njal's sons are jealous of Hoskuld's rising popularity, and it irks them that their father Njal appears to love their foster brother more than he loves them. It annoys these biological sons that Hoskuld was raised in their home as partial settlement of an earlier stage of a smouldering bloodfeud, which saw Hoskuld's father killed. Hoskuld is newly married and his young widow, Hildigunn, is aggrieved at her husband's brutal killing. She appeals to her uncle, the *goði* Flosi, the most prominent man of her family for help. It thus falls to Flosi to decide how to respond to the killing. Hildigunn wants blood revenge for

---

5   Including what is found in the seven volumes of the *Scriptores Rerum Merowingicarum*.

6   There are many fine studies of Icelandic/Norse women. See for instance Jenny Jochen, *Women in the Viking Age*. London 1991, and idem, *Women in Old Norse Society*, Ithaca 1995. Especially important is Sarah M. Anderson and Karen Swenson (eds.), *Cold Counsel: Women in Old Norse Literature and Mythology: Women in Old Norse Literature and Mythology*, New York 2002.

7   *Njal's Saga*, Magnus Magnusson and Hermann Pálsson (trans.), New York 1960, p. 240. The standard Icelandic edition is Einar Ól. Sveinsson (ed.), *Brennu-Njáls saga*, *Íslenzk fornrit*, 12, Reykjavík 1954, chap. 116.

her husband's death, and in the modern critical literature about feud in early Iceland, she, along with several other women displaying similar intransigence, have sometimes been taken to represent women in early Icelandic feud.

Hildigunn's fame rests in part on Flosi's chilling words about her coldness of her counsel. She seeks justice and the retribution for a wrong committed, while passionately defending her and her family's honour. Hildigunn's legacy is that of a powerful woman who surmounts the obstacles in her path and sets in motion revenge acts that result in the fatal burning of Njal and his sons. Carol Clover places Hildigunn within the larger context of feud: 'Just as women play a central role in funeral rites throughout the world, so they often play, in societies governed by the law of bloodfeud, a central role in the business of remembering and reminding and so perpetuating vendetta'.[8]

From the start, Hildigunn knows that Flosi is weighing his options in deciding whether or not he will help her. She is aware that leaders among his supporters will counsel Flosi to accept a negotiated settlement. Newly drawn into the conflict, he is not yet immersed in the full animosity of the feud. The victim is not Flosi's blood relative, but the husband of his niece. At this stage, he still has options to avoid vengeance honourably. Just before meeting with Hildigunn, a wise counsellor advised Flosi to: 'Take the course that will lead to the least trouble. This is because Njal and other good men will make generous offers of compensation'.[9]

In times of dispute and feud, Icelandic women were influential in forming the private consensus that underlay group decisions. Within the family, the importance of such influence, as in the case of Hildigunn, was considerable. What we need to determine, if we are to arrive at a balanced view of women involved in feud in early Iceland, is whether the vengeance-taking that Hildigunn advocated was the only choice for women in times of conflict. The following examples from the family and Sturlung sagas show women in a wide range of feud situations and at different times in feud cycles. Some, like Hildigunn, push for vengeance, but others dissuade family members from continuing reprisals.

It is also helpful to know that Icelandic women in land-owning families, both as individuals and members of their kin groups, had legal rights and

---

8   Carol Clover, "Hildigunnr's Lament", Sarah M. Anderson and Karen Swenson (eds.), *Cold Counsel: Women in Old Norse Literature and Mythology: Women in Old Norse Literature and Mythology*, New York 2002, p. 33.

9   This passage from chap. 115 and other passages from *Njal's Saga* are from the translation by Magnus Magnusson and Hermann Pálsson, cited above. At times I have made small changes.

responsibilities, which were in some respects comparable to those of men. To a degree unusual in continental medieval regions of the West, women maintained a measure of independence and control over their own lives, including their right to own property. According to *Grágás*,[10] Iceland's extensive law books, women, when acting as heads of households, were required to tithe 'in the same manner as men',[11] and like men they were subject to outlawry for a wounding or killing.[12]

Despite their influence in some areas, Icelandic women did not enjoy full legal or social equality with men. For example, women played no substantial role in the open political life of the country, and they did not serve as advocates at the local and national assemblies and courts, but women were not refused these rights. *Grágás* says nothing on the subject of women leading prosecutions, but in practice they did not. It also appears that women did not speak publicly at a *thing* or assembly. When present at assemblies, they probably attended as onlookers. The rules concerning judges mention only men,[13] and women did not serve as members of a *kviðr* (a verdict-giving panel). They were probably not allowed to act as legal witnesses.[14] Although a woman could inherit a chieftaincy (*goðorð*), she was ineligible to act as a *goði* and had to appoint a man to act on her behalf.[15] Almost all of these factors would have affected the actions of a woman such as Hildigunn, and the sagas assume that the audience understood this dense ethnographic setting.

Let's return to Flosi as he rides from his home in eastern Iceland toward Hildigunn's farmstead in southern Iceland. His grieving niece has summoned him to come speak with her as makes his way to the two-week Althing held annually at Thingvellir in Western Iceland. Flosi knows in advance what Hildigunn wants. She, for her part, prepares a high seat or throne chair in her home in order to inspire him to act like a great chieftain or even a king. Hildigunn is counting on Flosi's right in the eyes of the community to take

---

10 *Grágás* (here abbreviated as *GG*) was edited by Vilhjálmur Finsen and published in three volumes. Ia and Ib: *Grágás: Islændernes Lovbog i Fristatens Tid, udgivet efter det Kongelige Bibliotheks Haandskrift*, Copenhagen 1852. II: *Grágás efter det Arnamagnæanske Haandskrift Nr. 334 fol., Staðarhólsbók*, Copenhagen 18/9. III: *Grágás: Stykker, som findes i det Arnamagnæanske Haandskrift Nr. 351 fol. Skálholtsbók og en Række andre Haandskrifter*, Copenhagen 1883. At times, I also cite the modern Icelandic edition using the notation *GG* 1992, Gunnar Karlsson, Kristján Sveinsson, Mörður Árnason (eds.), *Grágás. Lagasafn íslenska þjóðveldisins*, Reykjavík 1992.

11 *GG* 1852 Ib: 206, chap. 255. 1879 II: 47, chap. 37. 1883 III: 44, chap. 28.

12 *GG* 1879 II: 350, chap. 318.

13 *GG* 1852 Ia: 38-39, chap. 20.

14 *GG* 1852 Ia: 161, chap. 89. 1879 II: 322, chap. 289.

15 *GG* 1852 Ia: 142.

revenge against the Njalssons. The vengeance taking falling upon Flosi is filled with uncertainty and danger. Flosi must decide whether to fulfil Hildigunn's expectations for satisfaction through the revenge process or to determine if the cost of blood-taking is too high.

Flosi has a long and complicated relationship with his ambitious and status-minded niece, and if we are to judge by the following passage, he has mixed feelings about her. With issues of honour and shame in the foreground, the saga portrays Hildigunn's preparations to force Flosi's support:

'I want all the men to be outside when Flosi rides in,' she said. 'The women are to clean the house and put up the hangings, and make ready a high-seat for Flosi'.

Soon Flosi came riding into the home-meadow. Hildigunn went to meet him.

'You are welcome, kinsman,' she said. 'My heart rejoices at your coming'.

'We shall eat here and then ride on,' said Flosi.

The horses were tethered. Flosi went inside. He sat down, and threw the high-seat away from him onto the dais.

'I am neither king nor earl,' he said, 'and there is no need to make me a high-seat. There is no need to mock me, either'. Hildigunn was beside him. 'It is a pity you are offended,' she said. 'We did this in all sincerity'.

Flosi replied, 'If you are being sincere with me and your motives are good they will speak for themselves and condemn themselves if they are ill meaning'.

Hildigunn laughed an icy laugh. 'This is nothing,' she said. 'We shall get closer yet before we part'.

She sat down beside Flosi, and they talked in undertones for a long time.

After that the tables were set up, and Flosi and his men washed themselves ... Then he sat down at the table and told his men to eat. At that moment Hildigunn came into the room and went up to Flosi, pushed her hair back from her eyes, and wept.

Flosi said, 'You are sad now, kinswoman, you are weeping. It is only right that you should weep over a good husband'.

'What redress will you get me?' she asked. 'How much help will you give me?'

Flosi replied, 'I shall press your claims to the full extent of the law or else conclude a settlement which in the eyes of all good men will satisfy every demand of honor'.

Hildigunn said, 'Hoskuld would have avenged you with blood if he were in your place now'.

'You are a ruthless woman,' said Flosi. 'It is clear now what you are after'.

Hildigunn said, 'Arnor Ornolfsson from Forsriverwoods never did your father as grave an injury as this, and yet your brothers Kolbein and Egil killed him at the Skaptafell Assembly'.

She walked from the room and unlocked her chest. She took out the cloak, the gift from Flosi, which Hoskuld had been wearing when he was killed, and in which she had preserved all his blood. She came back with the cloak and went up to Flosi without a word. Flosi had finished eating and the table had been cleared. She threw the cloak around his shoulders, and the clotted blood rained down all over him.

'Flosi, this is the cloak you gave to Hoskuld,' she said, 'and now I give it back to you. He was wearing it when he was killed. I call upon God and all good men to witness that I charge you in the name of all the powers of your Christ and in the name of your courage and your manhood, to avenge every one of the wounds that marked his body – or be an object of contempt to all men'.

Flosi threw off the cloak and flung it back into her arms. 'Monster', he cried. 'You want us to take the course which will turn out worst for all of us. 'Cold are the counsels of women (chap. 116).

Regarding Flosi's words, Sarah Anderson notes the social complexity of Flosi's statement. She emphasises that the vengeance inciting aspect of women rests in social custom rather than emotionality: 'Flosi regards Hildigunn's goading as monstrous, as a deviation from what is natural and appropriate; but, as lamenters and as whetters to revenge, women like Hildigunnr are engaging in one of the few speech acts represented by the literature as open to them, and they are speaking on behalf of the customs of their society – not in monstrous aberration from them'.[16] Despite Flosi's objections, Hildigunn gets her way. Flosi becomes enmeshed in a series of violent rounds that he comes to regret bitterly. Like Hildigunn, many women in the sagas demand blood vengeance. Frequently missed in the discussion surrounding women and feud in Iceland is an additional critical point: there are numerous, but often overlooked, examples of women who oppose blood vengeance. Rather than urging their men to engage in feud, these women counsel restraint and insist on reconciliation.

Does shifting emphasis from the admittedly spectacular examples of vengeance-seeking women, and focusing on a more balanced view of their roles in Icelandic feud, have consequences for the larger study of feud? The answer is yes. The Icelandic texts – extensive, varied, and detailed – are vital sources, not only for the comparative study of women and feud but also for our understanding of women as peace makers. We may even go further. As sources for the analysis of violence and peace-making within a pre-modern context, the sagas are a treasure. Iceland's medieval writings offer us some of the most wide-ranging information on non-tribal, quasi-modern feuding.

---

16 Sarah M. Anderson, "Introduction", Sarah M. Anderson and Karen Swenson (eds.), *Cold Counsel: Women in Old Norse Literature and Mythology*, New York 2002, p. xii-xiii.

To a significant degree, the value of the sagas as source material accrues because the information they contain approaches the type of ethnographic material collected by modern anthropologists. In one way, the sagas may even have an advantage over most indigenous ethnographic observational writings. Because anthropological observations cannot cover an adequate span of time, they rarely capture the full range of variability affecting the community under study. The sagas do not have this anthropological drawback regarding feud. Rather, they combine ethnographic immediacy with historical sensibility, capturing a wide range of variability and offering insight into the mentality and strategies of this culture group. In particular, they depict personal life and the constellation of factors that affect decisions and consensus at the heart of family and community life. Concerning the processing of feud, the sagas reveal ways in which women set in motion actions that escalate and prolong feuds as well as resolve and prevent them.

Many Icelandic texts show women acting with *hóf* (moderation). A significant example is found in *The Saga of the People of Weapon's Fjord* (*Vápnfirðinga saga*).[17] In this saga from the East Fjords, a blood feud that continues for two generations among kinsmen is resolved after Jorun, the wife of one of the parties forcefully expresses her wishes. At the time of Jorun's intervention, her husband, Thorkel, is recovering from wounds received in a failed ambush of his cousin Bjarni. Thorkel is seeking vengeance for Bjarni's killing of Thorkel's father Geitir in response to Geitir's killing of Bjarni's father. Here again vengeance continues for many rounds. According to our talking points, the saga is a classic example of feud. It begins with competition for power and access to resources, and continues through a long cycle of recurring violence replete with public score-keeping and deep-rooted hatred. It is also a telling example of how a feud can end, with the parties wearing themselves out and seeking settlement.

At the time of the passage quoted below, Thorkel's honour is at low ebb. He has been publicly humiliated by the utter failure of his springtime ambush. The attack not only brings about the deaths of several of Thorkel's own supporters, but the slow healing of his wound keeps him from the summer's farm work. Winter is coming and Thorkel is facing disaster. He has not put in a store of hay for his livestock, and he will have to kill off his precious cattle and sheep. With this loss, his wealth and status will severely drop. Having learned of Thorkel's problems, Bjarni, Thorkel's enemy and cousin, takes action. Bjarni makes an unexpected offer of assistance that may be interpreted in several ways. Either

---

17   Jón Jóhannesson (ed.), *Vápnfirðinga saga* (*The Saga of the People of Weapon's Fjord*), Reykjavík 1950.

it is humiliating to the point of calculated mockery or it is nobly generous. Thorkel hesitates. Perhaps his sense of honour, driven by shame, will not let him accept. His wife Jorun sees the matter differently, and she steps in. The passage begins when Bjarni's messenger arrives at Thorkel's farm:

Just as men sat down to table, Jorun was carrying in the food. The messenger walked up to Thorkel and told him the whole of Bjarni's message. Jorun stayed in the room and was listening to what he said. Thorkel made no answer.

'How can you be silent about this', said Jorun, 'when it is such a noble offer?'

'I am not going to give a hasty answer in this matter,' said Thorkel, 'for so handsome an offer would catch most men off balance'.

'What I should like,' Jorun told him, 'is for us to take ourselves off to Hof [Bjarni's farm] in the morning and meet Bjarni for such an offer seems to me in every respect honourable from a man of his character'.

'You shall have your way,' agreed Thorkel, 'for I have found over and again that you are both wise and kind'.

The next morning they left home, twelve of them together, and when their coming was seen from Hof, Bjarni was informed of it. He was overjoyed the moment he heard it: he went out to meet them and had a warm greeting for Thorkel. And once the kinsmen had a good talk together, they went into all their problems well and truly, and then Bjarni offered Thorkel atonement and the right to make his own award [for the killing of Bjarni's father Geitir] ...and they came together now in whole-hearted reconciliation (chap. 19).

Far from offering cold counsels, Jorun is a peacemaker. Her goal goes beyond simply ending the rounds; she also demands that the former enemies reconcile. She stipulates that Thorkel travel to Bjarni's farm and that they publicly display peaceful intentions. Hence the score keeping is ended. Neither inciting nor passive, Jorun is portrayed as an engaged participant in the decision-making process leading to peace. The story of Jorun offers considerable information about the private lives of a feuding family, and this is the type of information needed if we are to construct a historical understanding of the workings of feud. Bjarni's messenger talks to Thorkel, the man of the house, but the woman of the house acts on her right to intervene to the point where she takes charge.

This episode from the *Saga of the People of Weapon's Fjord* is found in a family saga, a text that was written down several generations after the events it describes. We can question whether Jorun's intervention is a literary invention. Luckily, we have a reliable historical source for a similar example of a woman's intervention within the decision-making arena. This source, which serves as a third example, is an episode from *The Saga of Thorgils Skardi* (Þorgils saga skarði), a thirteenth-century text called a 'contemporary saga' because it was written down close in time to the events described.[18] The incident involves Groa Alfsdottir, the long-time mistress of Gizur Thorvaldsson (d. 1268), a chieftain of the southern Haukdælir family, who at the very end of the Icelandic Free State rose to a commanding position when he became jarl or earl over large sections of Iceland.

Thorgil's Saga recounts that shortly after Gizur takes part in the killing in 1241 of the chieftain and saga author Snorri Sturluson, a fifteen-year-old boy from the Sturlung clan comes to live as a hostage in Gizur's household. The plan is to prevent the Sturlungs from attacking. The hostage named Thorgils, who later became a powerful chieftain, quarrels with another boy, Sam, over a game of *tafl*, (a kind of chess). The status of the boys is very different. Sam is Gizur's kinsman, whereas Thorgils is there without choice. As it turns out, Gizur is fond of Thorgils, whose position in the household is much like that of a foster son. The quarrel between the boys over the chess game escalates when Thorgils sweeps the game pieces off the board and strikes Sam on his ear. Because Sam's wound bleeds, the action is a serious insult if left uncompensated. Upon entering the room, Gizur reprimands Thorgils, who answers him in a challenging manner.

Gizur and Thorgils are verging on a quarrel when Groa intervenes. Groa, whom the saga refers to as *húsfreyja*, the mistress of the house, perceives the danger in the situation. Thorgils has acted violently while in their home. Everyone's honour is at stake, and Groa knows that if Gizur quarrels with Thorgils, the way will be open for a smouldering dispute which may claim lives. She takes Gizur aside, asking:

'Why are you so angry? To me it seems that it is you who will have to answer for it, even if he [Thorgils] does something that calls for compensation'.

Gizur replied, 'I do not want to listen to your opinion in this matter'.

She answered, 'Then I will, on my own, offer compensation, if that is what is necessary'. (chap. 1).

Like Jorun, the saga portrays the sharp-witted Groa as having a cooler head than the *húsbóndi*, the man of the house. The woman sees the makings of feud – insult, injury, shame, honour, and humiliation – and realises that, unless

---

18   Jón Jóhannesson, Magnús Finnbogason, and Kristján Eldjárn (eds.), *Þorgils saga skarða* in *Sturlunga saga*, vol. 2, Reykjavík 1946. *The Saga of Thorgils Skardi, Sturlunga Saga* (*The Saga of the Sturlungs*), Julia McGrew and R. George Thomas (trans.), 1-2, New York 1970-1974.

curtailed, animosity will fester and claims to vengeance will prevail. Typical of feud, almost everyone involved perceives the events in different terms, and as a consequence, the path is opened to a cycle of escalation. A prolonged quarrel between the boys or between Gizur and Thorgils would provide entry for third parties to intervene, harming the family.

One thing we know about feud is that slights rankle. In feuding cultures, it is crucial to settle immediately even the smallest dispute. In this instance, it is the woman who ignores the principle of retaliation and demonstrates her understanding of the politics of Icelandic feud. Like Jorun, Groa knows that reconciliation does not require the defeat of wrongdoers, but rather calls for a public declaration of peace sufficient to heal the breach. Groa first stops the escalation when Gizur yields to her; next she waits her time as she moves to reconciliation. The saga recounts that the matter was dropped, but 'Gizur was less friendly toward Thorgils than he had been earlier'. So matters continue until Groa intervenes at Christmas (in the year 1242) when she and Gizur reconcile the household with gifts: 'Before Christmas Groa had a green tunic made for Thorgils from new green cloth, while Gizur gave Sam a blue tunic that he had previously owned. And they were good friends ever after'.

In summary, the sagas offer considerable depth of information about feuding. The examples of Hildigunn, Jorun, and Groa illustrate diverse intentions and maneuvers within the different cycles of feud. Barred from public roles, these women, nevertheless, exercise influence. At this juncture, our understanding of the roles of women in the sagas might well be replaced with a broader and more balanced view. We conclude with a saga example in which a woman turns to self-help, relying on her own quick thinking.

The woman is Freydis, the daughter of Eirik the Red, the Icelander who colonised Greenland in the 980s. She is one of the first Norse women to voyage to the North American continent, and her troubles on this early eleventh-century voyage of exploration and attempted settlement at the far western end of Viking activity offer us an example of a woman relying on her own resources. Elsewhere the saga describes Freydis as a successful participant in feud. Her husband is the expedition's leader, and she kills innocent women, when she considers them her enemies.

Freydis ruthlessly finds ways to acquire power and leadership. She causes death and inspires action. Jenny Jochens has an interesting take on this point, which adds to our understanding of Freydis' actions. [19] Jochens writes: 'In

19   Jenny Jochens, "Vikings Westward to Vínland", Sarah M. Anderson and Karen Swenson (eds.), *Cold Counsel: Women in Old Norse Literature and Mythology: Women in Old Norse Literature*

the nineteenth century the Chinese men brought in to build railroads in this country (the US) suffered from a male sex ratio of 20,000. Male sexual demands were partially met by rendering the scarce Chinese women available to all the Chinese men through organized prostitution'.[20] This solution was not sought by the Norse. In Vínland the married men enjoyed the sexual mono-poly of their wives, leaving the rest to frustration. The mere accusation from Freydis – false as it turned out – that she had been molested by another man was enough to cause her husband to take action.

The following description from *The Saga of Eirik the Red* (*Eiríks saga rauði*)[21] takes place on the North American continent when *Skrælings* or Native Ame-ricans attack the Norse settlers. Although the Scandinavians are equipped with iron weapons of the Viking Age, the Native Americans, nevertheless, rout them. As Freydis comes out of her hut, she finds the *Skrælings* pursuing the fleeing Norsemen through the settlers' camp. Seeing the men retreating, she realises the seriousness of the situation and wastes no time:

'Why do you flee from such pitiful wretches, brave men like you? You should be able to slaughter them like cattle. If I had weapons, I am sure I could fight better than any one of you'.

The men paid no attention to what she was saying. Freydis tried to join them but she could not keep up with them because she was pregnant. She was following them into the woods when the Skrælings closed in on her. In front of her lay a dead Norse-man, Thorbrand Snorrasson, with a flint stone buried in his head and his sword beside him. She snatched up the sword and prepared to defend herself. When the Skrælings came rushing toward her she pulled one of her breasts out of the top of her dress and slapped it with the sword. The Skrælings were terrified at the sight of this and fled back to their boats and made off as fast as they could (chap. 11).

We can only guess why the *Skrælings* were so disconcerted at the sight of Freydis, with sword in hand and breast exposed, the saga tells us no more.

---

    and Mythology, New York 2002, p. 146.

20 Jochens cites Marcia Guttentag and Paul F. Secord, *Too many Women?*, London 1983, pp. 29-30.

21 "Eirik's Saga", *The Vinland Sagas: The Norse Discovery of America*, Magnus Magnusson and Herman Pálsson (trans.), Harmondsworth 1987, p. 100.

Conclusion

The sagas, rich sources of ethnohistorical material, augment our study of feud in early Europe, allowing us to follow conflicts well past 'two rounds'. This article works toward a definition of feud. It explores talking points behind a general definition and provides a definition of Icelandic feud. In so doing, it take into account many aspects and levels of the phenomenon. The four examples provided in the article, offer a balanced view of women's roles in Iceland's feuding culture and illustrate the value of the sagas as sources for the study of feud. Along with presenting women as inciters and escalators of feud, the sagas offer examples of women as peacemakers and as critical actors dampening reprisals. Hildigunn, Jorun and Groa defend their family honour, while Freydis takes matters into her own hands. In varying ways, all these women exercise power and change the course of events. The Icelandic writings expose the multiplicity of women's roles. They offer portraits of women involved in contention, coping with insult, injury, and limited resources while practicing a form of Realpolitik.

Faction and Feud in Fourteenth-Century Marseille

DANIEL LORD SMAIL

When King Jean II of France paid a visit to Marseille in January of 1351, all was not well in Provence. The recent experience of plague was bitter enough, but war, a more familiar enemy, was now looming on the horizon. The clouds of war were gathering even in March of 1349, in the very shadow of the plague: on the twenty-first of that month, the city council of Marseille approved a public proclamation forbidding any citizen who possessed crossbows from selling them to strangers. Shortly after, on the tenth of April, citizens were allowed to quicken their military blood through jousts, in the teeth of a century-old statute forbidding them to do so. The sense of crisis deepened swiftly. April 14: the council forbids all innkeepers who have sequestered the weapons of their foreign guests from restoring them to their owners. May 1: the defence of the city and the gates is being planned. Two days later, all citizens residing outside the walls of Marseille are invited to move within the walls, under penalty of losing all their possessions.[1] Late in 1350, tension mounts again. November 26: all inhabitants of Marseille between the ages of 14 and 70 are ordered to stand by, armed and ready to assemble at the Palace at the sound of the tocsin. On the same day, all hostellers are ordered to inscribe the names of their guests in a register at the tribunal. November 30: a night patrol is formed and placed under the orders of the newly created position of constable.[2]

Thus in 1351, the French king making his way through Angevin Provence to Marseille was surrounded by the threat of war and brigandage, a threat that would soon transform itself into a reality as the violence of the Hundred Years War spilled into the region. Such violence, in sporadic bursts, was typical of

---

1 Archives Municipales de la Ville de Marseille (hereafter AM) BB 20, fols. 99, 115, 117, 127, and 130. The author would like to thank Marc Bouiron, Conservateur du Patrimoine et Archéologue de la Ville de Nice, for his help in preparing the maps.
2 AM BB 21, fols. 79-80, 82.

the medieval landscape, and it was against the possibility of violence that city walls were raised. On the day that King Jean arrived in Marseille, the walls were festively adorned with the banners of craft guilds, set out to honour their distinguished guest. But even as he passed through a gate in the wall that separated the safe city from the violent hinterlands, the king himself was immediately swept along in a different current of violence. This was violence grounded in noble feud and neighbourly enmity, not in warfare or brigandage. Underneath and alongside the dais draped in red where, flanked by two horsemen, the king had settled himself in splendour and honour, strode nine men chosen to carry, accompany, and greet the king. These nine included the nobleman Peire de Jerusalem and his nephew, Peire the younger; also, the knight Johan Vivaut, the nobleman Peire Bonafos, and the knight Guilhem de Montoliu. All five were important members of the city council. All five were bitter enemies, members of two families or factions, the Vivaut and the de Jerusalem, at war with each other for at least four decades. Barely six months after the king's visit, on the evening of the feast of St. Mary Magdalene, a huge public battle (Provençal *briga* or *brega*) involving hundreds of men broke out between the two factions. And in May of 1356, the younger Peire de Jerusalem, pierced by swords and knives in twenty-one places, was lying dead between the walls of the city, slain by assassins while on his way to church. Those assassins included Amiel Bonafos, a Vivaut captain, whose father Peire had once stood alongside the victim as together they supported the dais of the king of France.

The great Vivaut/de Jerusalem hatred was the stuff of everyday lore in Marseille, and the uneasy symbolism of the January 1351 royal entry – a king carried aloft on the shoulders of enmity – would not have been lost on contemporary observers. Whatever their fulminations in favour of peace, kings had little power to suppress either the spirit or the practice of vengeance. The persistence of vengeance has long been taken as proof of the weakness of the late medieval state – in Bernard Guenée's phrase, *la justice impuissante*.[3] Yet to view blood vengeance as a sign of political impotence is to miss out on the fundamental ways in which the practice of vengeance suffused the legal culture of late medieval states and contributed to political processes. Though late medieval rulers spoke of peace and civility, patterns of royal administration selectively and perhaps unintentionally enabled forms of violence and hatred in the realm of civil and criminal justice. As I have argued elsewhere, civil litigants in fourteenth-century Marseille used courts to pursue their feud-like envies

3   Bernard Guenée, *Tribunaux et gens de justice dans le bailliage de Senlis à la fin du Moyen Âge*, Paris 1963, pp. 293-95.

and enmities in a forum that was safe, reasonably efficient, and fully public.[4] In criminal cases, denunciations and hostile depositions served much the same role in facilitating vengeance. A single illustration of the point will suffice. In July of 1341, a goatherd named Marin Morlan was brought before the court to answer to a charge of trespass. He protested that the man who denounced him to the court, Guilhem Sycart, was motivated by hatred of him and his sons (*Guillelmus Sycardi denunciator est inimicus eiusdem Marini et liberorum suorum*).[5] A witness, Ayglina Castellana, reported that Marin (or one of his sons) had wounded Guilhem's brother, Raymon.[6] This was a family-based feud, though expressed in forms that encompassed legal actions as well as bloodshed. Note how the failure to crush the spirit of vengeance that so patently motivated Guilhem Sycart can hardly be considered an error of governance or a sign of political impotence. To encourage people like Guilhem to pursue their vengeance using legal processes was to create a systematic dependency on the organs of state. Vengeance built court caseloads. Late medieval states, according to this model, did not crush the spirit of vengeance. They harnessed it.

This argument is persuasive only if enmity was an emotion and a practice available to the entire population, not just a monopoly of urban patricians. This was in fact the case. A range of evidence from late medieval Marseille shows that the inclination toward vengeance was ubiquitous among artisans, peasants, day labourers, fishermen, and goatherds; private citizens and public officials; adults and children; women and men; and layfolk as well as secular and regular clergy. These were people whose pursuit of vengeance filled court caseloads. Like Marin Morlan and Guilhem Sycart, they also engaged with their enemies from time to time via insults, threats, and bloodshed. Witness the actions of a shepherd named Guilhem de Bessa, who in 1361 came before a notary of the city of Marseille to announce the death of his employer, a man named Raymon de Ornhon. It turns out that Raymon and three henchmen had beaten Guilhem not too long ago, a humiliation that he did not forget. Pursuing vengeance (*volens habere vindictam*), Guilhem bided his time and then killed Raymon. Following the vengeance killing, he came to the city to have the announcement of vengeance achieved drawn up in the form of a notarised act. In the body of the act, he even indicated his intention to avenge himself

---

4   See Daniel Lord Smail, *The Consumption of Justice: Emotions, Publicity, and Legal Culture in Marseille, 1264-1423*, Ithaca 2003. The pattern has long been noted by historians of litigation.

5   Archives Départementales des Bouches-du-Rhône (hereafter ADBR) 3B 43, fol. 12r.

6   *Ibid.*, fol. 15r.

on the other three men involved in the beating.[7] The desire to have one's vengeance notarised is remarkable, indeed wholly unprecedented. But the underlying spirit of vengeance was common enough among shepherds and other ordinary folk.

That all Massiliotes could be motivated by the spirit of vengeance can be easily illustrated by compiling anecdotes like this. Such anecdotes exist in profusion in the court records from fourteenth-century Marseille. In this contribution, however, I would like to illustrate the social breadth of vengeful attitudes by means of a prosopographical analysis of the great Vivaut and de Jerusalem factions themselves. The factions were led by members of the urban patriciate, men who simultaneously held high office in the city council and other positions of government. But membership in both parties was swollen by lower-status individuals. Some were recruited as clients and servants. Others, significantly, allied themselves as autonomous individuals seeking greater resources in the pursuit of their own enmities. We should not look upon the Vivaut and de Jerusalem parties as feuding factions at war with each other and with the state. Instead, to borrow a model developed by Jacques Heers, we should see them as political parties, offering their members access to resources, including positions on the general council, the law courts, and possibly even tax farms.[8] The very enmities that drove factional recruitment were incorporated into political processes and political life.

The factional warfare between the two factions that captured the headlines in fourteenth-century Marseille cannot be known to us through a town chronicle or any other kind of pre-packaged narrative. Like most Provençal towns, Marseille had little use for the chronicles that were so popular in Florence and elsewhere on the Italian peninsula. The city council, in turn, proved squeamish about discussing any matters involving the factions. The veiled references that do exist in the registers of the council deliberations make sense only if one already knows of the existence of the enmity. The careful silence is perhaps not wholly surprising, since the council itself included a number of men belonging to the two factions.

To reconstruct the history of the warfare between the Vivaut and the de Jerusalem, therefore, we are almost wholly dependent on registers of criminal prosecutions, civil lawsuits, and appeals. These records survive only sporadically from the fourteenth and fifteenth centuries, guaranteeing at best a piecemeal

---

7   ADBR 381E 83, fols. 16v-17r, 27 Apr. 1361.
8   Jacques Heers, *Parties and Political Life in the Medieval West*, Amsterdam 1977.

history. Very little has been preserved from the thirteenth century, though we know that the court was producing registers from at least the mid-thirteenth century. Reading the extant court registers, which survive in sufficient density only after 1300, one has the impression of factional violence bursting on the scene, fully formed, in the early fourteenth century. This is probably an illusion, a product of the incomplete survival of records.

In their mid-fourteenth-century incarnations, the factions usually took their names from two of the oldest and most powerful noble families of Marseille, the Vivaut and the de Jerusalem. Thirteenth-century records are littered with references to significant predecessors from both families,[9] and both families were linked to streets or squares from an early date, their very names inscribed in the city's mental geography. The de Jerusalem lineage had made its fortune in armaments, and if the name is any indication probably included a crusader in their genealogy. The Vivaut had strong ties to the countryside in the fourteenth century—among other things, members of the family were the lords of the nearby village of Cuges. A third family, closely linked to the Vivaut faction, was the Martin, relative newcomers to power and prestige. The family's fortune lay in commerce; its rise to prominence began with an ancestor, the merchant Jacme Martin, who died a wealthy man in 1302.

Judicial registers record several dozen incidents of factional warfare between the 1330s and 1360s, ranging from isolated vengeance killings to the massive *briga* of 1351, which involved several hundred armed men.[10] These episodes did not fail to impress the popular imagination. 'It is very old, the hatred between the Vivaut and the de Jerusalem', remarked a witness, a nobleman named Montoliu de Montoliu, during the course of an interrogation.[11] The party of the de Jerusalem 'has always had tremendous ill-will for those of the Vivaut party', said another, the merchant Laurens Rostahn.[12] In this as in other ways, the enmity between the two families was modelled in a way not dissimilar to

---

9   On both families see Victor-L. Bourrilly, *Essai sur l'histoire politique de la commune de Marseille des origines à la victoire de Charles d'Anjou*, Aix-en-Provence 1925, *passim* (see index). See also Édouard Baratier and Félix Reynaud, *De 1291 à 1480*, vol. 2 of Gaston Rambert (ed.), *Histoire du commerce de Marseille*, Paris 1951, pp. 692-693; references to members of both families can be found in the index to the series.

10   Elsewhere I have discussed some of these incidents at greater length; see Daniel Lord Smail, "Telling Tales in Angevin Courts", *French Historical Studies*, 20, 1997, pp. 183-215.

11   ADBR 3B 811, fol. 66v: *antiquitus fuit rancor inter Vivaudos et illos de Jerusalem.*

12   *Ibid.,* fol. 69v: *semper habuerunt magnam inimicitiam contra illos de parte Vivaudorum.*

the feuds or enmities described in the epic poems and prose narratives of the age, where the central theme concerned the enmity between families.

Once we probe behind the language of the records, however, we find entities whose structures and modes of recruitment departed significantly from the kin-based rhetoric that shaped the perception of the feud. To begin with, both judges and other observers were fully aware that the most prominent lineages, the Vivaut, the Martin, and the de Jerusalem, did not act alone. A peace accord dated 24 March 1349, for example, spoke of the need for peace between men of the lineage of the Toesco (*de genere dels Thoesquos*) and a member of the lineage of the Englese (*unius de genere Anglicarum*). These were fishermen. Other cases make it clear that judges were aware of long-standing hatreds between the families of the Mercier and the de Serviers, between the Mercier and the de Jerusalem, and between the Martin and the de Jerusalem.[13] At the very least, therefore, the factional violence in and around the 1350s implicated seven agnatic groups. Moreover, a prosopographical reconstruction of the two factions, derived from lists drawn up by the courts during phases of criminal prosecution, shows that factional membership extended far beyond these seven agnatic cores. Some members were related through marriage or through their mothers' kin. The majority, however, were not related by any close bonds of kinship.

The great *briga* which took place on the evening of the feast of St. Mary Magdalene, on 22 July 1351, can be used to illustrate this point. Although members of the Vivaut, Martin, and de Jerusalem families were prominent in the battle, they hardly acted alone. The noble Guilhem de Montoliu played a major role among the Vivaut, and trials arising from subsequent incidents reveal that Amiel Bonafos was an important Vivaut captain. For the de Jerusalem, Isnart Eguesier and Peire Carbonel were deeply involved in the leadership. The peace treaty of 26 July 1351 that followed the battle listed the names of twenty men deemed most responsible for inciting violence. Members of the Vivaut, Martin, and de Jerusalem families accounted for only six of these twenty (Table 1).

More striking for what it reveals about the distribution of parties across agnatic lineages is a longer list of people known to have participated on behalf of the Vivaut and Martin in the battle of 1351, many of whom were assessed fines

---

13   ADBR 3B 820, fols. 16r-20r.

TABLE 1:   Main Figures in the *Briga* of 1351

Party of the Vivaut and Martin	Party of the de Jerusalem
Guilhem de Montoliu, knight	Peire de Jerusalem, senior
Johan Vivaut	Peire de Jerusalem, junior
Jacme Martin	Bernat de Cepeda
Amiel Bonafos	Isnart Eguisier
Johan Martin	Bertran Auriol
Peire de Lengres	Johan de Vaquiers
Laugier de Soliers	Bertomieu de Montels
Bertomieu Bonvin	Guilhem de Serviers
Peire Amat	Esteve de Fonte
Uguo Vivaut	Guilhem Audoart

source: ADBR 3B 820, fols. 19v-20r (the peace treaty of 26 July 1351)

at the conclusion of the initial criminal inquest (Table 2).[14] The sixty-one names on this list were distributed across forty separate families.[15] Twenty-eight surnames were unique, and, with the exception of the Martin, no group of agnates surpassed three in number. Only eleven men belonged to the twin agnatic cores of the Vivaut/Martin party.

Despite the tendency of officials to talk about the *pars Vivaudorum et Martinentorum*, the Vivaut and Martin party was an untidy agglomeration of men whose agnatic ties to one another were minimal. Although the de Jerusalem party is not so well documented, the same appears to be true. The patrilineages, in fact, had considerable difficulty recruiting among their own members. Fifteen or twenty men bore the Vivaut name between 1337 and 1362, and only three were clearly involved in factional violence. As many as thirty or forty men belonged to the de Jerusalem lineage, yet only two or three participated in fighting.[16]

---

14 This list has been reconstructed from two sources: 1) the list of defendants found at the beginning of the transcript and at other points throughout the case; 2) testimony from members of the party concerning who was participating.

15 Edward Muir also finds a broad array of surnames among the clans of Renaissance Friuli; see Edward Muir, *Mad Blood Stirring: Vendetta and Factions in Friuli during the Renaissance*, Baltimore 1993, p. 85.

16 The Martin surname was so common that it is next to impossible to say with confidence who may have been related to whom. The Vivaut and de Jerusalem names were much less common.

TABLE 2: List of Participants in the Vivaut and Martin Party in 1351

Name and profession	Fine	Name and profession	Fine
Peire Amat	100 l.	Peire de Lengres, squire	none
Carle Athos	200 l.	Arnaut Marinier, mariner	none
Lois Athos, son of Carle	none	Bernat Martin	none
Lois Athos	none	Guilhem Martin, squire	200 l.
Raymon Audebert, notary	none	Johan Martin	200 l.
Johan Aycart	200 l.	Jacme Martin	200 l.
Bernat de Batut	100 l.	Monet Martin	none
Berengier Baxiator, fuller	none	Peire Martin, banker	200 l.
Raymon Beroart	none	Peire Martin	none
Guilhem Blasin, painter	none	Guilhem Mercier	100 l.
Bonfil Bocaran, buckler	none	Johan Mercier	none
Amiel Bonafos	200 l.	Primar Mirapeis, jurist	none
Jacme Bonafos, mariner	100 l.	Arnaut de Montoliu	none
Augier Bonpar	none	Guilhem de Montoliu, knight	200 l.
Augier Bonpar	none	Johan Naulon	100 l.
Bertomieu Bonvin, squire	100 l.	Uguo Ode, merchant	none
Lois Bonvin	none	Jacme Peire	none
Esteve de Brandis	100 l.	Berengier Pictor, painter	none
Periton Catalan	none	Johan Quatrelinguas	none
Johan Cayrellier	none	Guilhem Seguier	none
Uguo Dode, cleric	none	Laugier de Soliers, noble	100 l.
Johan Englese, fisherman	100 l.	Johan de Strelhe, apothecary	none
Jacme Englese, fisherman	200 l.	Guilhem dal Temple, noble	100 l.
Guilhem Englese, fisherman	none	Isnart dal Temple	none
Raymon Faber	none	Raymon de Vaudroma, noble	none
Guilhem de Sant Felis	none	Antoni Vassall	none
Johan Fustier	none	Nicolau Vassall	none
Uguo Jacme	none	Guilhem Vivaut, noble	200 l.
Johan de Laureis	100 l.	Uguo Vivaut, noble	200 l.
Raymon de Laureis	100 l.	Johan Vivaut, noble	200 l.
Johan de Laureis, fisherman	none		

source: ADBR 3B 811

Given the limited role played by agnation, we must seek elsewhere for the principle that joined unrelated men together. Some of the faction leaders were related to one another through marriage. A variety of sources reveal that an axis of marriage joining the Vivaut, the Bonafos, and the Martin lay at the heart of the Vivaut and Martin party (Figure 1). Other cognatic and affinal linkages too numerous to relate, moreover, suggest complex webs of relations

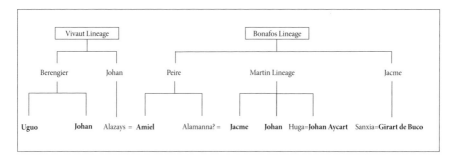

FIGURE 1:   Vivaut Bonafos Martin intermarriages.
Note: Only partial family trees are provided here. Names in bold indicate the men who participated in the *briga* of 1351.

among the leaders. Among the leaders of the factions, agnatic ties may have played the role of the warp in the fabric, but it was marriage that provided the woof, joining the party's leaders horizontally.

Yet although marriage connected the leadership of the party, it was patronage or alliance with lesser families that added much of the bulk. Both parties filled out their ranks by recruiting heavily among men of lower and middling status. Some of these men were clearly servants, members of the households or *familia* of prominent participants. One such armed servant was Guilhem Verdelhon, the arms-bearer (*scutifer*) of the de Jerusalem captain Isnart Eguesier. Another was Raymon Chaudon, the arms-bearer of Peire Martin. But a large number of people associated with the parties in one way or another were tradesmen, artisans, or professionals of one kind or another. The range of professions is extremely broad. Among the Vivaut clients we find, in addition to twenty-some nobles, twelve fishermen, mariners, or other members of sea-going professions, four peasants, one caulker, one reamer, one painter, one butcher, one fuller, one baker, one buckler, six apothecaries, two cobblers, three drapers, one banker, twelve merchants, fifteen notaries, and three jurists. The de Jerusalem party, in turn, included not only fifteen nobles but also a barber, a mason, a farrier, a grocer, a miller, a fisherman, a clothier, two judges, two butchers, three drapers, three notaries, nine peasants, and ten merchants.

Several features in these lists stand out. First, the Vivaut were far more inclined to attract associates from among the sea-going professions; the de Jerusalem party, in turn, included more urban peasants. This sharp distinction stands to reason: most members of the sea-going professions lived west of the plaza of the Vivaut in an area evidently dominated by the Vivaut and their allies, whereas the de Jerusalem were centred on the street of the de Jerusalem, closer to the agricultural hinterland and certainly nearer to areas where labourers predominated among neighbourhood populations. Second, all the apothecaries found to have participated in factional warfare belonged to the Vivaut party, and the Vivaut had or were thought to have had strong allies in the Spicery, the neighbourhood associated with the apothecaries. Other evidence reveals that the de Jerusalem were linked to more members of the cloth trades such as drapers and tailors than the list implies.

The simple names *pars Vivaudorum* and *pars de Jerusalem*, therefore, mask a great deal of social complexity. To the extent that the factions were based on kinship at all, they conjoined loosely affiliated bilateral kindreds linked most prominently by ties of marriage. Friendship and clientage played significant roles. Recruitment was geographically broad. Membership was constantly shifting, as alliances fell in and out of use. In all respects, affiliations followed social cleavages based on particular friendships and hatreds, individually calculated strategies, and accidental or incidental alliances.[17] Kinship, and especially agnatic kinship, was but one of the many principles that could serve as a basis for recruitment. The parties, in other words, were never enduring structures with fixed memberships. They were constantly being reinvented. What Edward Muir has said about the clan of Renaissance Friuli applies well to the faction of medieval Marseille: we should understand it 'more as a dynamic process than as a fixed structure'.[18] And this dynamism is nowhere more visible than in the imagined geography of the feud.

In their testimony, the defendants in the trial that followed on the heels of the *briga* of 1351 created a mental geography that carefully partitioned the city into territories controlled by the Vivaut and the de Jerusalem and by their allies. The eponymous families were each linked to prominent city streets. The plaza of the Vivaut, for example, was located in the administrative district (*sixain*) known as Accoules. The street of the de Jerusalem was located in the *sixains* of Draparie and St. Jacques. Perceptions of the feud were powerfully moulded by this geography, an axis of hatred running east-west along the north shore of the

---

17 Recent studies of feuding and vendetta observe the same phenomenon. See William Ian Miller, *Bloodtaking and Peacemaking: Feud, Law, and Society in Saga Iceland*, Chicago 1990, pp. 188-89. The situation of the feud was thus directly comparable to what historians now understand to be the messy and unsystematic alliances that characterised the Guelf and Ghibelline loyalties in Italy. See the recent discussion of this in Carol Lansing, *The Florentine Magnates: Lineage and Faction in a Medieval Commune*, Princeton 1991, pp. 180-184.
18 Muir 1993, p. xxiv.

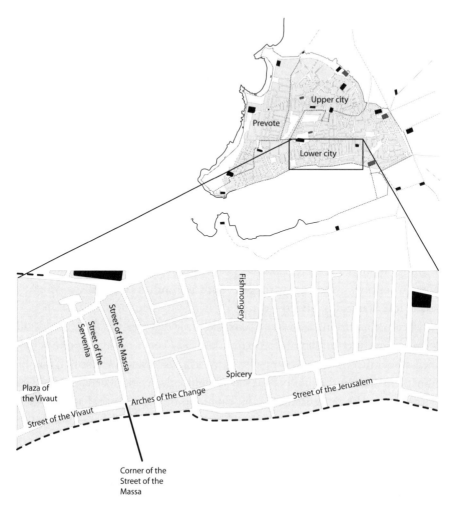

Figure labels (top map): Upper city, Prevote, Lower city

Figure labels (detail map): Fishmongery, Street of the Massa, Street of the Servenha, Street of the, Plaza of the Vivaut, Arches of the Change, Spicery, Street of the Jerusalem, Street of the Vivaut, Corner of the Street of the Massa

FIGURE 2:   The Geography of the *Briga* of 1351.

harbour. From testimony in the original inquisition transcript, it is clear that the invading de Jerusalem were thought to have offended the residential space of the Vivaut. This would explain why most defendants took care to describe their movements through named streets on the fateful evening. Guilhem Vivaut, alias Raolin, described how he was waiting in a house belonging to Johan Vivaut, and how he left the house, meeting up with others 'at the head of the street of the Vivaut where fruits are sold' (*in capite carrerie Vivaudorum ubi vendentur fruche*).[19] Others described how the party then moved off down

19   ADBR 3B 812, fol. 24r-v.

the street of the Vivaut toward the Arches of the Change, at the corner of the street of the Massa.[20]

The testimony of Bertomieu Bonvin is particularly suggestive regarding territorial identity.[21] While he was participating in a council being held in the house of the heirs of Berengier Vivaut to discuss what to make of the peace offered to them, he heard the cry 'A las armas! a las armas!'. After arming himself, he rushed to the corner of the street of Guilhem Tomas (identical to the street of the Massa) which he described as 'inside their boundaries' (*accessit ad locum cantoni Guillelmi Thomacii intra eorum confinias*). The defendant Bernat de Batut also spoke of boundaries, although in his deposition the boundary was located at the corner of the street of Guilhem del Alans[22] (a third name for the street of the Massa).[23] Several witnesses remarked that Peire de Jerusalem was first spotted a few blocks away, in the Spicery and slightly nearer in the Change, although all reports suggest that the conflict eventually took place at the so-called boundary.[24]

Depositions from other trials also make clear that territory was considered a convenient way to identify people. Asked how he was able to identify two men as members of the Vivaut party, a de Jerusalem associate testified that he 'saw them daily in the plaza of the Vivaut with arms'.[25] Similarly, two further witnesses for the de Jerusalem in this case supported the claim that most men on the street of the Spicery, midway between the two enclaves, belonged to the Vivaut/Martin party: they observed that most of the street had risen up on behalf of the Vivaut during the *briga*.[26] This was a street where allies of the Vivaut, called the Mercier, dominated.

Yet despite all this talk, the geography of the enmity was not as simple as those involved liked to think. The broad distribution of the participants throughout various families in Marseille was mirrored in geography by a city-wide basis of recruitment that greatly obscured the imaginary axis that ran from the plaza of the Vivaut to the street of the de Jerusalem. Figures 3 and 4

---

20 *Ibid.*, deposition of Johan Aycart, fol. 26r; deposition of Laugier de Soliers, fol. 27r; deposition of Carle Athos, fol. 28r-v.
21 *Ibid.*, fol. 30v.
22 This identification was particularly odd because the merchant and draper Guilhem del Alans was an ally of the de Jerusalem.
23 *Ibid.*, fol. 34r.
24 E.g. *ibid.*, deposition of Johan Naulon, fol. 39r: *vidit aliquos de parte Petri de Jerusalem in Spiciaria et in Cambiis.*
25 ADBR, 3B 812, fol. 21r: *quod cotidie erant in platea Vivaudorum cum armis.*
26 *Ibid.*, fols. 17v and 21r.

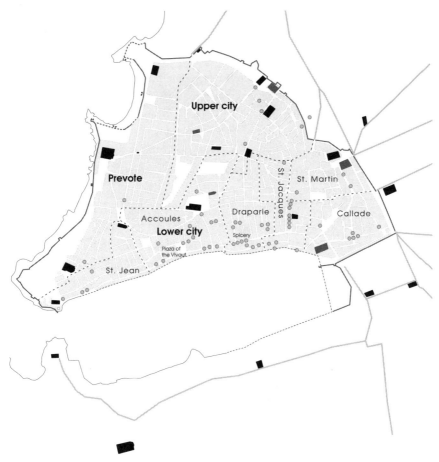

FIGURE 3:   Approximate Location of Residences of Vivaut Party Members.

take lists of *all* those who were identified in various mid-fourteenth-century records as members respectively of the Vivaut and de Jerusalem parties and plots the geographical distribution of their likely residences, where known.[27]

Although the maps suggest that certain streets were relatively homogenous – streets such as St. Jacques de Corregaria and the area around the plaza of the Vivaut for the Vivaut party; and the street known as Corregaria (not to be

27   Here and elsewhere I have relied on a prosopographical index containing some 14,000 names of people who lived in Marseille between 1337 and 1362. For a description of this research enterprise, see the appendix to Daniel Lord Smail, *Imaginary Cartographies: Possession and Identity in Late Medieval Marseille*, Ithaca 1999.

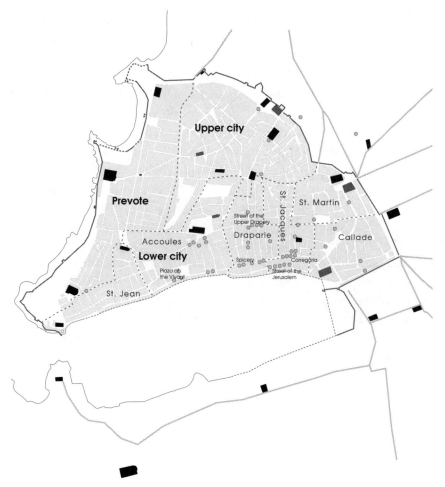

FIGURE 4:   Approximate Location of Residences of de Jerusalem Party Members.

confused with St. Jacques de Corregaria to the north; this street was located
at the eastern end of the street of the Lower Drapery), the eastern end of the
street of the de Jerusalem, and the street of the Upper Drapery for the de
Jerusalem faction – other streets show a great deal of overlap, notably in the
Spicery. Property belonging to the Martin family was at one point in time
located predominantly in the street of the de Jerusalem itself. On the level of
the *sixains*, the six basic administrative quarters into which the city was divided,
the Vivaut/Martin party shows a slightly greater concentration in the *sixains*
of St. Jean and Accoules, whereas the de Jerusalem were associated more with
the *sixains* of St. Jacques and Draparie. Yet the distinctions are very slight.

What lies behind the broad distribution of residences at this particular moment in the mid-fourteenth century? The answer to this question brings us to the subject of the social breadth of vengeance in fourteenth-century Marseille. The great hatred between the Vivaut and the de Jerusalem was a prominent feature of medieval Marseille. But theirs was not the only feud. Throughout the city, in neighbourhoods and among people of all social backgrounds, existing hatreds periodically erupted in episodes of violence and bloodshed and sometimes made their way into the courts. Hostile gestures created memories of grievances and the obligation to respond. Though the available sources make it difficult to say whether it was common for assaults to echo back and forth for generations in the manner of the classic feud, there is no question that injuries of different kinds routinely evoked simple reprisals. A classic example was the 1403 vengeance killing of a caulker named Johan Areat by Jacme Albin, a smith. In his defence, the smith argued that the vengeance killing was legitimate, since a year earlier, Johan had killed Jacme's brother. Moreover, the victim was still under the ban of contumacy and had not made peace with his victim's family, as required by law.[28]

Note the professions of the two men involved: a caulker and a smith. In this case, the smith felt no compunction about claiming the right to exercise legitimate vengeance. The eight extant notarised peace acts from mid-fourteenth-century Marseille that arose from killings or severe injuries all involved people from undistinguished backgrounds: shepherds, carpenters, butchers, bakers, peasants, day labourers, curriers, and so on.[29] Other records reveal that people thought capable of participating in hatreds included children, members of religious orders, servants and former slaves, and many, many women.

These were petty enmities, not nearly on the scale of the great Vivaut/ de Jerusalem enmity. But they mattered a great deal to the people involved, to the point where people cherished their enmities as if they were family heirlooms. In pursuit of hatred, they often sought additional resources that would allow them to best their adversaries. Often enough people involved in petty enmities turned to their own neighbours and friends, and the scale of the hatred escalated as others were drawn into it. In some especially interesting cases, however, it is clear that the individuals involved in neighbourhood

---

28 ADBR 3B 140, fols. 229r-273v, case opened 11 July 1403.
29 See ADBR 381E 38, fols. 19v-21r, 25 Apr. 1337; 381E 393, fol. 121v, 1 Mar. 1344; 381E 79, fols. 67v-68r, 9 June 1353; 381E 79, fol. 125r-v, 8 Dec. 1353; 381E 86, fols. 35r-37v, 29 May 1354; ADBR 355E 290, fols. 20r-21r, 4 Apr. 1355; 355E 35, fol. 62v, 6 Aug. 1357; AM II 42, fols. 60r-61v, 10 Apr. 1349.

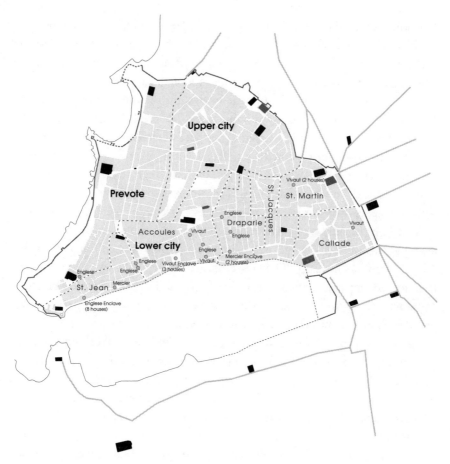

FIGURE 5: Approximate Location of All Houses Belonging to the Vivaut and Their Allies, the Englese and the Mercier.

enmities turned to the Vivaut and de Jerusalem factions. Both factions offered considerable resources – friends, allies, even legal advisers in the form of notaries, lawyers, and judges. Both offered protection from enemies. Above all, factional membership guaranteed that one's own murder would be avenged by one's factional colleagues. In Marseille's urban context, where mortality was high and the world of kin was relatively small, relatives were sometimes in short supply and not always in a position to avenge a death. Factional membership served as a kind of vengeance-insurance policy.

The hatred between the Vivaut and the de Jerusalem, therefore, acted as an alternative forum for justice, and petty neighbourhood feuds sometimes accreted to the Vivaut/de Jerusalem axis, losing their own autonomy in the process. The geographies of the maps above are muddied precisely because they

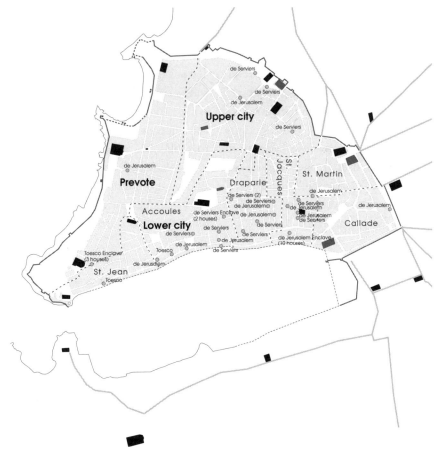

FIGURE 6: Approximate Location of All Houses Belonging to the de Jerusalem and Their Allies, the Toesco and the de Serviers.

reveal the geographical origins of these petty hatreds. The best-known examples are those provided by the feuds pitting the Englese against the Toesco and the Mercier against the de Serviers. The Englese and the Mercier were clients or allies of the Vivaut. Their enemies were allies of the de Jerusalem. Their respective hatreds were spawned by residential proximity (compare Figures 5 and 6). Both the Englese and the Toesco were fisherfolk, and the prominent members of the family lived in family enclaves located at the western end of the *sixain* of St. Jean. The Mercier and the de Serviers, in turn, lived in fairly close proximity to one another in the *sixain* of Draparie: the Mercier in the Spicery; the de Serviers in the Fishmongery. Consider a second time the maps identifying the residences of Vivaut and de Jerusalem faction members (see Figures 3 and 4). The maps look almost identical because both factions recruited members out of petty neighbourhood adversaries, ensuring that both factions were represented in most quarters of the city.

That the gravitational pull of the great hatred between the Vivaut and the de Jerusalem was drawing in petty hatreds may be seen in legal disputes. Several court cases from the period seem to have arisen from disputes that were originally based either in neighbourhood conflicts or in professional disputes but were, over time, absorbed into the great feud. The analysis of these cases is complicated, so in the interests of space I shall discuss only one of these at length. The patterns in this case are similar to those found in two or three other cases, and suggest a plausible model for understanding the process of factional recruitment.

Guilhem Tomas was a fairly prominent merchant who lived in an area known as the Spur, probably named after a house- or tavern-sign in the neighbourhood. A man by the same name shows up in records as early as 1341; by the early 1360s, someone of this name was elevated enough to have participated on one of the committees of the city council. This is very likely to be the same man, since he lived in the same administrative district as our Guilhem (the *sixain* of St. Jacques), and the only other Guilhem Tomas from the period was a fisherman of relatively low status. Guilhem was important enough that a number of addresses were identified in relation to his residence. By way of example, in a confraternal record from the early 1350s a man named Guilhem Bernat was identified as living 'before (the house of) Guilhem Tomas, at the Spur' (*denant Guilhem Tomas a Lesperon*).[30]

Guilhem's equally prominent neighbour was a public notary named Guilhem de Belavila. This Guilhem received his notarial license on 9 June 1340 and was probably of much the same age as Guilhem Tomas. As a notary, he kept registers of many kinds of contracts on behalf of clients, though none, as it happens, are still extant. De Belavila was also nominated to serve at least one year-long stint as a notary of the criminal court, a position accorded only to relatively senior and respected notaries.

By the 1350s or early 1360s, the two men were among the most prominent residents of the Spur and it appears that in their jockeying for position and influence they ran afoul of each other. Matters came to a head in May of 1365 when de Belavila and his brother-in-law Fulco Robaut killed Tomas during the course of a fight that took place on the street of the Spur, in front of

---

30 See ADBR 2HD E7 for a number of examples of this kind.

TABLE 3: Factional Allegiance of the Members of the City Council, by *Sixain* of Residence

Sixain	Councilors affiliated with the de Jerusalem party	Councilors affiliated with the Vivaut party	Unaffiliated with any party	Degree of factionalisation (%)
St. Jean	1	1	19	10
Accoules	7	6	20	39
Draparie	8	6	38	27
St. Jacques	8	7	19	44
St. Martin	2	4	21	22
Callade	2	4	24	20
Total	28	28	141	28

Source: AM BB 21

their own houses and witnessed by all the neighbours. During the course of the subsequent trial, we learn that Tomas was a committed member of the de Jerusalem faction. De Belavila, in turn, was attached to the Vivaut. There is no way of knowing how far back this factional association went. Tomas had married a woman named Johana de Fonte, whose maiden name suggests kinship with a family whose menfolk supported the de Jerusalem faction. In 1356, de Belavila had given testimony in a court case in favour of a Vivaut party captain. But the enmity also bears a strong local flavour. Witnesses for both sides spoke eloquently of petty neighbourhood hatreds involving the wives and female friends of both men. A plausible scenario is that, as the rivalry deepened over the course of the 1350s, Tomas was drawn into the orbit of the de Jerusalem by virtue of his wife's relations. De Belavila, in turn, was pushed into the arms of the Vivaut. Whatever the situation, the Spur, by 1365, was riven by an enmity that had become overtly factionalised.

A similar model may explain what happened in the case of the Toesco and the Englese in St. Jean and the Mercier and the de Serviers in the area of the Spicery and Fishmongery. The muddied geography of the Vivaut/de Jerusalem feud acts as a kind of indirect proof for the assertion that feuds or enmities were practiced up and down the social spectrum. The major families did not recruit members solely among their own neighbours, thus dividing the city into distinct regions. Instead, the factional members can be found throughout the city, as neighbourhood adversaries like Guilhem de Belavila and Guilhem Tomas sought to escalate their own enmities by pursuing the resources offered by the factions.

The powerful gravitational pull of the great Vivaut/de Jerusalem enmity suggests a situation where a lawless city was made even more lawless by the sinister activities of renegade patricians. It is certainly true that the power of the Angevin kings and queens was weakening over the course of the fourteenth century. Vivaut partisans considered the de Jerusalem party to be a savage band of men inspired by the devil and contemptuous of all civility. The feeling was entirely mutual. Given this situation, accusations of lawlessness are only too common in Marseille's fourteenth-century court records, since both parties frequently used the courts to get back at one another and stuffed their accusations and depositions with moralising comments. In point of fact, however, neither the Vivaut nor the de Jerusalem were outsiders to the sphere of civic governance, since both were well represented on the city council. Records listing the members of the city council, moreover, reveal that factional allegiance was roughly balanced from one *sixain* to the next, so that no given faction dominated any of the *sixains* (Table 3).

In a sense, it may be accurate to view the factions as the prototypes for political parties. Hence the powerful symbolism of the royal entry of 1351, where both political parties shared responsibility for carrying aloft the body of the king, the representation of the state.

The structures of violence characteristic of mid-fourteenth-century Marseille are not like the classic feuds studied by anthropologists and historians. They bear greater resemblance to the factional warfare of the Later Middle Ages and Early Modern Era.[31] Although the feuding agnatic cores of the Vivaut and de Jerusalem families were important to factional membership and recruitment strategies, the agnatic cores had long since been swamped by the addition of other families. In size, each faction counted more than a hundred members at any given moment, a significant grouping in a city of no more than 20,000 around the middle of the fourteenth century. Yet although it would be fair to say that the practice of feuding was evolving in the fourteenth century – is there ever a time when customs of vengeance are not in transformation? – this observation is not meant to minimise the significance of vengeance in late medieval Massiliote society. The two major factions of mid-fourteenth-century Marseille grew large not because their captains recruited gangs of thugs or servitors whose services were rewarded by a daily wage. Instead, ordinary folk – fishermen, artisans, agricultural workers, merchants, and men-of-law –

---

31 See, among others, Muir 1993, and Osvaldo Raggio, *Faide e parentele: Lo stato genovese visto dalla Fontanabuona*, Turin 1990.

engaging in their own family feuds selectively chose to ally themselves with certain factions so as to pursue their own enmities more efficiently.

The sources do not make it easy to witness this transformation in particular cases, though the case of Guilhem Tomas and Guilhem de Belavila is one of several that provides some insight into the nature of the process. More relevant to the arguments made here is the observation that the Vivaut and the de Jerusalem attracted members from all over the city, often from the very same neighbourhoods. As this suggests, local neighbourhood enmities pitting individuals of low to moderate social status were absorbed into greater factional enmities. This was a political process, as individuals sought access to resources made available to them by the larger factions. In this transformation we may see the origins of political parties, a process that was driven, ultimately, by the widespread practice of enmity in late medieval society.

Italian Medieval Vendetta

TREVOR DEAN

In an article written in 1996, Andrea Zorzi, one of the leading historians of Italian medieval crime and justice, argued for the existence of a 'culture of vengeance' in Italy in the period from the thirteenth to the fifteenth centuries.[1] He advanced four main aspects of this culture: a language of conflict that was dominated by notions of friendship and enmity; the positive value attributed to vengeance by almost all the great thinkers; vengeance having a central place in works of civic education; and feuds (*faida*) not just as expressions of personal hatred, but as mechanisms to protect family honour.

My own study of revenge has taken a rather different path. My article published in 1997, in ignorance of Andrea Zorzi's arguments above, was conceived in a spirit of opposition to the dominance in Italian historiography of the Florentine experience, and to a conception of revenge that limited its incidence and social environment to the family.[2] Most of the older and more recent studies of Italian vendetta have, with some exceptions,[3] been about Florence,[4] and Zorzi too is a Florentine historian. Most have accepted a construct

---

1   Andrea Zorzi, "Conflits et pratiques infrajudiciaires dans les formations politiques italiennes due XIIIe au XVe siècles", Benoit Garnot (ed.), *L'infrajudiciaire du Moyen Age à l'époque contemporaine*, Dijon 1996, esp. pp. 23-24.

2   Trevor Dean, "Marriage and mutilation: vendetta in late medieval Italy", *Past & Present*, 157, 1997, pp. 3-36.

3   Edward Muir, *Mad Blood Stirring: Vendetta and Factions in Friuli during the Renaissance*, Baltimore 1993. On the same theme, see also Furio Bianco, "*Mihi vindictam*: aristocratic clans and rural communities in a feud in Friuli in the late fifteenth and early sixteenth centuries", Trevor Dean and K.J.P. Lowe (eds.), *Crime, Society and the Law in Renaissance Italy*, Cambridge 1994.

4   I. Del Lungo, "Una vendetta in Firenze: il giorno di San Giovanni del 1295", *Archivio storico italiano*, 4:18, 1886, pp. 355-409. Umberto Dorini, "La vendetta privata al tempo di Dante", *Giornale dantesco*, 29, 1926. Anna Maria Enriques, "La vendetta nella vita e nella legislazione fiorentina", *Archivio storico italiano*, 7:19, 1933, pp. 85-146, 181-223. Thomas Kuehn, "Honor and conflict in a fifteenth-century Florentine family", *Ricerche storiche*, 10, 1980, pp. 287-310, and now in his *Law, Family and Women: Toward a Legal Anthropology of Renaissance Italy*, Chicago 1991. Matthew Taylor, "Pace con onore: un esempio del declino della ven-

ITALIAN MEDIEVAL VENDETTA   135

of revenge that is essentially familial. This is echoed in recent anthropological studies: Kelly's typology of the practice of vengeance mainly concerns varieties of 'kin-based vengeance obligations'.[5] The Florentine construct has two essential elements, both related to the possession or ownership of revenge: injuries to one member of a family are said to belong to all the kin; and vendetta is said to be an obligation on kinsmen and transmitted down the generations.

So I argued, conversely:

1. That revenge was not confined to family contexts. When we look across a range of late-medieval narrative sources, we find vendetta embedded in warfare between all sorts of social groups, not just families, but, for example, between armies and cities too. Revenge could play both positive and negative roles in conflict: on the one hand, supporting just war, or inspiring soldiers to fight; on the other, being generated after battle by the ferocity of the fighting or the treatment of prisoners of war. Moreover, within those social groups we often find the individual exacting his own revenge, without reference to ownership by kin.

2. That within families there was no over-riding obligation to pursue vengeance, and no automatic coagulation of family solidarity. Revenge had to be deserved; families could choose the vendettas they wished to pursue; and families could be pulled apart as well as together by the exercise of vengeance.

3. That there were significant differences in law and practice across Italy. Florentine law and practice was more elaborately developed than those in other parts of Italy: the Florentines' law on revenge attacks is unintelligibly complex, their frame of reference for vendetta being more familial than elsewhere. Moreover, against the view – again based on the Florentine experience – that vendetta was respected by the law, lawyers and the law-courts, I have argued that in some other cities vendetta was criminalised, and that there are examples of prosecutions and penalties for revenge attacks.[6]

---

detta a Firenze nel primo Quattrocento", *Archivio storico italiano*, 553, 1992, pp. 775-804. Alessandro Valori, "Famiglia e memoria: Luca da Panzano dal suo "Libro di ricordi": uno studio sulle relazioni familiari nello specchio della scrittura", *Archivio storico italiano*, 560, 1994, pp. 261-97.

5   Raymond Kelly, *Warless Societies and the Origins of War*, Ann Arbor 2000, p. 60, as quoted in Pamela J. Stewart and Andrew Strathern, *Violence: Theory and Ethnography*, London 2002, p. 111.

6   Dean 1999, pp. 8-10. Trevor Dean, "Violence, vendetta and peacemaking in late medieval Bologna", *Criminal Justice History*, 17, 2002, pp. 1-17, esp. pp. 4-5.

4   That different political structures might act either to encourage or to stifle the memory of injuries. Preserving the memory of injuries received is central to vendetta and, in contrasting the operation of memory in Florentine and non-Florentine accounts of revenge killings, I argued that political context played an important role in the operation of selective memory. As has recently been observed: 'revenge may operate either to control levels of killings or to accelerate them, depending on the political and historical contexts'.[7]

My work has thus focused on vendetta, and not feud, because it is the more observable phenomenon in late-medieval Italian texts. Vendetta is clearly vengeance, retaliation for specific injury, whereas there was no word corresponding to 'feud' or 'bloodfeud': instead writers use the terms 'enmity', 'hatred' or 'war' (*inimicitia, odium, guerra*).

A second strand in my approach to vendetta has been an interest in the revenge *narrative*. In that same article in 1997, I examined the issue of topoi in the narrative origins and conclusions of cycles of revenge: in particular, the ways in which revenge cycles were presented as starting in marriage disputes, and as closing in the mutilation of revenge targets. In the following years, I benefited from reading Natalie Davis' article on Montaillou, which exposed the narrative structure of depositions, and her *Fiction in the Archives*, which treats petitions for pardon as constructed tales which fall into certain types according to gender, social rank and occupation. Petitions thus use story-telling techniques to transform actors and actions into forms that the authorities would recognise as justifying pardon.[8] By the time I came to write about revenge in my book *Crime in Medieval Europe*, such an approach had been reinforced by Claude Gauvard's incomparable study of petitions for pardon in the France of King Charles VI, and the way that she treats these as a source that gives us not a crime or a criminal or a victim, but only images of them in accordance with the needs of pardon: in other words these are narratives adapted to their audience. What we are left with is not an objective account of a crime, but a tale spun within the limits of contemporary credibility.[9] So petitions for pardon can be placed against fictional accounts of revenge to reveal the points of contact, the similarities between fictional and 'factual'

---

7   Stewart and Strathern 2002, p. 113.

8   Natalie Zemon Davis, "Les conteurs de Montaillou", *Annales*, 34, 1979, pp. 61-73. Idem., *Fiction in the Archives: Pardon Tales and their Tellers in Sixteenth-century France*, Oxford 1987.

9   Claude Gauvard, *'De grace especial': Crime, état et société en France á la fin du Moyen Age*, Paris 1991, pp. 66-68.

narration: both are exercises in persuasion, both are constructed around a small group of themes, both share elements in the culture of revenge such as incitement and escalation.[10]

It is the issue of narrative structure that I want directly to address here. To do this, I have selected revenge narratives – mostly of a familial kind – from three chronicles. These sources are: the Sienese chronicles (*Cronache senesi*) from the fourteenth century; the chronicle of Count Francesco di Montemarte, from the chronicles of the city of Orvieto; and the chronicle of Giovanni di maestro Pedrino, from fifteenth-century Forlì. Now, a historian should at this point provide some information about these authors, and about the cities in which they wrote, as a means of establishing context.[11] So, we might note the range presented here in the type of city, the type of regime, and the social status of the authors. Siena was a one-time big commercial centre, now fading.[12] Forlì was a small agricultural town. Orvieto was a disturbed and depopulated city, profoundly damaged by both the Black Death and the movement of the papacy to Avignon.[13] Siena was one of the surviving republican city-states, whereas Forlì had long been ruled by a single family, and Orvieto was undergoing the turbulent transition from city-state to lordship. Equally varied is the authorship of these chronicles: one was written by a count, one by an artisan, and one by an anonymous bourgeois. This group of chronicles thus represents fairly faithfully the social and political world beyond Florence. We might expect that these chroniclers would voice different perceptions of vendetta in their narratives. This is partly true, but it does not seem to be related to the social situation of the authors. This essay will examine those differences, by focusing on four aspects: the narrative construction of victim innocence, the appropriateness of the target, the moral framework of responses by observers, and the marginalisation of women.

10   Trevor Dean, *Crime in Medieval Europe*, London 2001, pp. 96-98.
11   Bernard Guenée, "Introduction", Jean-Philippe Genet (ed.), *L'historiographie médiévale en Europe*, Paris 1991, pp. 13-18, at p. 14. Idem, "Histoires, annales, chroniques: essai sur les genres historiques au Moyen Age", *Annales*, 28, 1973, pp. 997-1016, at p. 998.
12   Giuliano Pinto, "'Honour' and 'profit': landed property and trade in medieval Siena", Trevor Dean and Chris Wickham (eds.), *City and Countryside in late Medieval and Renaissance Italy*, London 1990.
13   See recently David Foote, "In search of the quiet city: civic identity and papal state building in fourteenth-century Orvieto", Paula Findlen, Michelle M. Fontaine and Duane J. Osheim (eds.), *Beyond Florence: The Contours of Medieval and Early Modern Italy*, Stanford 2003, and Daniel Waley, *Medieval Orvieto*, Cambridge, 1952.

1. The narrative innocence of the victim

Take these six short revenge narratives from the fourteenth-century Sienese chronicles.[14]

I. [1311] Pazzino Pazzi, one of the major leaders ruling Florence, and loved by the people, went out hawking on horse without a guard, and was killed by Paffiera Cavalcanti, treacherously, so it was said, because Pazzino was not on the look-out for them ['non si guardava da loro']. This was in revenge for Maso Cavalcanti: Pazzino was blamed for having him killed.

II. [1321] Francesco, called 'friar', the son of Messer Vanni Sinibaldi, going home to the Salimbeni palace [in Siena] on Tuesday evening 29th December ... was attacked by Balsino di Francesco Tolomei, with some accomplices, one of whom wounded him. From his wounds Francesco died. Francesco had not been on the alert, because there was peace between them for past injuries. For this deed, Balsino and the others were banished [by the commune].

III. [1322] Giovanni, called 'Bottone', the son of Messer Salimbene arranged to have some armed men from Florence, who came secretly, entering Siena in twos and threes just as the gates were closing. It was said that these men were sent to him by a Florentine citizen who was a friend of the Salimbeni family. The armed men stayed hidden in the Salimbeni palace. On a Tuesday evening in April, Giovanni, with some of his kinsmen and with the armed men, took up position on the piazza of the Tolomei family, securing all the exits. He then went to the rear of the Tolomei palace and placed ladders up to the windows. He and his men then entered the palace, broke down some doors and killed Mino, Tondo and Prina, the sons of the deceased Messer Meo Tolomei. Meanwhile, a clamour arose and the podestà's family took up arms, and the government rang the alarm bell, such that most of the *popolo* turned out, and if Giovanni had stayed any longer, he and his men would have been killed by the *popolo*. Giovanni and his men left Siena and went to Rocca. Giovanni did this deed out of revenge for Francesco di Messer Vanni Salimbeni, his kinsman. His houses were destroyed [by the commune] and he was declared a rebel.

IV. One night in June, Agnolino Bottone, Stricca di Messer Giovanni, and Meo di Cione, all members of the Salimbeni, concealed some armed men in a cellar outside Lucignano, with the connivance of the priest of the parish (which belonged to Messer Francesco). On the following morning, Messer Francesco Tolomei, and his son and nephews, left Lucignano for a walk. At that point the soldiers came out of their hiding place and attacked them, cutting Francesco to pieces, wounding his son and one

---

14   Alessandro Lisini and Fabio Iacometti (eds.), "Cronache senesi", *Rerum italicarum scriptores*, 2nd ed., 15, pt 6, Bologna 1931-, pp. 316, 389, 391, 505, 512, 530.

of his nephews. Another boy who was with Francesco, Pietro Piccolomini, was also wounded and died shortly afterwards; he had not been recognised by the Salimbeni. During the assault, Agnolino, Stricca and Meo arrived with some horsemen, and cut the head off Francesco's corpse. They also cut [mutilated?] many of the bodies, and then returned to the castle in Tentenano.

V. Four members of the Piccolomini entered the castle of Malavolti and killed Rigolo, who was playing chess. They had thought to find Messer Guasta there. And they did this to avenge the wounding of Naddo [Piccolomini].

VI. 25 December: Messer Salimbene degli Scotti, a Sienese nobleman, went with some kinsmen to eat with some Tolomei. They were attacked by Vanuccio de' Saraceni ... with twenty armed men: they wounded Messer Salimbene many times, out of personal vendetta. Within a few days, he was dead.

These narratives use markers of innocence in the same way as petitions for pardon. Just as petitions suggest that, as Natalie Davis puts it, the supplicant was taken by surprise while going about his daily business or his festive pleasure in a peaceable manner,[15] so too some revenge narratives stress the innocence and peaceableness of one party, and the guilt and guile of the other. They spin a tale of innocence overpowered by cunning. One could say that these tales are focalised on the victim. So, when the Sienese chronicler notes that victims of revenge attacks 'went out hawking on horse without a guard ... not on the look-out', 'had not been on the alert, because there was peace between them for past injuries', was simply 'playing chess', or was going to a Christmas dinner, he is presenting the revenge as a violation of sacred time (peace, game-time, Christmas). The same stress on innocence applies to chronicle narratives that include deception by the avengers: again, the Sienese chronicle speaks of the attackers as 'armed men from Florence, who came secretly ... stayed hidden', or as 'some armed men [concealed] in a cellar ... with the connivance of the priest of the parish'. Secrecy, concealment, connivance of those who should be outside revenge-taking, all reinforce this focalisation.

---

15   Davis 1987, pp. 43-44.

2. Appropriate revenge targets

Here I want to examine just one narrative, from the Orvieto chronicle. Control of Orvieto in the mid-fourteenth century was contested between two factions. In a battle between these factions, Luca di Vannozzo was captured and taken prisoner.[16]

[1350] In this time, the sons of Messer Ermanno with some cavalry and infantry, went to attack Sermognano. They took it, and they had Cecco di Niccolò and fifteen other citizens, who were there, killed … In one raid, they captured Luca di Vannuzzo, the son of a bastard of the sons of Messer Buonconte. Because he [Luca] was a powerful man, Benedetto di Messer Buonconte had great affection for him, and he was taken prisoner to Torre. There, Niccolò di Cataluccio de' Bisenzo killed him. For this reason, Luca's brother, Conte, having as his prisoner Pietro di Corrado di Messer Ermanno, a boy of seven years, took him to the Piazza del Popolo, and killed him, cutting his throat as if he were a kid-goat. And he did this despite the fact that his sister was married to Buonconte di Ugolino di Messer Buonconte. This was regarded as a thing of the greatest cruelty and barbarity, to kill an innocent boy in this fashion.

Noticeable here is the use of a child as a revenge-target and the perception of a relation of alterity (human/animal) between avenger and boy-victim. This is evidently deliberate, a way of conveying the inhumanity of using children as revenge targets. This calls to mind a similar comment in the chronicle of another Tuscan city, Pistoia, following the mutilation in revenge of a youth of unspecified age by distant members of his own family: it was 'considered by everyone to be too cruel and severe a thing, to shed their own family's blood'.[17] Public opinion regarded certain revenges as too cruel, severe or barbarous.

3. Revenge tale as exemplum

Chroniclers could present revenge narratives with an explicit moral message, in the manner of the exempla used by medieval preachers. In doing so, they report the attitudes of an asserted common morality, drawing its points of reference either from the Bible, or from proverbs, or from common report, *fama*. I have elsewhere indicated the exemplary features of a narrative story in

---

16   Luigi Fumi (ed.), "Cronica del conte Francesco di Montemarte", in *Ephemerides urbevetane*, *Rerum italicarum scriptores*, vol. 15, pt 5, Città di Castello 1903-, p. 225.

17   Trevor Dean, *The Towns of Italy in the later Middle Ages*, Manchester 2000, pp. 185-186.

the Graziani chronicle from Perugia.[18] In the chronicles taken for the present study, the chief example comes from the Forlì chronicle of Giovanni di maestro Pedrino.[19]

[1434] Discord had sowed its seed so that now the bad harvest had to be reaped. A family of peasants, the sons of Jacobo da Poggio, arrived to take revenge for one of Jacobo's sons who had been killed by the family of Varano Turchi, a year previously. They left Castrocaro, where they lived, and, with the support of some adherents, assailed their enemies in Poggio, wounding some and killing the 'principal' who had killed Jacobo's son. They then sought to return to Castrocaro, but found their way blocked by Varano and his family, both men and women, and by force they wounded more men than they intended. And a woman was killed. Their allies disappeared, and two of Jacobo's three sons were wounded, and later died at Castrocaro. And in this way, they avenge badly their shame, those who add to the evil: of Jacobo's four sons only one now survives.

The framing statements of this narration – of reaping the harvest sown by discord, and of adding to evil by bad revenge – illustrates reference to biblical and proverbial texts. The introductory sentence echoes a passage from *Hosea*, 'they have sown the wind and shall reap the whirlwind'; the ending re-states a proverb, which was current already in the thirteenth century and known in northern Europe as well as in Italy.[20] This proverb counters the pressure to take vengeance by warning of the moral and human costs of escalation.

4. Narrative marginalisation of women

My aim here is to investigate the allocation of roles in a narrative according to the sex of the character. Writing recently about 'Women's influence on revenge in ancient Greece', Fiona McHardy has argued that, although women are said not to fight in feuds, and killing a woman in a feud is said not to be honourable, Greek women did participate in feuds, in three ways: by raising children to avenge their father's murder, by influencing the kin to take revenge,

---

18   Dean 1999, p. 32.
19   Giovanni di maestro Pedrino depintore, *Cronica del suo tempo*, Gino Borghezio and Marco Vattasso (eds.), Rome 1929, vol. 1, p. 477.
20   Dean 1999, p. 18. James W. Hassell, *Middle French Proverbs, Sentences and Proverbial Phrases*, Toronto 1982, p. 137.

and by making calls for vengeance.[21] Women are associated in both ancient Greek history and modern Mediterranean culture with issuing persistent calls for revenge, and with preserving the memory of unavenged wrongs. The role women assume in the origins of medieval Italian revenge is rather different, and the key difference lies in agency. I have elsewhere examined two forms of this – the broken marriage promise and aggression in defence of wronged women[22] – but in the narratives I am using here, marginalisation works in other ways: first, by referring to women only at the beginning or end of revenge stories; and second, by minimising women's role in the process of revenge-taking. Women thus provide only the occasions for revenge-takers to strike; they represent cross-cutting ties which revenge-takers disregard; and if they do suffer injury, they are nameless additions to detailed lists of male victims.

Thus, the Forlì chronicler tells one revenge story in the following way:

[1425] A castellan had taken a daughter of an inhabitant of the castle. The father complained, but no disciplinary action was taken. So, to take his revenge, this man arranged to betray the castle to Florentine troops. Though the troops entered, they could not take the castle, because aid swiftly arrived. The castellan seized the man and had him executed.[23]

As we have seen, the same chronicler, narrating a different revenge story, gives names and kin-relationships for all the men killed or injured, but of the female victim says merely 'And a woman was killed'.

Moving to Orvieto, we have two cases of marginalisation in the course of revenge attacks. The origin of the enmity lay in an action of war: Cecco, the son of Conte Farolfo, was wounded and taken prisoner. He surrendered to Silvestro Gatti, the lord of Viterbo, who was his kinsman, and who had him mounted on his horse. But Neri de' Baschi, apparently in revenge for the killing of one of his own kinsmen, wounded Cecco in the back with a dagger, killing him. A revenge attack was then planned when the son of Silvestro, the main revenge target, came to Orvieto to be married.

21 Fiona McHardy, "Women's influence on revenge in ancient Greece", Fiona McHardy and Eireann Marshall (eds.), *Women's Influence on Classical Civilization*, London 2004, pp. 92-114.
22 Dean 1999, pp. 16-17.
23 Borghezio and Vattasso 1929, vol. 1, p. 122.

[1330] And after a while, Silvestro's son, Giovanni, concluded a marriage agreement in Orvieto with the son of Messer Buonconte, and came to be married. Ugolino di Buonconte was in the habit of going at night to a woman's house, and Giovanni went with him. The sons of count Farolfo's son, Ugolino, heard of this, and one night, near the church of San Francesco, they challenged Giovanni, and he was killed. And Ugolino di Messer Buonconte was fatally wounded in the face, despite the fact that he was many times asked by the attackers to withdraw and to leave this affair to them, but he refused, and so the enmity endured between the sons of Messer Buonconte and our family for a long time, until the commune of Orvieto made us make peace and marry Ugolino's son, Francesco, to Giovanna di Cecco.

Here women provide the occasion twice over: the marriage brings the revenge target into the city, and a nocturnal escapade brings him into the street. Women also supplied the means, through marriage, to create cross-cutting ties that, as Gluckmann argued,[24] had the potential to restrain vendetta.

Still in Orvieto, for a second case of marginalisation we return to the seven-year-old boy killed on the Piazza: the chronicler comments that the killer did this *despite the fact* that his sister was married to one of the opposing faction leaders – a case, we might note in parenthesis, of cross-cutting ties failing to function as restraints. From start to finish of revenge narratives, women are thus present, but at the margins and in the background.

Conclusion

The narrativised innocence of the victim, comments on the unsuitability of some revenge targets and moralised framing of revenge tales were all ways in which chroniclers distinguished between 'illegitimate, threatening violence' and 'proper "ordering" violence'.[25] They also seem to reflect a practice that had gone beyond individual revenge towards bloodfeud: a 'transition to kin group member liability – in which the malefactor is the preferential but not the only recognized target of vengeance'.[26] It was not, however, the case

---

24 Max Gluckman, "The peace in the feud", *Past and Present*, 8, 1955, pp. 1-14.
25 Valentin Groebner, *Defaced: The Visual Culture of Violence in the Late Middle Ages*, New York 2004, p. 16.
26 Kelly 2000, p. 60.

that 'any member of the killer's group is susceptible to vengeance' – women, children, other kinsmen were all regarded as non-targets. So, if there was a dominant culture of vengeance, there was also a counter-culture, visible in modes of writing about vendetta and expressing disapproval and criticism, not acceptance or tolerance.

Values and Violence: The Morals of Feuding in Late Medieval Germany[1]

HILLAY ZMORA

At the beginning of *The Peloponnesian War*, Thucydides has the Athenians enumerate the three main reasons why men go to war: 'fear, honor, and interest'.[2] Recently, another eminent historian of that war argued that in many major conflicts in history some aspect of honour was a decisive cause, whereas 'considerations of practical utility and material gain' played only a small role.[3] Whether, and in what manner, these observations on wars apply to the feuds of fifteenth- and sixteenth-century German nobles is, to judge by the scholarly literature, a matter over which historians are likely to have a quarrel.[4]

1   I thank Sheilagh Ogilvie and Joachim Schneider for their comments on earlier drafts of this article.

2   *The Landmark Thucydides: A Comprehensive Guide to the Pelopennesian War*, Richard Crawley (trans.), Robert B. Strassler (ed.), New York 1996, 1.76.2 (p. 43).

3   Donald Kagan, *On the Origins of War and the Preservation of Peace*, New York 1995, p. 8.

4   Several competing interpretations and explanatory models have been proposed in recent years: Werner Rösener, "Zur Problematik des spätmittelalterlichen Raubrittertums", Wilhelm Maurer and Hans Patze (eds.), *Festschrift für Berent Schwineköper zum 70. Geburtstag*, Sigmaringen 1982, pp. 469-488. Regina Görner, *Raubritter: Untersuchungen zur Lage des spätmittelalterlichen Niederadels, besonders im südlichen Westfalen*, Münster in Westfalen 1987. Gadi Algazi, "'Sie würden hinten nach so gail.' Vom sozialen Gebrauch der Fehde im 15. Jahrhundert", Thomas Lindenberger and Alf Lüdtke (eds.), *Physische Gewalt. Studien zur Geschichte der Neuzeit*, Frankfurt a.M. 1995, pp. 39-77. Idem, *Herrengewalt und Gewalt der Herren im späten Mittelalter: Herrschaft, Gegenseitigkeit und Sprachgebrauch*, Frankfurt a.M. 1996. Joseph Morsel, "'Das sy sich mitt der besstenn gewarsamig schicken, das sy durch die widerwertigenn Franckenn nitt nidergeworffen werdenn'. Überlegungen zum sozialen Sinn der Fehdepraxis am Beispiel des spätmittelalterlichen Franken", Dieter Rödel and Joachim Schneider (eds.), *Strukturen der Gesellschaft im Mittelalter. Interdisziplinäre Mediävistik in Würzburg*, Wiesbaden 1996, pp. 140-167. Hillay Zmora, *State and Nobility in Early Modern Germany: The Knightly Feud in Franconia, 1440-1567*, Cambridge 1998. Cf. Klaus Graf, "Gewalt und Adel in Südwestdeutschland. Überlegungen zur spätmittelalterlichen Fehde", on-line

The question of the difference between war and feud has been one aspect of the fundamental debate over the nature of the feud and what it reveals about the social and political world in which it inhered. Otto Brunner famously contended that 'all wars within Christendom must be understood as feuds, in a legal sense'.[5] This is too sweeping a statement. For it might be argued that, if it is indeed quite difficult to tell feud from war with regard to earlier times, the military renaissance of the late medieval and early modern period had rendered the contrast between war and lower forms of violence unmistakable.[6] The emergence, or resurgence, of a military culture which can be characterised as Western (re)introduced massed, well-drilled armies arrayed in close-ordered ranks and fighting shock combats to the bitter end.[7] This approach to war-making – which the Marshal de Saxe was later to describe generically as 'l'ordre, et la discipline, et la manière de combattre'[8] – was a far cry from the 'typical' feud.

Yet, as far as the *Reich* is concerned, these military-historical arguments overshoot the mark. The *Reich* did not experience the crucible of furious, interminable and devastatingly expensive wars in which the modern states were forged in the Late Middle Ages in Western Europe. It matters little in this respect that the Swiss style of warfare was known well in Germany and that experiments with comparable, innovative formations and tactics were made in the late fifteenth century.[9] No great battles were fought on German soil in this period. In terms of intensity, magnitude, organisation, mobilisation of resources, or historical importance, there were no Ravennas, Marignanos, or Pavias here. And military conflicts within Germany, between its multiple constituent powers, remained modest. On the other hand, it was

---

  (http://www.geschichte.uni-freiburg.de/mertens/graf/gewalt.htm) 2000. See also Christine Reinle, *Bauernfehden: Studien zur Fehdeführung Nichtadliger im spätmittelalterlichen römisch-deutschen Reich, besonders in den bayerischen Herzogtümern*, Stuttgart 2003, pp. 276-277.

5   Otto Brunner, *'Land' and Lordship: Structures of Governance in Medieval Austria*, Howard Kaminsky and James Van Horn Melton (trans.), Philadelphia 1992, p. 35.

6   Brunner was of course aware that armed conflicts were of different scope. But such dissimilarities do not necessarily vitiate his point: wars were great feuds, feuds small wars. He did point out that by the end of the Middle Ages war and feud could practically be distinguished, *ibid.*, p. 34.

7   See Thomas Arnold, *The Renaissance at War*, London 2001, esp. pp. 69-100, and the magnificent Victor Davis Hanson, *Why the West Has Won: Carnage and Culture from Salamis to Vietnam*, London 2001.

8   Quoted by John Keegan, *A History of Warfare*, London 1993, p. 11.

9   Harald Kleinschmidt, "Disziplinierung zum Kampf: Neue Forschungen zum Wandel militärischer Verhaltensweisen im 15. und 16. Jahrhundert", *Blätter für deutsche Landesgeschichte*, 132, 1996, pp. 173-200, pp. 175-182. Arnold 2001, pp. 82-83.

precisely in such 'provincial' atmosphere, in the small landscapes disturbed but not transformed by the violent movement of modern state formation, that feuds proliferated. It must then be conceded in advance of any analysis of the causes and aims of feuds that if Brunner's claim is grotesque with regard to Christendom at large, it does make better sense with regard to the south and south-west of Germany. In this geopolitically highly fragmented area, with its puny territorial states, its kaleidoscopic jumble of ill-defined, intermingled and competing jurisdictions, wars and feuds had more resemblances and intimate relationships than elsewhere. It is hard to imagine, for instance, a French king deigning to conduct a feud against an untitled *gentilhomme*; it was nothing out of the ordinary for a German prince to be engaged in a feud against this or that local nobles. An otherwise perceptive observer, Philippe de Commynes noted with evident perplexity that 'there are [in Germany] so many fortified places and so many people inclined to do evil and to plunder and rob, and who use force and violence against each other on the slightest pretence, that it is almost incredible. For a single man with only a valet to attend him will defy a whole city and even attack a duke, so that he will have a better excuse to rob him, by using a small castle on a rock, where he can retire and where he has twenty or thirty horsemen'.[10] Moreover, given the nature of territorial contests in these politically incoherent zones, wars often appear as little more than concatenations of feuds, feuds as integral parts of – or apologies for – war.[11]

German realities, then, make it difficult to demarcate the feud, and hence to define and explain it. However, one hallmark of a great many feuds, which hitherto has not received attention commensurate with its significance, was not a characteristic of wars: the rivals were more often than not part of the same local or regional social setting, and were regularly linked to each other by multi-stranded social and economic ties. They frequently knew each other all too well already before they came to blows. Their feuds punctuated what was an ongoing relationship. This simple and ubiquitous fact was a crucial factor: it did a good deal to shape the methods employed in feuds as well as to inform their causes and motives. It may thus serve not simply to differentiate feuds from wars, but also as an interpretative key.[12] Now to stress this difference

---

10 Samuel Kinser (ed.), *The Memoirs of Philippe de Commynes*, 1-2, Isabelle Cazeaux (trans.), Columbia, SC 1969-1973, vol. 1, pp. 354-355.

11 See Zmora 1998, pp. 96-100.

12 The feuds at issue here are primarily those between nobles, and to some extent also those between nobles and their princes. The interpretation suggested below is thus of limited scope: it is not intended as an overall explanation of feuding, but to contribute to the elucidation of one important aspect of feuding. It does, however, apply also to some feuds against cit-

is not to deny that the Thucydidean triad of 'fear, honor, and interest' was equally operative in feuds. But it does suggest that this amalgam of non-rational impulses and rational calculations should be analysed in the formative context of the inimical intimacy in which so many feuds were rooted. This is the aim of the pages that follow, which focus on the motivational role of values and morals in feuds.

Several telling examples are contained in the *Geschichten und Taten* of the Franconian nobleman Wilwolt von Schaumberg.[13] Written in the early years of the sixteenth century by his relation Ludwig d.J. von Eyb,[14] the 'biography' of Wilwolt was conceived with a view to educating the young in the values and ideals of the nobility.[15] Given its expressly didactic purpose on the one hand, and its protagonist's evident taste for feuding on the other, the *Geschichten und Taten* is rich with information on the expectations and attitudes associated with, and expressed in, noblemen's agonistic conduct towards each other. Thus, at a tournament in Mainz, this paragon of nobiliary virtues accused one Martin Zollner (von Rothenstein) of dispossessing a woman relation of his of her inheritance. At first, Wilwolt and Zollner only exchanged harsh words. Then Wilwolt became worried that if he left it at that he would be held in contempt. He spent the rest of the day recruiting followers, and the night working out his tactics. When the games opened the next day he managed to corner Zollner and gave him a thrashing. This was not the end of the matter, for now Zollner became concerned about his honour and felt that he had to do something to redress the balance. So when Wilwolt made his way home, Zollner confronted him brandishing a spear, shouting and taunting. Wilwolt feared indignity if he put up with such an affront, and reached for his own spear. Only the intervention of their companions prevented a bloody conclusion there and then.[16]

---

ies, though in a modified form that takes account of the different kind of relationship between the parties.

13   Adalbert von Keller (ed.), *Die Geschichten und Taten Wilwolts von Schaumburg*, Stuttgart 1859.
Wilwolt (or Willibald) was born c.1446 and died in 1510: Oskar Freiherr von Schaumberg,
Neuaufstellungen der Stammtafeln des uradelig fränkischen Geschlechts von Schaumberg, Bamberg
1953, table VI.

14   For Ludwig d.J. von Eyb, see Eberhard Freiherr von Eyb, *Das reichsritterliche Geschlecht der
Freiherren von Eyb*, Neustadt a.d. Aisch 1984, pp. 137-148. Ludwig's sister was married to
Wilwolt's brother: *ibid.*, p. 148.

15   Keller 1859, p. 5. Cf. Hartmut Boockmann, "Ritterliche Abenteuer – adlige Erziehung", idem,
Fürsten, Bürger, Edelleute: Lebensbilder aus dem späten Mittelalter, Munich 1994, pp. 105-127,
pp. 107-109.

16   Keller 1859, pp. 48-51. For Martin Zollner and the dispute over inheritance, see Werner
Spielberg, "Martin Zollner von Rothenstein und seine Sippe", *Familiengeschichtliche Blätter*,

This episode suggests the difficulty of disentangling the material and symbolic motives of feuding and ranking them in order of importance. What began as a dispute over the property rights of a woman, to whom both parties were related, quickly mutated into a violent clash between men in which honour and reputation were at stake – and from here to a full-blown feud the distance was rather short.[17] Wilwolt and Zollner evidently took their honour and reputation very seriously. And both felt they were under pressure from a certain public to pick up the gauntlet or lose face. The sequence of events brings out the crucial importance of the non-rational, symbolic dimension of feuding.

These non-rational aspects of feuding predominate and animate the various writings which feuders produced for public consumption and which remain a staple documentary source. An integral part of the feuding process, these self-justifying accounts evince the same anxiety about the opinion of others that weighed so heavily on Wilwolt and Zollner. It is therefore revealing that they make use of a passionate moral language of right and wrong, of norms and their infringement. The feuding nobles explained and defended their actions in terms of justice, probity and honour, and denounced their opponents as acting out the opposite set of qualities and motives. Of the cold language of self-interest and expedience they availed themselves relatively little.

It would be incorrect to dismiss this rhetorical strategy as nothing more than conscious dissimulation on the part of feuders. The very fact that they regularly justified themselves by invoking a uniform set of notions of right conduct suggests that these notions represented moral standards by which their behaviour was evaluated and judged. Feuders clearly felt compelled to conform, or to appear to conform, to a pattern of behaviour which these standards publicly circumscribed and sanctioned. That feuding nobles are certain to have internalised these moral standards to unequal degrees is immaterial. What mattered were the external constraints imposed by the social setting of feuds, and these ensured that the room for individual simulation and deception was limited. This was so because the public to whom the feuders appealed and

---

15, 1917, pp. 129-136 (part 1) and 167-180 (part 2). Zollner was district governor in Wallburg, an indication that he was a prominent noble: Staatsarchiv Würzburg, Literaliensammlung des Historischen Vereins von Unterfranken und Aschaffenburg, MS f. 1044, Samstag vor dem Sonntag Voc.Joc. [29 April] 1486. Staatsarchiv Würzburg, Libri diversarum formarum, no. 15, pp. 82-83.

17 A younger relation of Wilwolt, Adam von Schaumberg, took up the claim upon coming of age, and bullied Zollner into accepting a settlement on his terms: Keller 1859, p. 51.

whose opinion significantly affected the outcome consisted of people whom it was not easy to mislead over the motives and the details of a local conflict.

The point here is not the veracity of the feuders' accounts of their feuds. It certainly was not beneath them to stretch the imagination and bend the facts. The point is that the majority of feuds between Franconian nobles occurred within the boundaries of a moral community. This is a fact which poses a fundamental problem of interpretation. Nobles engaged in feuds were not simply people who commonly knew each other, nor merely people who shared values and norms. They were people who often, directly or indirectly, depended on each other in a variety of ways. Local nobles were each other's main marriage partners, and so had to keep their relationship with neighbouring families in good repair; they were each other's main suppliers of credit and loan guarantees; they relied on each other to provide patronage in princely courts and in cathedral chapters; they needed each other as witnesses and advocates in legal proceedings or infrajudicial dispute settlements; and, not least, they turned to each other as allies and helpers in feuds. And yet it is precisely with the people with whom they cultivated such vital ties that nobles tended to have feuds.

The mutual dependence and the need to think about tomorrow explain the relative mildness with which noblemen acted against each other in feuds. The violence they exercised was directed mostly against property and the tenants of the rival noble, much less often against his person. For one thing, killing a rival noble in feud was counterproductive: it defeated the immediate objective of forcing a claim on him, and in addition entailed risks of revenge or punishment. For another, it was normatively beyond the pale.[18] But if shared values and mutual dependence help account for the relative restraint which noblemen exhibited in feuds against fellow nobles, they seem by the same token to make it difficult to explain why noblemen waged those feuds in the first place. The question, to put it simply, is why would noblemen tend to feud against the very people from whose goodwill they had so much to gain and from whose enmity so much to lose. Feuds were not isolated, one-shot encounters between strangers, but normally part of an iterated interaction between neighbours, relations and acquaintances.[19] In other words, they occurred in

---

18 Brunner 1992, p. 68. Thomas Vogel, *Fehderecht und Fehdepraxis im Spätmittelalter am Beispiel der Reichsstadt Nürnberg (1404-1438)*, Frankfurt a.M. 1998, pp. 227-229.

19 Cf. Oliver Volckart, "The Economics of Feuding in Late Medieval Germany", *Explorations in Economic History*, 41, 2004, pp. 282-299. Although Volckart emphasised that 'feuds were mostly waged by members of the nobility who were socially and economically dependent on each other in many and diverse ways', p. 290, he nevertheless reached the inconsequent

a social environment which on the face of it could be expected strongly to discourage feuds: first, the geographical proximity made retaliation easy and must have constituted something of a deterrent. Secondly, the availability of mutual friends and kin could serve to facilitate mediation and accommodation. Thirdly, and for the same reasons, feuds involved the peril of estranging quite a few people with whom one had, or could have, multiple ties – economic, social, cultural – whose severance would have dire consequences.[20] In addition, there are strong indications that feuds were, in economic terms, a loss-making business, a fact of which nobles were unlikely to be oblivious.[21] The costs of feuds were thus considerable in several crucial respects.

Given these costs and their specific sources, the fact that a large number of feuds occurred between people inhabiting the same social and moral universe must serve as a point of departure for an attempt to understand the feud in terms of the morals and values that informed them. To wit, one has to seek an explanation in terms of ethical principles and perceptions precisely because the material bonds of interdependence between nobles not only often failed to mitigate against feuds, but, on the contrary, actually motivated and precipitated them. A case in point is unpaid debts, a prevalent cause of feuds.[22] The incentive behind such feuds is apparently plain: to coerce the debtor to repay the sum outstanding, an undertaking rendered all the more justified by the absence or weakness of institutions capable of enforcing contracts. However, the social context of credit transactions between nobles suggests that things were not quite that simple. The first thing to note is that nobles did not lend money to just anyone. They typically lent to those they knew or to those their kin and friends knew. Of the 24,584 Gulden debt of Hans-Georg von Absberg in 1523, slightly more than 15,000 Gulden were owed to fellow nobles. And looming large among the latter were his son (5,000 Gulden),

conclusion that '[if] the many and diverse problems of enforcing contracts between strangers are considered, it becomes plausible that the threat of feuding helped actors to take credible commitments, thus contributing to solving the problem of transacting over time and space', p. 295, and that '[f]euds helped stabilize exchange by turning the one-shot Prisoner's Dilemmas posed by non-simultaneous transactions between strangers into iterated games where the cheated party had the chance to punish the defector", p. 296.

20   Cf. Alexander Jendorff and Steffen Krieb, "Adel im Konflikt: Beobachtungen zu den Austragungsformen der Fehde im Spätmittelalter", *Zeitschrift für Historische Forschung*, 30, 2003, pp. 179-206, p. 197.

21   Markus Bittmann, *Kreditwirtschaft und Finanzierungsmethoden: Studien zu den Verhältnissen des Adels im westlichen Bodenseeraum*, Stuttgart 1991, esp. pp. 109-110.

22   Janine Fehn-Claus, "Erste Ansätze einer Typologie der Fehdegründe", Horst Brunner (ed.), *Der Krieg im Mittelalter und in der Frühen Neuzeit: Gründe, Begründungen, Bilder, Bräuche, Recht*, Wiesbaden 1999, pp. 93-138, pp. 115-116.

his son-in-law (1,500 Gulden), and the margraves of Brandenburg-Ansbach (2,000 Gulden).[23] The mountainous debt impelled the Absbergs to sell their castle Vorderfrankenberg. One of the buyers was the prominent *financier gentilhomme* Ludwig von Hutten. A list of his debtors drawn up in 1548 names, apart from Margrave Kasimir (4,000 Gulden), Bernhard von Hutten for 2,000 Gulden, Lorenz von Hutten for 1,000, and several other local nobles.[24] Loans were not unalloyed financial transactions. They were multi-stranded, mixing political, social and economic considerations, often in this very order.[25] And they linked nobles to each other and to princes in a dense web of reciprocal relations. When in 1524 Albrecht von Vestenberg asked for a repayment of 2,000 Gulden he had lent to the margrave of Brandenburg, he explained that he himself owed 2,000 Gulden to Count Wilhelm of Henneberg who now wanted his money back in order to pay off his own debt of 2,000 Gulden to another nobleman.[26]

Nobles were thus simultaneously creditors and debtors. Accordingly, the consequences of defaulting were bound to have a ripple effect. If a nobleman was not repaid or reimbursed in time, that could make it difficult for him to repay his own debts. And this in turn could bring about two unpleasant outcomes: one was a damage to his creditworthiness; the other was the likelihood that he too would become a target of other noblemen seeking to enforce their contractual claims.[27] In such circumstances, the decision to

---

23   Staatsarchiv Nürnberg [henceforward StAN], AA-Akten, no. 1402, fols. 126r-129r. See also Alfred Wendehorst and Gerhard Rechter, "Ein Geldverleiher im spätmittelalterlichen Franken: Philipp von Seckendorff-Gutend", Uwe Bestmann, Franz Irsigler, and Jürgen Schneider (eds.), *Hochfinanz, Wirtschaftsräume, Innovationen: Festschrift für Wolfgang von Stromer*, 1-3, Trier 1987, vol. 1, pp. 487-529, 509-511.

24   Richard Schmitt, *Frankenberg: Besitz- und Wirtschaftsgeschichte einer reichsritterschaftlichen Herrschaft in Franken, 1528-1806 (1848)*, Ansbach 1986, p. 386, n. 1.

25   Ludwig von Hutten (father of the above-mentioned Ludwig) pointed out in a pamphlet against Duke Ulrich of Württemberg, that he had lent the duke 10,000 Gulden free of interest, although he could have invested them elsewhere with profit: Eduard Böcking (ed.), *Ulrichi Hutteni, equitis Germani, Opera quae reperiri potuerent omnia*, 1-5, Leipzig 1859-61, vol. 1, p. 77.

26   StAN, AA-Akten, no. 728, prod. of Donnerstag nach Matthei [22 September] 1524. In 1487 Margrave Friedrich settled a debt of 1,000 Gulden to Hans von Haldermannstetten Stettner genannt, by designating him creditor for the 1,000 Gulden owed to himself since 1485 by Arnold von Rosenberg: StAN, Gemeinbücher, Tom. V, fols. 48r-v.

27   Brunner 1992, p. 11. Fehn-Claus 1999, p. 118. Alexander Patschovsky, "Fehde im Recht. Eine Problemskizze", Christine Roll (ed.), *Recht und Reich im Zeitalter der Reformation. Festschrift für Horst Rabe*, Frankfurt a.M. 1997, pp. 145-178, at p. 177.

wage a feud was not senseless. Alternative avenues for seeking redress[28] risked being taken for cowardice or weakness or indeed for downright dereliction of duty. Feuds, on the other hand, by the very real costs and dangers they implicated, demonstrated one's good faith and signalled moral seriousness and uncompromising commitment that could make the desired impact on other actors – reassuring creditors, warning debtors, impressing neutral third parties.[29]

A similar set of pressures and motives was at work in conflicts relating to lordship rights, another very widespread cause of feuding in Franconia and elsewhere. What is often striking in these disputes is the apparent asymmetry between the negligible pecuniary value of the rights in question and the intransigence and intense moral indignation that the feuders displayed. As one noble put it during an intra-familial dispute over a fishpond: 'I want to show myself in this such that one should see that it means much to me and want either to be ruined or die for it or to maintain my ancestral and paternal property and my wife's property'. A few years earlier, his rival stated his position in no less trenchant terms: 'it is proper for me to defend myself when one unjustly takes away my property … I have always heard that one should fight and die for one's paternal inheritance before one allows it to be taken away'.[30] The biologist Robert Trivers noted in a now famous article that 'much of human aggression has moral overtones. Injustice, unfairness, and lack of reciprocity often motivate human aggression and indignation. … A common feature of this aggression is that it often seems out of all proportion to the offenses committed'. He explained this feature thus: 'since small inequities

---

28 On the use of *Scheltbriefe* by creditors to impugn the honour of debtors or guarantors who did not keep their word, see Guido Kisch, "Ehrenschelte und Schandgemälde", *Zeitschrift der Savigny-Stiftung für Rechtsgeschichte GA.*, 51, 1931, pp. 514-520. Eduard Philippi, "Die Fehde des Herrn Nickel von Minkwitz im Jahre 1528", *Zeitschrift für preussische Geschichte und Landeskunde*, 3, 1866, pp. 541-551. Julius Traugott Jacob Könneritz, "Verbürgung für Nicol von Minckwitz durch Einreiten 1530", *Archiv für die sächsische Geschichte*, 8, 1870, pp. 102-117. For a graphic example, Franz Heinemann, *Der Richter und die Rechtspflege in der deutschen Vergangenheit*, Leipzig 1900, Beilage 8, where a cow befouls the coat-of-arms of Heinz von Guttenberg; the caption reads: 'hie ist die gleichnuss Heinczen von Gutenberg insigels da mit Er die lewt umb das Ir betreugt'.

29 Cf. Fehn-Claus 1999, p. 115, n. 103.

30 StAN, Ansbacher Historica, no. 210, prod. of Palmtag zu Abend [29 March] 1488 ('… so wil ich mich darinen bewysen das man sol sehen das es mir leit ist und wil dar ob verderben oder sterben oder wil mein anherlich vetterlich und weyplich gut behaltten und zu mein handen prengen'). *Ibid.*, prod. of Montag Antonii [17 June] 1485 ('zimpt mir so mir einer das meyn an recht nymt zu weren … wan ich albeg gehort habe, einer soll umb sein vetterich [sic] erbe streyten und sterben ee und er im das nemen laße').

repeated many times over a lifetime may exact a heavy toll in relative fitness, selection may favor a strong show of aggression when the cheating tendency is discovered'.[31]

This logic fits disputes over lordship rights in Franconia very well indeed. The foundation of noble status, lordship in late medieval and early modern Franconia was not a solid, monolithic, cohesive entity. Rather, it was a composite structure, the sum total of diverse rights, a *summa iurium*. This meant that any one of its constituent elements could be alienated from one lord by another. Failing to respond forcefully to the threat of alienation of one element, however paltry in itself, was likely to be seen by other lords as a sign of impotence, of a flagging will, of demoralisation. Quiescence or placatory measures were unlikely to bring tranquillity. On the contrary, in the competitive world of armigerous lords they were likely to breed contempt, whet appetites and feed aggression. And this in turn could lead to the disintegration and eventual collapse of lordship.[32] Hence any dispute over lordship rights was potentially critical, and it was quite sensible for nobles to respond to challenges vigorously, sometimes in seemingly disproportionate manner. Baron Friedrich of Schwarzenberg, for instance, confronted the menace of a neighbour engaged in local empire building by offering, spectacularly, a duel to decide which of them was the lord over the disputed area and tenants. The proposal was made in a printed pamphlet, presumably intended to be disseminated far and wide among the regional nobility.[33] More dramatic was the feud which Christoph Fuchs von Bimbach started in 1462 against the prince-bishop of Bamberg over grazing rights.[34] The chronicler of this feud that led to a war between princes noted that the annual income from the disputed right was a mere three Gulden. He could not help concluding that 'this was the beautiful Helen over which the two princes ... went to a veritable Trojan War'.[35] Nobles such

---

31   Robert Trivers, "The Evolution of Reciprocal Altruism", *Quarterly Review of Biology*, 46, 1971, pp. 35-57, p. 49. Cf. Robert Wright, *The Moral Animal: Evolutionary Psychology and Everyday Life*, New York 1994, pp. 205-209.

32   Hans von Egloffstein complained that, because of a protracted conflict with Nuremberg, he had to evacuate his home 14 times in a space of 18 years, and was eventually forced to put it up for sale: Staatsarchiv Bamberg, Hofrat Ansbach-Bayreuth, no. 579, prod. of Freitag nach Egidii [4 September] 1545.

33   I have used the copy Geheimes Staatsarchiv, XX.HA: Hist. Staatsarchiv Königsberg, Herzogliches Briefarchiv, A 4, 29 January 1534 (K. 191).

34   The cartel of defiance in Staatsarchiv Würzburg, Standbücher, no. 717, fols. 257r-v.

35   Lorenz Fries, *Chronik der Bischöfe von Würzburg 742-1495*, vol. 4, *Von Sigmund von Sachsen bis Rudolf II. von Scherenberg (1440-1495)*, Ulrike Grosch, Christoph Bauer, Harald Tausch, and Thomas Heiler (eds.), Würzburg, 2002, pp. 205-223.

as Fuchs and Schwarzenberg had not only to react to current threats, but to anticipate future ones as well. They feared a situation encapsulated in a maxim of which one feuder reminded fellow nobles in 1470: 'he who sustains the damage must often suffer the scorn as well'.[36] Hence they felt constrained to maintain formidable reputation – that invisible and intangible palisade against prospective encroachers. However, such edgy behaviour entailed immediate costs, whereas the benefits were to be reaped, if at all, only in the future. And it is here that honour played a pivotal role, which also explains the emphasis nobles laid on it and on its inculcation in the young.[37] For concern with personal and family honour helped them summon the rage, the angry determination that enabled them to make the necessary sacrifices in the present, to put up a credible show of aggression, and thus to bridge the gap between the current costs of such conduct and its future reputational benefits.[38]

Feuding, then, was not merely a direct action undertaken to counter or enforce claims. It was also a way of communicating to the aristocratic community one's personal traits, disclosing one's moral characteristics, one's commitment to the values and norms that helped define membership in the local or regional nobility. This is probably one reason why nobles sometimes chose to feud even when the option of legal action or arbitration was open to them:[39] litigation apparently did not, in certain circumstances, convey the right message to the aristocratic public who observed and appraised the performance of the disputing parties. An example is provided by a feud which took place in 1519 between Baron Johann of Schwarzenberg and Hans-Georg von Absberg. Schwarzenberg at first agreed to appear before the margrave

---

36 StAN, AA-Akten, no. 738, Prod. 6.

37 The nobles' concern with honour is formally evident in statutes of noble societies enjoining members to defend each other's honour and to inform each other of defamations that come to their notice: Herbert Obenaus, *Recht und Verfassung der Gesellschaft mit St. Jörgenschild in Schwaben: Untersuchungen über Adel, Einung, Schiedsgericht und Fehde im fünfzehnten Jahrhundert*, Göttingen 1961, p. 82. Cyriacus Spangenberg, *Hennebergische Chronica: Der uralten löblichen Grafen und Fürsten zu Henneberg, Genealogia, Stamm-Baum und Historia, ihrer Ankunfft, Lob und denckwürdigen Tathen, Geschichten und Sachen wahre und gründliche Beschreibung*, Meiningen 1755, p. 435.

38 For general theoretical considerations of this pattern of human behaviour, see Robert H. Frank, *Passions within Reason*, New York 1988, pp. 83, 84, 88-89, 169, 211. Cf. Matt Ridley, *The Origins of Virtue*, Harmondsworth, 1996, pp. 127-147. Cf. also Ernst Fehr, Urs Fischbacher, and Simon Gächter, "Strong Reciprocity, Human Cooperation, and the Enforcement of Social Norms", *Human Nature*, 13, 2002, pp. 1-25, p. 18.

39 Cf. Fehn-Claus 1999, pp. 99, 117. Julius R. Ruff, *Violence in Early Modern Europe, 1500-1800*, Cambridge 2001, pp. 76-77. Stuart Carroll, "The Peace in the Feud in Sixteenth-Century France", *Past and Present*, 178, 2003, pp. 74-115, at p. 85.

of Brandenburg for adjudication, but later retracted. In a letter to Margrave Kasimir he explained that, since Absberg had in the meantime perpetrated some more hostilities against his tenants, it would now be a disgrace if he, Schwarzenberg, came before the prince all the same.[40] It may well have been prudent for nobles to be conciliatory, but it may equally well have been reckless to appear to be so. In brief, one had to know when and how to carry out a feud. Nobles who failed in these tests of will and skill risked incurring disesteem that could have adverse effects in many other areas of aristocratic existence. Failure could indicate that one was a pushover, and therefore useless as an ally, an unattractive marriage partner, or an unreliable client or servitor – in short, more a liability than an asset. Failure to risk a feud, when the situation called for it, could foreclose essential opportunities for social exchange in other circumstances.

It is in this context, finally, that the nature of the feuders' self-justifying accounts is to be understood. It is not for nothing that they were couched predominantly in a moral idiom, and that the feuding nobles defended themselves and accused their opponents in terms of ethical values rather than in terms of practical utility. The accounts they wrote and circulated were of a piece with their belligerent actions. The aim of the feuders was to project themselves as moral beings, and to present their opponents as immoral ones, as false nobles from whom any self-respecting nobleman would distance himself.

Feuds, in other words, were about attracting as well as about deterring. Precisely because they reflected certain values and norms, because they required making sacrifices, because they appeared to be driven by passions rather than by mere rational calculations, feuds could signal that the feuder was a man of principle, a man of honour, a moral person who could be trusted by others to do the right thing even at a personal cost to himself. A virtuous man like that would surely cooperate and keep faith even in situations where he could gain more by defecting. Feuds, whatever their proximate reasons and immediate ends, could help nobles position themselves favourably in the aristocratic network of relations on which their status and fortunes so heavily depended. It is not only that one could not withstand or win feuds without supporters and allies; it is perhaps equally true that one could not win allies and supporters unless one was prepared to feud and, crucially, was believed to be so. Hence failure to respond to challenges, or a humiliating defeat, could result in grave damage to one's reputation and standing with other nobles, and could diminish one's chances of success in other areas of aristocratic life.

It is in this context, finally, that the nature of the feuders' self-justifying accounts is to be understood. It is not for nothing that they were couched predominantly in a moral idiom, and that the feuding nobles defended themselves and accused their opponents in terms of ethical values rather than in terms of practical utility. The accounts they wrote and circulated were of a piece with their belligerent actions. The aim of the feuders was to project themselves as moral beings, and to present their opponents as immoral ones, as false nobles from whom any self-respecting nobleman would distance himself.

---

40 StAN, Fehdeakten, no. 69, prod. 10.

To be on the safe side, they often perorated with a concrete appeal – sometimes fortified with veiled threats – to deny the other party any assistance of whatever nature. Their ultimate end was to mobilise support, and to bring the adversary to heel by morally isolating him. An instructive example is again provided by Wilwolt von Schaumberg. He picked a feud with Konrad Schott – who was later to make a name for himself as a ruthless feuder[41] – and the two slugged it out for a couple of years. Then the duke of Saxony intervened, being the feudal overlord of both, and the two nobles were summoned to appear before him. Schott worked hard to solicit support among the nobility. Yet when the audience took place no one wanted to take up the cudgels for him. So there he stood alone, having nobody to speak for him. He broke down in tears 'like a child' and begged the prince for mercy. The fact that, during the feud, Schott managed to field some artillery pieces gave him no decisive edge over Wilwolt; the fact that he did not manage to garner the moral support of fellow nobles was his undoing.[42] Wilwolt's biographer, except for playing up Schott's dishonourable demeanour and moral flaws, does not expand on how his hero succeeded in discrediting and undermining his antagonist so effectively. One can only conjecture that Wilwolt's triumph had something to do with the fact that he came from a large and distinguished family, whereas Schott did not.

Be that as it may, what clearly emerges from this episode, as from many other feuds, is that force did not in itself suffice to win such conflicts. Force without morality, or the semblance of morality, was nearly as ineffective as morality without the capacity and will to use force. Morality was an inseparable feature, and an indispensable instrument, of feuding. Feuding nobles knew that full well, hence all those angst-ridden, angry written accounts that make modern historians happy. But, as has been argued, and as Wilwolt's feuds suggest, it was also the case that physical violence had roots in the moral sensibilities and perceptions of the noble community. And precisely because they derived from and expressed values and morals, feuds could and did serve much larger ends than simply winning disputes and enforcing claims. Nobles possessing the subtle arts of amalgamating the symbolic and the material could utilise feuds as a vehicle for reinforcing or acquiring prestige, preserving or making a name, and thus for maintaining one's social position or indeed upgrading it. As Wilwolt's biographer put it, in 'the land of Franconia [feuds]

---

41   Joseph Baader (ed.), *Verhandlungen über Thomas von Absberg und seine Fehden gegen den Schwäbischen Bund 1519 bis 1530*, Tübingen 1873, p. 71, n. 1. Rochus Freiherr von Liliencron (ed.), *Die historischen Volkslieder der Deutschen vom 13. bis 16. Jahrhundert*, 1-4, Leipzig 1865-69, vol. 2, pp. 351-353, no. 193.
42   Keller 1859, pp. 70-74.

seldom ceased, whereby barons and nobles who were at loggerheads captured fortified places, burned down villages, and seized cattle'. Wilwolt 'served determinedly his good companions who asked for [his help] in these affairs'. And this is how he 'made a big name (*groß geschrai*) for himself and earned recognition from the princes and the knightage'.[43] Feuds launched him on the brilliant military career that made him an edifying example for young nobles, and a most proper subject of a biography.

---

43   *Ibid.*, p. 60.

Peasants' Feuds in Medieval Bavaria (Fourteenth-Fifteenth Century)[1]

CHRISTINE REINLE

When dealing with the scholarly discourse on feuding in mediaeval Germany, one is faced with various preconceived ideas: Be it the common stereotype of the mounted knight fighting his more or less wicked enemy, be it the popular figure of the 'robber-knight' pillaging merchants and terrorising the people,[2] or be it even the literary character of a righteous but stubborn outlaw struggling for his right as did Michael Kohlhaas.[3] Among these clichés, however, there is

---

1 A similar but more detailed version of this article has recently been published in German: Christine Reinle, "Von Austreten, Landzwang und mutwilliger Fehde: Zur bäuerlichen Fehdeführung in Altbayern im Spätmittelalter", *Zeitschrift für Geschichtswissenschaft*, 52, 2004, pp. 109-131. This article is based on my postdoctoral thesis: Christine Reinle, *Studien zur Fehdeführung Nichtadliger im römisch-deutschen Reich unter besonderer Berücksichtigung der bayerischen Herzogtümer (13.-16. Jahrhundert)*, University of Mannheim 1999; now published as: Christine Reinle, *Bauernfehden: Studien zur Fehdeführung Nichtadliger im spätmittelalterlichen römisch-deutschen Reich, besonders in den bayerischen Herzogtümern* (VSWG Beihefte 170), Stuttgart 2003. Because of the documentation given there, the notes can be restricted to a minimum here. Concerning the English version of this article, I would like to thank Sebastian Schäfer (Bochum) for proofreading. The following article was finished in June 2004; later published articles – especially Hans-Henning Kortüm, "'Wissenschaft im Doppelpass'? Carl Schmitt, Otto Brunner und die Konstruktion der Fehde", *Historische Zeitschrift*, 282, 2006, pp. 585-617 – could not be taken into account here, because this would have extended this article too much. The discussion with Kortüm shall be continued elsewhere.

2 The 'robber-knight' is a popular motif common both in scholarly articles and in literature. The concept it stands for, however, has recently been challenged. Cf. Regina Görner, *Raubritter: Untersuchungen zur Lage des spätmittelalterlichen Niederadels, besonders im südlichen Westfalen*, Münster 1987, pp. 3-6. Kurt Andermann, "Raubritter – Raubfürsten – Raubbürger? Zur Kritik eines untauglichen Begriffs", Kurt Andermann (ed.), *"Raubritter" oder "Rechtschaffene vom Adel"? Aspekte von Politik, Friede und Recht im späten Mittelalter*, Sigmaringen 1997, pp. 9-29, esp. pp. 9-11. Klaus Graf, "Feindbild und Vorbild: Bemerkungen zur städtischen Wahrnehmung des Adels", *Zeitschrift für die Geschichte des Oberrheins*, 141 (Neue Folge 102), 1993, pp. 121-154, esp. pp. 136-144.

3 Hans Kolhase (U 1540), a burgher of the Brandenburgian town of Kölln. He waged a long lasting feud because of some claims he was unable to force through by negotiations. Kolhase

no place whatsoever for feuding peasants. It is only a single well-known work, Heinrich Wittenwiler's early fifteenth-century comic verse novel *Der Ring*,[4] that tells us about two villages waging a feud – and ruthlessly mocks them for the very reason that they dared to feud.

This attitude corresponds with the predominant opinion in historical research: Historians, too, refuse to accept the idea that townsfolk or even commoners,[5] let alone peasants, could have possibly waged feuds. In the nineteenth and early twentieth century, the historians of law constructed a model according to which there were two different kinds of feuds in the German Middle Ages: the noblemen's feud (also known as knightly feud) on the one hand, and the blood vengeance or bloodfeud on the other hand. Serving as a paradigm for the concept of feuding, the knightly feud can be defined as a means of violent self-help. Yet, it was considered perfectly rightful as long as it followed some definite rules: Provided that the enemies had tried and failed to achieve a peaceful agreement by attending an arbitration hearing or some other kind of trial, the feud that followed was regarded as rightful if the intention behind it was based on a just cause. In that case, any person entitled by their social origin to instigate a feud had indeed the right and possibly even the obligation to defend themselves against a potential infringement of their rights by means of violent self-help, i.e. by feuding.

Formal rules had to be observed as well in order to guarantee the legitimacy of a feud. Especially important was the obligation to challenge the enemy before the fighting began (*Absage*, Lat. *diffidatio*). Usually, feuds aimed at damaging the economic basis of the enemy, thus forcing him to give in. Hence, aggressive acts like robbery or arson were customary elements of feuds, although they were considered crimes outside the legal context of feuding. Wounding or

---

became famous in a novel by Heinrich von Kleist (*Michael Kohlhaas*, Berlin 1810) – maybe nearly as famous as was Rob Roy in Scotland. Cf. Hartmut Boockmann, "Mittelalterliches Recht bei Kleist: Ein Beitrag zum Verständnis des *Michael Kohlhaas*", *Kleist-Jahrbuch 1985*, pp. 84-108. Malte Dießelhorst, "Hans Kohlhase – Michael Kohlhaas", *Kleist-Jahrbuch 1988/89*, pp. 334-356. Malte Dießelhorst and Arne Duncker, *Hans Kolhase: Die Geschichte einer Fehde in Sachsen und Brandenburg zur Zeit der Reformation*, Frankfurt a.M. 1999.

4 Heinrich Wittenwiler, *Der Ring: Frühneuhochdeutsch-Neuhochdeutsch: Nach dem Text von Edmund Wießner ins Neuhochdeutsche übersetzt und hrsg. von Horst Brunner*, Stuttgart 1991, durchges. und bibl. erg. Ausg. 1999. Wittenwiler was probably born a noble. He is supposed to have also been an advocate at the court of the Bishop of Constance. His well-known work *Der Ring* is the object of a very controversial debate, which cannot be discussed here.

5 I am using 'commoner' in the restricted sense of anyone below the ranks associated with the nobility.

killing the enemy, though, was rather the exception than the rule.[6] Castles, too, were destroyed in fundamental conflicts only, for instance when the prince of a territory campaigned against a rebellious noble, or when either the captains of an alliance to secure the Public Peace (*Landfriedenshauptleute*) or town councils had to intervene against notorious offenders of the peace. In the vast majority of cases, however, nobles engaged in a feud attempted to dodge battles and avoided destroying castles – destruction was generally considered a punishment whereas feuding was supposed to be a competitive contest and as such was an option available to nobles willing to come to terms with each other.

To sum up: The knightly feud was a possible reaction to any violation of rights. However, it could be waged exclusively by the aristocracy or the gentry. In contrast, in cases of 'vendetta', i.e. when blood had been shed, everyone was granted the right to take revenge.[7] Even Otto Brunner, a severe critic of the traditional history of law, denied that commoners could have possibly waged feuds. He recognised that in the society of mediaeval Germany violence did not necessarily disagree with Right. But he claimed that this order was valid for noblemen only. Consequently, he considered commoners who waged feuds to be dubious characters or even criminals.[8] Above all, Gadi Algazi declared feuds to be a privilege exclusively enjoyed by lords, who, according to him, more than accepted that the damage they caused each other also helped them to keep their subjects subjugated.[9] Sources dating from the late fifteenth and early sixteenth century, however, evidently contradict these opinions, as they mention peasants like Peter Paßler from Tyrol,[10] who waged feuds the same way as noblemen did. These cases are not only quite similar to those

---

6   Otto Brunner, *Land und Herrschaft: Grundfragen der territorialen Verfassungsgeschichte Österreichs im Mittelalter* (5th edition), Wien 1965, pp. 41-55, 73-86, 95-101.

7   Hans Fehr, "Das Waffenrecht der Bauern im Mittelalter", *Zeitschrift der Savigny-Stiftung für Rechtsgeschichte. Germanistische Abteilung*, 35, 1914, pp. 111-211, esp. pp. 145f. For more details on the blood revenge cf. Paul Frauenstädt, *Blutrache und Totschlagssühne im Deutschen Mittelalter: Studien zur Deutschen Kultur- und Rechtsgeschichte*, Leipzig 1881, *passim*. Rudolf His, *Das Strafrecht des deutschen Mittelalters: Zwei Teile* Weimar 1920, pp. 264 ff.

8   Brunner 1965, pp. 64-73.

9   Gadi Algazi, "Social Use of Private War: Some Late Medieval Views Reviewed", *Tel Aviver Jahrbuch für deutsche Geschichte*, 22, 1993, pp. 253-273. Gadi Algazi, "'Sie würden hinten nach so gail'. Vom sozialen Gebrauch der Fehde im 15. Jahrhundert", Alf Lüdtke and Thomas Lindenberger (eds.), *Physische Gewalt: Studien zur Geschichte der Neuzeit*, Frankfurt a.M. 1995, pp. 39-77. Gadi Algazi, *Herrengewalt und Gewalt der Herren im späten Mittelalter: Herrschaft, Gegenseitigkeit und Sprachgebrauch*, Frankfurt a.M. 1996.

10 The conflict between Peter Paßler and his enemies first began as a feud but later resulted in the Tyrolean Peasant War, cf. Reinle 2003, pp. 157-173.

of feuding townsfolk, they also closely resemble those of noblemen who still continued to wage feuds after the practice had been banned by the Imperial Law which established the so-called Perpetual General Peace of Worms in 1495. This was the starting point for my research, which was finally completed in 1999. Based on some well-documented examples I explored first of all the typical behaviour patterns in feuding, the usual reasons for starting a feud and its common course. Secondly, I examined a number of serial sources since I wanted to demonstrate that the results of the micro-studies could indeed be generalised. For this purpose, the well-preserved records produced by Lower Bavaria's financial administration proved to be particularly useful. Thirdly, the results had to be interpreted. Let us assume that the feuds waged by commoners were a widespread social practice: Were they, then, considered a customary right or simply a frequently committed crime, similar to theft or infanticide? A final problem occurred a short time ago: Only recently in 2000 and 2003 Jan Peters and Monika Mommertz have shown that commoners in Brandenburg still waged feuds until the sixteenth and early seventeenth century.[11] That raises the question of the similarities and differences between the late mediaeval peasants' feuds in Bavaria and the early modern commoners' feuds in Brandenburg.

I

The first example to be examined has been thoroughly documented: the feud waged by a peasant named Hans Örtel. As both his case and my other examples lead us to Bavaria, I will have to start with two remarks on its political order in the Late Middle Ages. First: In 1392 the dukedom of Bavaria was divided into four parts, which later became independent princely states. Two of them were situated in Upper Bavaria (Bavaria-Ingolstadt and Bavaria-Munich) and two in Lower Bavaria (Bavaria-Landshut and Bavaria-Straubing). In each case, the names refer to the respective capital. By the middle of the fifteenth century, only two of these dukedoms had survived – namely Bavaria-Munich and Bavaria-

---

11 Jan Peters, "Leute-Fehde: Ein ritualisiertes Konfliktmuster des 16. Jahrhunderts", *Historische Anthropologie*, 8, 2000, pp. 62-97. Monika Mommertz, "Von Besen und Bündelchen, Brandmahlen und Befehdungsschreiben: Semantiken der Gewalt und die historiographische Entzifferung von 'Fehde'-Praktiken in einer ländlichen Gesellschaft", Magnus Eriksson and Barbara Krug-Richter (eds.), *Streitkulturen. Gewalt, Konflikt und Kommunikation in der ländlichen Gesellschaft (16.-19. Jahrhundert)*, Köln 2003, pp. 197-248. Both articles are based on the sources of the jury of Brandenburg (*Brandenburger Schöppenstuhl*).

Landshut. Second and more important to know: Concerning the law, there was a crucial difference between Upper and Lower Bavaria: Upper Bavaria possessed a written law, the so-called *Rechtsbuch Kaiser Ludwigs/Oberbayerisches Landrecht* (Emperor Louis' Code of Law/Upper Bavarian Territorial Law).[12] In contrast, the legal order in Lower Bavaria was mainly based on common law and oral tradition.

Let us return to Hans Örtel.[13] His father had already been in dispute with the collegiate church in Habach in Upper Bavaria, arguing about the property right concerning a certain strip of land. Assuming he was the rightful owner, Hans Örtel the Elder had tried to fight his case before the duke's district court (*herzogliches Landgericht*). Interestingly enough, he always won when it was the district jury (presided by a noble ducal official) that cast the judgement. Every single time, however, when the canons appealed to the ducal Aulic Court in Munich, they succeeded in getting a different judgment there – one in favour of their cause. When Hans Örtel the Elder eventually died, his family accused the canons of being guilty of his death, claiming that it resulted from the anguish they had caused him. Furthermore, Örtel's relatives complained that they themselves were deeply distressed by the clerics too. Now in 1505, Hans Örtel's son Hans took the case over. But unlike his father, he decided to wage a feud. Having left the country, he sent a declaration of enmity (*Absage*, Lat. *diffidatio*), a challenge he had written by a teacher, to the canons and immediately opened hostilities with a surprise attack on the monastery. During his feud, Örtel preferably robbed horses, but once he even kidnapped a parson, holding him to ransom. It is striking that he deliberately refrained from committing arson, declaring that the burning impoverished the common people.[14] In addition, he more than once tried to come to terms with his enemies by sending them messages and offering negotiations.

---

12   Hans Schlosser and Ingo Schwab, *Oberbayerisches Landrecht Kaiser Ludwigs des Bayern von 1346: Edition, Übersetzung und juristischer Kommentar*, Köln 2000.

13   The sources documenting this case – extant in Bayerisches Hauptstaatsarchiv München, Codex KÄA 4101 – were first mentioned by Ernst Lupprian, "Bayerisches Recht im Mittelalter", *"Gerechtigkeit erhöht ein Volk": Recht und Rechtspflege in Bayern im Wandel der Geschichte: Ausstellung des Bayerischen Hauptstaatsarchivs mit Unterstützung des Bayerischen Staatsministeriums für Justiz und der Landesnotarkammer Bayern, München, 15. September – 18. November 1990*, Neustadt an der Aisch 1990, pp. 21-46, esp. no. 20 pp. 44-46. Concerning the case itself cf. Reinle 2003, pp. 133-157. Reinle 2004, pp. 115-117.

14   Having been caught, Hans Örtel stated during an interrogation that he agreed with one of his assistants who dissociated himself from the usual methods of feuding: *Wir wellen nit prennen, dan es macht arm leyt*, cf. Reinle 2003, p. 154.

Of course, Örtel could not dare to conduct his feud from his farm. After his attacks he therefore had to rush into hiding, seeking shelter in particular beyond the river Lech, which divided Bavaria from the region of Swabia. However, he always returned to continue his feud. Örtel was supported by a small group of (mostly seven) men including one mercenary. Usually, they congregated immediately before their strikes and split up shortly after. But Hans Örtel also received help from the common people, who provided him with food and intelligence. Moreover, the followers of his families also volunteered to carry out certain actions.

Caution was always necessary of course. Ducal Riding Officers hunted the gang and would punish them if they got hold of them. After about one year, in 1506, Hans Örtel and two of his companions were caught. Whereas one of them was able to escape, the other was first tortured and then sentenced to death. Hans Örtel had to suffer torture as well. Nevertheless he might have been incredibly lucky under the circumstances: He was not arrested by the officials of the duke of Upper Bavaria themselves but by men of the bishop of Augsburg, i.e. by forces of a prince of the Empire who was not involved in the conflict himself. Then, a certain burgher of the Bavarian town of Weilheim near Habach, who had stood security for Hans Örtel before the beginning of the feud and who thus knew the entire case, intervened on his behalf to Emperor Maximilian, whose servant he was. The emperor, then, intervened to the bishop of Augsburg. After this episode, the sources do not mention Hans Örtel any longer. It is well possible that the bishop pardoned him as a favour to the emperor.

The case of Hans Örtel shows some remarkable features typical for both the course of feuds in general and for the feuds waged by commoners (and especially by peasants) in particular. Some of them have already been mentioned above. In order to define them more specifically, six crucial characteristics of mediaeval feuding in Germany have to be considered. First: If an act of aggression offended a right that was demanded by the person being attacked, the struggle had first to be taken to a court of law or at least to an arbitrator before the actual feud could begin. Second: Certain declarations of discontent were supposed to warn the enemy before a feud. Possibly, these declarations were followed by further threats. Third: If the conflict escalated through the course of a feud, the party starting the feud committed the more or less formal act of the so-called 'going out' (*Austreten*), which was specific to peasants' feuds.[15] In many cases this actually meant leaving the country or at least the

---

15   The term *Austreten* means 'to break the peace', 'to wantonly feud and offend' or even to deliberately 'enforce a claim by violence and without authorisation'. Cf. Maria Rita Sagstetter,

home region, especially if the feuding parties had resorted to acts of violence. Fourth: The actual declaration of feud, the official act of challenge (*Absage*, Lat. *diffidatio*) was an equally formal event, which was prescribed by an Imperial Act to secure the General Peace in 1187-8. According to this *Brandstifterbrief*, three days had to pass after a challenge had been delivered before hostilities could actually begin. Thus, it was a breach of law when Hans Örtel did not completely respect this rule and attacked the monastery in Habach faster than the canons could have recognised the declaration of feud. Fifth: The particular strategy Hans Örtel and his followers employed and the techniques they used, e.g. inflicting damage or committing robbery and arson. As mentioned above, these means were customary in noblemen's feuds as well. Sixth: The intention of a feud was thus neither to hurt nor to kill, but to force the enemy into negotiating, to make him accept one's own position or at least to consent to some compromise. Finally, we have to mention the mediators who intervened between the conflict parties. Although they did not play a decisive role in Hans Örtel's case, they were important in others.

II

Concerning my second point, evidence that this pattern of feuding was very common in rural Bavaria is provided by three different kinds of sources: First, by administrative and legislative texts; second, by the records of the dukedom of Bavaria-Landshut; and third, by certain charters that contain oaths to keep the peace instead of taking revenge for a punishment once suffered. These *Urfehden* will be ignored here since they make up only a comparatively small number of feud cases. As they are not specific to Bavaria, the administrative and legislative documents can also be dealt with in short. During the fifteenth

---

Hoch- und Niedergerichtsbarkeit im spätmittelalterlichen Herzogtum Bayern, München 2000, p. 258, n. 153 ("Austreten' bedeutet Friedbruch (das 'Heraustreten' aus einer Friedens- und Rechtsgemeinschaft) durch mutwilliges Befehden und Angreifen oder eigenmächtig- es und gewaltsames Durchsetzen von Rechtsansprüchen unter bewußter Umgehung des Rechtsweges und sogar in gezielter Konfrontation gegen die Obrigkeit'). See also *Deutsches Rechtswörterbuch*, 1, Weimar 1914-1932, col. 1127. Peters 2000, pp. 65f., n. 26, defines *Austreten* as a term which refers to leaving a community or family. Thus it was a serious way to flee – it necessarily meant leaving the area of legal protection for a free but unprotected sphere of activity ('Austreten' bezeichnete in prägnanter Weise das Verlassen einer Kommunität, Gemeinschaft, Familie und damit einen gravierenden Schritt von Flucht, der zugleich aus dem rechtlichen Schutzbereich hinausführte und den Betreffenden in einen freien, aber un- geschützten Handlungsbereich hineinführte.').

century, similar documents came into use in each territory of the Empire. In Bavaria, they contained both the so-called *Landgebote* and the so-called *Landesordnungen*. The *Landgebote* were ducal orders issued to the officials of a district, regulating many administrative, judicial and military details. The *Landesordnungen* (1474, 1501, and 1508) were, however, comprehensive compilations of law and order, setting out more general rules valid for the entire territory. The only aspect I would like to emphasise concerns a particular similarity between the *Landesordnungen* and the *Landgebote*: Both contain a large number of regulations on robbery, arson and so forth. These regulations used to be interpreted as inhibitions against ordinary crime but actually aimed at suppressing the customary practice of non-knightly feuding. In a similar way, the late thirteenth- and early fourteenth-century territorial prescriptions for securing the public peace (*Landfrieden*) hint that violent self-help and commoners' feuds were a frequent practice.[16]

However, it is more important that from the beginning of the 1440s onwards the dukes of Bavaria-Landshut developed a particular method of pardoning people who had been sentenced to severe punishment: They compiled a catalogue of crimes that were supposed to result in a death sentence but that now could also be punished by commuting that death penalty, turning it into the obligation to pay a fine. This change was possible in Lower Bavaria because there, Right was not fixed by the codification of Emperor Louis (*Kaiser Ludwigs Rechtsbuch*, mentioned above) and thus could be handled more flexibly.[17] The dukes delegated the right to pardon to their deputies, the *vicedomini* (*Viztume*) and later passed it on to other high officials, the *Landschreiber*. Accordingly, after 1446 the crimes the *vicedomini* were authorised to pardon were called *Viztumhändel* and the corresponding fines *Viztumwändel*.[18] Fortunately, the records (i.e. the calculations) that were kept to check the dukedom's revenues, including the *Viztumwändel*, have been well-preserved until today.[19]

---

16 Cf. Reinle 2003, pp. 73-74, 75-103, 240-244 for more details.

17 Cf. Walter Ziegler, *Studien zum Staatshaushalt Bayerns in der zweiten Hälfte des 15. Jahrhunderts: Die regulären Kammereinkünfte des Herzogtums Niederbayern 1450-1500*, München 1981, pp. 194, 223.

18 Concerning the *Viztumhändel* cf. Klaus Peter Follak, *Die Bedeutung der "Landshuter Landesordnung" von 1474 für die Niederbayerische Gerichtsorganisation*, München 1977, pp. 35-58. Idem, "Entstehung, Funktion und Bedeutung der Viztumhändel im spätmittelalterlichen Niederbayern", *Verhandlungen des Historischen Vereins für Niederbayern*, 103, 1977, pp. 71-84. Sagstetter 2000, pp. 233 ff., 240 ff.

19 The following records are of special relevance: Bayerisches Hauptstaatsarchiv München, *Ämterrechnungen bis 1506*, no. 120-142 (Landschreiberrechnungen des Rentmeisteramts Burghausen, 1470-1507; documentation has gaps, though). *Ämterrechnungen bis 1506*, no.

Hence, we have clear evidence both of the frequency and of the typical course of commoners' feuds. We can prove that at least 258 peasants' feuds were conducted during a period of about 57 years.[20] Furthermore, the records tell us a great deal about the misdemeanants themselves, about their offences and the fines imposed on them. Interestingly enough, not only feuders were punished but also a lot of their supporters and sympathisers – a consequence which shows precisely that feuding was widely accepted among the rural population. Then, we learn that not every feud necessarily led to violence and damage. In approximately 86 per cent of all cases there was only a challenge, possibly followed by the escape of the feuder and obviously accompanied by negotiations or by the intervention of impartial persons.[21] Moreover, evidence is given that in about forty cases the enemy of the feuder was the lord of the land or another person or institution superior in rank. Commoners' feuds, then, were not fought amongst commoners only.[22] Finally, from the 1490s onwards the records contain a lot of information about ducal efforts to totally suppress feuds and to prosecute feuders. At that time the ducal administration altered its politics. From this point onwards, there was a fundamental change in how peasants' feuds were dealt with for suddenly no further profit could be gained from fining feuders to compensate for a corporal punishment or the death sentence. Instead, money actually had to be spent to track feuders down, to tempt them into leaving their hideout (which was often abroad, particularly in Bohemia) and returning to Bavaria, where they eventually could be captured and punished.[23]

313-360 (Summarische Rechnungen des Rentmeisters im Oberland 1450-1504; one gap which concerns the year 1500). *Ämterrechnungen bis 1506*, no. 459-498 (Landschreiberrechnungen des Rentmeisteramts Landshut, 1453-1506, has gaps) and no. 1577 (Landschreiberrechnung des Jahres 1438, copy from 1625). Considering the Bavarian records in general cf. Ziegler 1981, pp. 7-25. Georg Vogeler, "Die Rechnung des Straubinger Viztums Peter von Eck (1335) und ihre Stellung im mittelalterlichen Rechnungswesen Bayerns", *Archivalische Zeitschrift*, 82, 1999, pp. 149-224. Concerning the Vitztumwändel that are documented in those records cf. Ziegler 1981, pp. 95f., 127, 194, 205, 214, 223, 257. Reinle 2003, pp. 69-73, 228-240.

20 Reinle 2003, pp. 253f.
21 *Ibid.*, p. 259.
22 *Ibid.*, *Bauernfehden*, pp. 311-314.
23 *Ibid.*, pp. 322, 336-339.

III

Concerning my third point: Regarding these more or less intensive efforts that were taken to punish feuders – either by fining them or by sentencing them to death – the actual nature of commoners' feuds might remain doubtful: What kind of social practice was feuding? Was it indeed a customary right or rather a misuse?

Answering this question is anything but easy, yet I suppose that there is a lot of evidence in favour of feuds being a customary right, one which was merely suppressed before noblemen's feuds were. Firstly, in their form and their function commoners' feuds were quite similar to noblemen's feuds. And therefore they followed an identical social logic and belonged to the same juridical framework. In particular, they were closely connected to the defence of rights: Contrary to the hitherto positions of historical research, commoners' feuds were not restricted to waging a blood vengeance but could well maintain all kinds of rights. Secondly, peasants' feuds were broadly accepted by the social environment of the feuding persons. Commoners waging a feud were likely to find a lot of help. Their supporters sometimes belonged to the better educated or more privileged social strata such as teachers or parsons. Even noblemen occasionally supported these feuds. One must admit, though, that it is impossible to determine for each case whether someone voluntarily supported a feud or rather did so since they might have felt pressured or menaced. Thirdly, the fact that mediators did exist is supposed to be an argument for the large social basis of feuding. Since negotiating was considered a way to support feuds, mediators and negotiators risked being punished as well. But nevertheless they undertook their task and tried to bring about reconciliation between the opponents. Ultimately, the particular way the dukes of Bavaria-Landshut turned individual death sentences into the obligation to pay fines can be regarded as some kind of compromise: On the one hand, it allowed the dukes to raise the claim to secure the General Peace and to establish (new) written rules, while, on the other hand, they silently accepted that what they opposed (i.e. the practice of feuding) was indeed a deeply-rooted custom.

The question why peasants preferred waging a feud to going to a court of law cannot be discussed here in detail. There are some reasons for that, just let me mention the peasants' distrust of the lordships' courts and their discontent with the usually expensive legal procedures. However, let me also stress a certain mentality that might be typical for pre-modern times: the wish to solve one's conflicts without involving the lordship and his authorities, to personally take revenge and thus to protect one's honour, to demonstrate one's own ability to defend a social position, and finally the common understanding of violence as the appropriate answer to any offence.

IV

Having put forward these theses, my fourth and last thought follows. I would like to show that the feuds waged by commoners were not limited to one particular area but existed everywhere in the Empire (and, by the way, also in France[24]). There are examples from every region: From Dithmarschen in the very North to the Alsace in the Southwest, from the territory of the archbishop of Cologne to Swabia and Franconia.[25] But as far as I know no region features as dense an accumulation of surviving records from the Late Middle Ages as Bavaria. In other territories one can find normative sources only – such as single orders or prescriptions, which are, what is more, possibly not as old as those from Bavaria. Contrasting records that reflect the actual practice of feuding do not exist. However, jurists like Benedikt Carpzov (1595-1666) were able to discuss in their works some problems of the feuds waged by commoners, thus these feuds must obviously have still been happening even in early modern Germany.[26] This practice of an early modern feuding has also been shown only recently by Jan Peters and Monika Mommertz. Both dealt mostly with the records of the jury of the town of Brandenburg (*Brandenburger Schöppenstuhl*). Interestingly, the records that Peters and Mommertz used belonged to a similar context as Carpzov's records, for Carpzov was not only a professor at Leipzig University but also a member of the famous jury of Leipzig (*Leipziger Schöppenstuhl*).[27] It was juries such as these that local courts had to refer to before they were permitted to torture deviant persons. Using the trial records, Peters and Mommertz were able to construct a pattern of early modern commoners' feuding which was almost identical to the one described

---

24 Philippe de Beaumanoir, *Coutumes de Beauvaisis: Texte critique publié avec une introduction, un glossaire et une table analytique*, Amédée Salmon (ed.), 1-2, Paris 1899f., no. 1671-1672. I would like to thank Michael Gelting (Copenhagen) who gave me this hint.

25 Reinle 2004, p. 125f. offers examples.

26 Wolf Recktenwald offers examples for feuding in early modern Saxony too. Recktenwald dealt with crimes against the public order in Kursachsen, mainly scrutinising them from a legal point of view. He analysed the substantive law (*materielles Recht*), classified various types of crime and compared them with real crime. He refused to subscribe to the view of feuding as a legitimate social practise. Cf. Wolf Recktenwald, *Verbrechen gegen die öffentliche Ordnung in Kursachsen zur Zeit Benedict Carzovs*, Diss. jur., University of Bonn 1956, pp. 56-65, 117-130.

27 Benedict Carpzov (*1595-1666) was a member of the Brandenburgian jury (*Brandenburger Schöppenstuhl*) for almost 40 years, an ordinary professor at the Faculty of Law at Leipzig University and the author of various important legal works. His study on criminal law and criminal proceedings, the *Practica Nova Imperialis Saxonica rerum criminalium in partes III divisa*, Wittenberg 1652, became especially famous. Cf. Reinle 2003, pp. 117, 119-121 for Carpzov's position towards feuding.

above. What finally will be discussed now, are the slight differences that – according to the evidence in literature – seem to exist between the Bavarian and the Brandenburgian case. Whether these differences really exist, though, has still to be shown in the sources.

Firstly, in a remarkable number of feuds in early modern Brandenburg it seems that the 'going out' (*Austreten*) was a merely symbolic declaration of protest against a real or a pretended injury – a formal challenge serving as a means of communication rather than a real action. Consequently, not every single Brandenburgian feuder had to leave their home and flee into hiding. Instead they could stay and pursue their aims, ideally forcing their foe to accept their own point of view or at least to agree on some compromise.[28] Therefore, this was obviously a method also available to women who struggled for a certain right.[29] In late mediaeval Bavaria, on the other hand, women were hardly ever actively involved in any feud[30] – although, as supporters they played a bigger role.

Secondly, a somewhat delayed development of the administration in Brandenburg might have given feuders the chance to act quite openly. The introduction of laws against feuding does not seem to have started until the Perpetual General Peace of Worms, i.e. about one hundred years later than in Bavaria.[31] And whereas Bavarian feuders had to face strict governmental measures, in Brandenburg they were prosecuted by the local authorities only. Although here, too, the lordship tried to obtain intelligence on feuders and to hunt them down,[32] these actions supposedly were far less effective than those in Bavaria.

From the Late Middle Ages onwards Bavaria was able to profit from a comparatively well-functioning administration, which deprived the local lords of their right to use severe corporal punishment or to sentence people to death. And it also transferred the duty to prosecute severe crimes to officials like the *Viztume* and *Landschreiber*, who had to be informed about the misdeeds of the population by local officials. They even placed a number of informants within local society.[33] In Brandenburg, however, it was the task of the local courts of law to proceed against feuders – even if they had to turn to the above-mentioned juries to use torture. Because of this partly decentralised or even

---

28 Mommertz 2003, pp. 229f., 232, 236f.
29 *Ibid.*, pp. 220f., 224f., 229 ff.
30 Reinle 2003, p. 322f.
31 Peters 2000, pp. 62 f., 65-68. Concerning the legal situation in Saxony cf. p. 67.
32 *Ibid.*, pp. 66, 69.
33 Reinle 2003, p. 316f.

partly dysfunctional law system, commoners' feuds in Brandenburg might have had the chance to survive through one more century.

Thirdly, although I was unable to find out what penalty all the Brandenburgian feuders might have expected in the end, it seems that they were not charged until they had lost the backing of their social environment – thus it is impossible to guess how many feuders might have succeeded in prolonging their feuds without any traces being left in the sources. Even more important is the fact that, in defiance of the legal prescriptions, juries by no means sentenced all the feuders to capital punishment.[34] Unfortunately, the scholarly literature lacks information on the number of cases in which juries either suggested the death sentence or decided to temper justice with mercy. Perhaps, the non-serial character of the trial records forbids any such statement at all. Conclusively, however, both the frequency and the seriousness of the punishment of early modern Brandenburgian feuders cannot be decided at the moment.

Finally, in early modern times it was typical to closely associate menaces caused by violence with those caused by magic.[35] The latter, however, played no role at all in the commoners' feuds of the Late Middle Ages.

V

To conclude: Commoners' feuds were a widespread phenomenon in late mediaeval and early modern Germany. They followed firm rules, and with regard to their form and function, they completely resembled the feuds of noblemen, also in their character as a customary right. Because the feuds waged by commoners were criminalised earlier than knightly feuds, they appear in the sources solely as crimes. The fact that many commoners continued to feud in defiance of prohibition and punishment, shows that they tried to preserve their traditional customs against the social and legal demands of the developing early modern state. This might even be regarded as some kind of active resistance. Peasants' feuds demonstrate in particular the importance of violence in the conflict management of early modern times, clearly illustrating that violence and a struggle for right and justice were quite compatible. Using force was not a privilege reserved for noblemen, since the nobility and social collectives (e.g. cities, monasteries, etc.) could fall victim to feuds too. Moreover, at least as far as early modern evidence shows, public opinion could suddenly turn against a

---

34 Peters 2000, pp. 69, 70, n. 46, 73 ff., 91; Mommertz 2003, pp. 243f.
35 Peters 2000, pp. 65, 80, 83, 92; Mommertz 2003, pp. 219f., 241.

nobleman threatened by a common feuder: If the said nobleman failed to prove that he had given no reason to be attacked, he – although a victim himself – was likely to be fully blamed for the feud and its consequences.[36] Therefore, the question of violence is far less important than the power to define what must be regarded as legal or illegal and the power to actually enforce these rules. Accordingly, it was the formation of the early modern state that put an end to commoners' feuds.

---

36 Even in the 19th century, arson was still considered an acceptable method for the underprivileged to take revenge. Their victims were denied compassion as it was a common understanding that they themselves were to be blamed for letting the conflict escalate. Cf. Regina Schulte, *Das Dorf im Verhör: Brandstifter, Kindsmörderinnen und Wilderer vor den Schranken des bürgerlichen Gerichts: Oberbayern 1848-1910*, Reinbek bei Hamburg 1989, pp. 50f., 65. Otto Ulbricht, "Rätselhafte Komplexität: Jugendliche Brandstifterinnen und Brandstifter in Schleswig-Holstein ca. 1790-1830", Andreas Blauert and Gerd Schwerhoff (eds.), *Kriminalitätsgeschichte: Beiträge zur Sozial- und Kulturgeschichte der Vormoderne*, Konstanz 2000, pp. 801-829, esp. pp. 803, 811.

Feud in Late Medieval and Early Modern Denmark

JEPPE BÜCHERT NETTERSTRØM

Since the 1970s Danish historians have given attention to the existence of feud in medieval and early modern Denmark. In the following I intend to give an impression of the main results of Danish scholarship on the subject with emphasis on the fifteenth and sixteenth centuries. I will give some examples of the feuds that were waged by the aristocracy in late medieval Denmark and then sum up some common features of these noble feuds. After that, I will treat peasant feuds and the dynamic relationship between noble and peasant feuding. Finally, I discuss the causes of the elimination of the feud system in Denmark during the sixteenth century.

In 1971 the legal historian Ole Fenger published his dissertation entitled *Fejde og mandebod* (Feud and Blood-money) which was a milestone in research on feud in medieval and early modern Denmark.[1] Fenger was inspired by Otto Brunner's anti-anachronistic project with its emphasis on the great importance of feud in late medieval Germany, and he was also inspired by the peace-in-the-feud theory of legal anthropology. Using this as a sort of theoretical framework, Fenger was able to study the Danish legal system from a new perspective, and he brought about a fundamental understanding of the great significance of feud in medieval and early modern Denmark.

Fenger pointed out that the rules concerning homicide and other violent crimes found in the provincial law-books of the first half of the thirteenth century were based on a system where law-rules were sanctioned by private feud and vengeance rather than by any central authority. King and church worked as feud regulating institutions, but these predecessors of modern State were yet far from capable of replacing feud as a means of retribution against law-breakers.

---

1   Ole Fenger, *Fejde og mandebod. Studier over slægtsansvaret i germansk og gammeldansk ret*, Copenhagen 1971.

Feuding as well as peace-making was based on kinship obligations, and in Denmark the kinship structure was bilateral with equal rights and duties on the father's and the mother's side. In the case of a homicide, the kinsmen of the victim had the legal right and a moral duty to demand blood-money or take revenge. The kinsmen of the killer had the obligation to assist in paying blood-money and negotiate a peaceful solution with the relatives of the deceased. If the killer and his kin refused to pay blood-money, the killer was declared an outlaw. This meant that the relatives of the deceased, and anyone else for that matter, were allowed to kill him without having to pay blood-money. It seems to have been Fenger's view that this feud system functioned in high medieval Denmark just as it did in other medieval societies and in tribal societies with a weak or non-existing central authority.

The analysis of feud in high medieval Denmark only formed a small chapter in Fenger's book. Fenger moved on to analyse the legislation up until the end of the seventeenth century. Since there was almost no new legislation on violent crimes during the late medieval period, the medieval laws concerning manslaughter remained in force until the reformation of 1536. At that time, the medieval system of compensation and reconciliation was radically changed as the death penalty was introduced in all cases of wilful homicide committed by peasants and common townsmen.

Cases of homicide committed by noblemen, however, continued – in principle – to be regulated by the medieval laws, until these were substituted by the absolute monarchy's *Danish Law* of 1683. According to Fenger this corresponded to the aristocratic right of declaring honourable feuds that was codified in 1468 and included in the coronation charters from 1513 until the advent of absolutism in 1660. This noble privilege was partly associated with the constitutional system, as the right of the nobility to dethrone a tyrannical king was based on the nobility's right of waging a feud against their ruler.

Fenger also studied the legal practice of the post-reformation era and showed that even among peasants and common townsmen, feud continued to exist for a much longer time than what had been recognised in earlier legal history. The blood-money system continued to work among nobles and in some cases among commoners, and the royal power did not always take full use of the instruments of punishment prescribed by its own ordinances.

In 1971, the same year as Fenger's dissertation was published, the late medieval historian Troels Dahlerup wrote a famous article on the Danish nobility of the Later Middle Ages. Here, Dahlerup mentioned that noble feuds worked as a catalyst of social stratification among the aristocracy – a process of stratification that was a consequence of the late medieval demographic and agrarian crisis. Feuds were not only waged by desperados of the lower aristocracy but often by members of the higher aristocracy. The German 'robber-knight' thesis would not match the case of Denmark, but this does not mean that the crisis of the low nobility was insignificant in connection with the noble feuds. The feuds played a part in the formation of patron-client relations between wealthy estate owners and lower nobles impoverished by the agrarian crisis. In times of feud between the high nobles, the low noble clients flocked around the principal feuders to get protection and to get an income as armed retainers.[2]

Recently, Dahlerup has presented a more detailed analysis of the noble feuds of the fifteenth century, for instance the feud between the nobleman Lage Brok and the Rosenkrantz family that was waged in the region of Djursland during the 1460s and 1470s. One of the most dramatic incidents of this feud took place when Lage Brok laid siege to Otte Nielsen Rosenkrantz' manor with 16 of his retainers for a whole day. Other than that, the feud mainly consisted of sporadic clashes between armed bands of the principal feuders and of assaults on peasants belonging to the opposing party. On one occasion around 1460, Lage Brok pursued one of Otte Nielsens low noble servants and tried to kill him, and in 1468, Lage Brok single-handedly killed a citizen of the market town Randers that was under Rosenkrantz protection. These incidents, and the fact that Lage Brok's servants were often convicted as outlaws, have shaped the notion in modern historiography that Lage Brok was an extraordinarily hot-tempered and lawless character. But Troels Dahlerup has shown that Lage Brok merely tried to secure his lordship against the expanding Rosenkrantz family by using the only methods available – methods that were traditional and widely accepted as legitimate. The reason why the retainers of Lage Brok and not those of the Rosenkrantz family were condemned as criminals and outlaws by the local hundred courts was that Otte Nielsen Rosenkrantz controlled these courts in his capacity of royal officer of the entire area of Djursland.[3] When, during a peace meeting in 1464, Lage Brok put forward his accusations against the Rosenkrantz family, they were ignored and not even put into writing because all Rosenkrantz actions had been 'carried out according to the law'.[4]

2   Troels Dahlerup, "Danmark", *Den nordiske adel i Senmiddelalderen. Struktur, funktioner og internordiske relationer*, Copenhagen 1971, pp. 45-80.

3   Troels Dahlerup, *De fire stænder, 1400-1500. Gyldendal og Politikens Danmarkshistorie*, 6, Copenhagen 1989, pp. 276-278. On this feud, see also Jeppe Büchert Netterstrøm, *Fejde og magt i senmiddelalderen. Rosenkrantzernes fejder med biskop Jens Iversen og Lage Brok 1454-1475*, unpublished PhD Thesis, Århus 2007.

4   Konrad Barner, *Fra de ældste Tider til Begyndelsen af det 16. Aarhundrede. Familien Rosenkrantz's Historie*, 1, Copenhagen 1874, Diplomatarium, no. 112.

It is also interesting that Erik Ottesen Rosenkrantz occupied the highest royal office in the kingdom of Denmark, that of steward of the realm, during his feud with Lage Brok.[5] It seems that the members of the Rosenkrantz family used their royal offices to legitimise their own feuding.

The Rosenkrantz family appears somewhat less innocent when one considers that Otte Nielsen Rosenkrantz toward the end of the feud was accused of instigating a murder plot against Lage Brok.[6] And the Rosenkrantz family's reputation as extraordinarily pious and beneficial toward the church diminishes when one considers that they had already in the 1450s feuded with the bishop of Århus. This feud between the bishop of Århus and Otte Nielsen Rosenkrantz is, by the way, just one of many examples of the fact that the leaders of the church took an active part in the feud culture of late medieval Denmark.[7] The best example of this is the feud that was waged around 1490 between the bishop of Roskilde and the Cistercian abbey of Sorø. This feud culminated when no less than 80 armed servants of the bishop assaulted a village owned by the abbey. The bishop's men looted the village and captured some of the serfs belonging to the abbey and put them in 'narrow dungeons where they could hardly breathe', as the lament of the abbey goes.[8]

In the following I am going to focus on some common features of noble feuds in late medieval Denmark.

One thing the noble feuds of the fifteenth century had in common was that they were more or less controlled with regard to the use of violence. The feuders seem to have exercised a certain degree of restraint. There was a great difference between the clashes and raids of noble feuds and the large military operations of public warfare – even though it is telling that contemporary terminology did not distinguish between private and public war: they were both called *fejde*.[9]

The exercising of restraint in noble feuds may be explained by a number of factors. First of all, the aim of noble feuding was not the complete annihilation of the opponent. When a nobleman waged a feud, the intention was to force his opponent to comply with a legal claim or to displace local power balances

---

5   William Christensen, *Dansk Statsforvaltning i det 15. Århundrede*, Copenhagen 1903, p. 681.
6   Barner 1874, no. 137-138.
7   Dahlerup 1989, pp. 274-276.
8   Dahlerup 1989, pp. 281-288. Recently treated in Per Ingesman, *Provisioner og processer. Den romerske Rota og dens behandling af danske sager i middelalderen*, Århus 2003, pp. 295-317.
9   Fenger 1971, p. 503.

in his own favour.[10] Furthermore, noble feuders did not act in isolation from the surrounding society: they depended on the support of kinsmen and friends, and these would often see an interest in persuading the feuders to make peace.[11] And, although the weakness of State is characteristic of the period, late medieval Denmark did not entirely lack a central authority. The king would often observe the noble feuds and try to influence the participants to make peace. These factors put pressure on feuding noblemen to negotiate truces or make peace – or at least restrain themselves when feuding. The relative restraint of violence in late medieval feuds can generally be taken as a warning against seeing medieval violence as verifying Norbert Elias' civilising process theory, according to which the curbing of aggressive outbursts was a product of early modern state making.[12] There was a certain element of civility in feuding, however foreign such kind of civility may seem from a modern point of view. The noble feuder was expected to control his feelings and not act impulsively. The Rosenkrantz family profited morally from the fact that, when the parties met at a peace meeting in 1460, the young Lage Brok became infuriated and 'ran wrathful (*vred*) and contumaciously out of court' and refused the arbitration settlement to which he had earlier agreed to subject himself.[13] Obviously, the Seven Deadly Sins of Catholic doctrine provided the moral and religious script for this condemnation of Lage Brok's lack of self-control. In spite of the relative restraint of violence and aggressive emotions, noble feuds were serious enough to affect late medieval society profoundly. It must have been a change of significant proportions that the Danish aristocracy, for one reason or the other, gradually ceased to wage large-scale private feuds during the first decades of the sixteenth century.

Another common feature of the noble feuds was that litigation and feuding were complementary, not mutually exclusive. Using the law courts for negotiations or law-suits did not preclude resorting to violence, and litigation (thus) seems to have been an incorporated part of the feud culture. Moreover, feuding noblemen often manipulated the law courts to legitimise violence, and they used their special judicial privileges to damage each other. I have already

---

10 This point is often made in German research on feud, e.g. Christine Reinle's contribution to the present volume. It seems to be appropriate in the case of Denmark as well.

11 This argumentation is, of course, inspired by Max Gluckman's peace-in-the-feud theory. On this, see the Introduction to the present volume. For a Danish late medieval example, see below n. 15.

12 On Elias, the civilising process and emotions in relation to feuding, see the introduction to this volume.

13 Barner 1874, no. 105.

mentioned this aspect in connection with the feud between Lage Brok and the Rosenkrantz family. Another example is the feud between the bishop of Roskilde and Sorø abbey, where the parties alternately used their religious powers and their influence on ecclesiastical as well as secular law courts to ban and outlaw each other's servants. As the late medieval historian Per Ingesman has recently shown, this feud even included a lengthy law-suit before the Papal Supreme Court in Rome that lasted for several years until a settlement was reached in 1493 with the Danish king as mediator.[14]

Of course, the abuse of law courts and judicial privileges in noble feuds was in principle unacceptable to the royal power and the church that had introduced them for the very purpose of keeping the peace. But as long as these two authorities of late medieval society were unable to enforce their legal systems, noble feuders used them to their own advantage. The king even promoted some noble feuders against others for political purposes instead of using the legal system to suppress feuding as such.

This can be observed during the first years of the Brok-Rosenkrantz feud when the king indirectly and covertly supported the Rosenkrantz family against Lage Brok. The reason was that Lage Brok and his cousin and nearest in kin, Axel Lagesen Brok, belonged to an aristocratic alliance headed by the Gyldenstjerne family which stood in opposition to Christian I's policy towards Sweden. The three Nordic kingdoms Denmark, Sweden and Norway had, since the end of the fourteenth century, been joined in a personal union, the so-called Kalmar Union, but at the time of Christian's election as king of Denmark and Norway, the Swedes had elected an indigenous noble to the throne of Sweden, making the ascent to power in Sweden the prime goal for Christian during the first two decades as king of Denmark. The Gyldenstjerne party intermarried with Swedish nobles and, together with parts of the Scanian aristocracy headed by the Thott family, which owned estates and held fiefs at both sides of the Danish-Swedish border, they promoted a policy of negotiation and reconciliation toward the Swedish nobility which demanded privileges and constitutional guarantees in return for electing Christian. The Rosenkrantz family, on the other hand, had no estates or fiefs in Sweden and thus supported the more belligerent policy of King Christian.[15] The link between these political

---

14 Cf. n. 8.

15 On the Nordic union and the noble parties in the reign of Christian I, see Poul Enemark, *Kriseår 1448-1451. En epoke i nordisk unionshistorie*, Copenhagen 1981 and Jens E. Olesen, *Unionskrige og Stændersamfund. Bidrag til Nordens historie i Kristian I's regeringstid 1450-1481*, Århus 1983. It should be added that a branch of the Gyldenstjerne family apparently broke off from the political course followed by the rest of the family group when the powerful

divisions and the Brok vs. Rosenkrantz feud can be seen, for instance, from the fact that when Lage Brok issued declarations of truce during the feud, the body of co-guarantors was made up of members of the Gyldenstjerne and Thott families and other noblemen belonging to their party.[16] There can be no doubt that they saw an interest in damaging the Rosenkrantz family politically by supporting its blood enemy. Likewise, there can be no doubt that the king looked the other way when the Rosenkrantz family used the royal powers invested in them to damage Lage Brok who was partly regarded as representative of a subversive section of the nobility. The direct causal relationship between political conjunctures and the course of local feuds may not be seen clearer anywhere else than in this feud. In 1466, a shift of policy toward negotiations with the Swedish aristocracy was forced through by the Gyldenstjerne-Thott party which also demanded of the king that he stripped the Rosenkrantz family of some of its powers. Otte Nielsen Rosenkrantz lost his royal fief which was handed over to the bishop of Århus and at the same time the Rosenkrantz party lost the large fief of Koldinghus in south-eastern Jutland which was handed over to Lage Brok.[17] A couple of years later, Lage Brok was finally granted the right (*birkeret*) of setting a manor court over his servants in the parishes closest to his manor. His demand to hold such a court and thus immunise his manor from the influence of Otte Nielsen Rosenkrantz – the royal officer of the area – had been one of the main causes of the feud, since the Rosenkrantz family had done their utmost to disrupt Lage Brok's attempts to buy peasant holdings belonging to the crown and local low noble landowners in order to close off his estate, which was a precondition for

---

Henrik Knudsen Gyldenstjerne had his daughter married to Erik Ottesen Rosenkrantz some time at the beginning of the 1450s. According to a late family tale, Henrik Knudsen had tried to make a king of his son, Knud Henriksen, but he was thrown aside by the election of Christian I, so the marriage alliance represented a dramatic shift of policy on behalf of Henrik Knudsen. Knud Henriksen was, however, Lage Brok's uncle and during the first half of the feud he appears as guarantor and negotiator for Lage Brok. In reality, however, his in-law relation to Otte Nielsen and Erik Ottesen was more important to him since his possession of estates and royal fiefs was based on the alliance between his father and his sister's father-in-law and their close connection to the king. Knud Henriksen then had ties to both the sides of the feud and had an interest in settling the dispute and keeping the truces and peace agreements. He nicely embodies the typical Max Gluckman-peacemaker. Perhaps his death in 1467 was a factor in the escalation of the feud in its closing years. Netterstrøm, *Fejde og magt*, 2007.

16   Barner 1874, no. 104-107, 109-111 and 133.
17   On the changes within the royal fief system around 1466, see Harry Christensen, *Len og magt i Danmark 1439-1481*, Århus 1983, pp. 96-134.

achieving the right to hold a manor court.[18] From now on, the Rosenkrantz family was not as strong in local politics and Lage Brok intensified his feuding activities. During the 1470s, however, a major setback in the king's quest for seizing Sweden made a unified Danish aristocracy more necessary than ever, which put pressure on both parties to stop the feud. This happened in 1475 when Erik Ottesen Rosenkrantz declared that he had promised Lage Brok peace and friendship and that he had made the same promise to the king.[19]

It is possible to show that many of the known feuds in Jutland during the 1450s, 1460s and 1470s were in some way related to these political conflicts. In north-western Jutland, Mourids Nielsen Gyldenstjerne, half brother to Axel Lagesen Brok (Lage Brok's cousin), feuded with the bishop of Børglum, Jep Friis who had succeeded Mourids Nielsen's father's brother to the diocese in 1453, diminishing the local power of this family. According to a verdict of the king's court of 1457, the bishop's retainers killed Mourids Nielsen's low noble vassal, Anders Thommesen, and, according to peace acts from 1471 and 1475, Mourids Nielsen's retainers killed one of the bishop's low noble servants, Henrik Kalf. Jep Friis, who was closely associated with King Christian, allied himself to the Rosenkrantz party. In the 1450s he thus assisted the Rosenkrantz family in their feud against the bishop of Århus. During the 1460s Mourids Nielsen Gyldenstjerne feuded with the royal officer of the hundred Hanherred, in which Mourids' manor was situated, a nobleman by the name Las Dan. The king had probably placed him there as a counterweight against the local power of Mourids and in order to signal his political superiority over the Gyldenstjerne family. In the 1450s, Las Dan had feuded against Anders Nielsen Banner, a local magnate married to the sister of the leader of the Gyldenstjerne party, Niels Eriksen Gyldenstjerne, whose brother Erik Eriksen was married to a daughter of the Swedish nobleman, Karl Knutsson, who had been elected king of Sweden to the great detriment of King Christian. Extant from the feud between Las Dan and Anders Nielsen Banner are documents relating to a property conflict managed by the court system and a report of the killing of Anders Nielsen's ploughman by Las Dan's servants. Las Dan is found in the records as a supporter of the

---

18   Jeppe Büchert Netterstrøm, "Øvrighederne, bønderne og fejden i Danmarks senmiddel-alder", Agnes S. Arnórsdóttir, Per Ingesman and Bjørn Poulsen (eds.), *Konge, kirke og sam-fund. De to øvrighedsmagter i dansk senmiddelalder*, Århus 2007, pp. 301-328. On Lage Brok's attempt to aquire the right of having his own manor court as background of the feud but with a more traditional evaluation of its parties, see Erik Ulsig, *Danske Adelsgodser i Middelalderen*, Copenhagen 1968, pp. 220-221.

19   The peace promise, Barner 1874, no. 141. For a full investigation of the feud, see Netterstrøm, *Fejde og magt*, 2007.

Rosenkrantz family. In 1470 he was removed from Hanherred and replaced by Mourids Nielsen as royal officer. This was probably a consequence of the same strengthening of the Gyldenstjerne party that boosted Lage Brok and damaged the Rosenkrantz family. Finally, in 1474, Mourids Nielsen appeared in the Brok vs. Rosenkrantz feud in a truce made by Lage Brok in a way that suggests that Mourids was directly involved in the feud, and at the same time he made a lawsuit against Erik Ottesen in a case concerning property – a conflict which, however, did not apparently lead to the use of violence. It also is possible to fit a number of conflicts that are not seen to have entailed violence at all into the major political conflicts and alliance patterns of the period.[20]

Political motives thus lay behind much feuding in late medieval Denmark, probably also in many instances where the cause of conflict is no longer clear. But such 'political' motives cannot be seen as a common feature of noble feuding in late medieval Denmark, unless one takes property disputes and conflicts over agrarian resources to be a matter of *local* politics. Even in conflicts that were affected by fluctuations in high politics, very local and very material factors often determined the outbreak, course and termination of feuding. Even though there was a political background to the Brok-Rosenkrantz feud, it was still very much a feud between neighbouring estates over the power to control and command local resources and local people. Many a noble feud may have been about nothing else than such local rivalry. But one can say that it was a common feature that such feuds over land and peasants tended to become political because the typical feuder would attempt to forge alliances by making 'friendships' with the political enemies of his local rival.

Another aspect that was common to many noble feuds in late medieval Denmark was that the noble feuders committed acts of violence and intimidation against the peasants subject to the opposing party. This has already been mentioned in connection with the feuds Brok vs. Rosenkrantz and the bishop of Roskilde vs. Sorø Abbey, and many more colourful examples of noblemen assaulting, abducting, plundering, threatening, and even killing each others' peasants could be added.

This important aspect has recently been examined by the late medieval historian Bjørn Poulsen, who has been inspired by Gadi Algazi's theory on the social use of private war in late medieval Germany. According to Algazi, the use of violence against peasants in noble feuds created a need of protection among the peasants – a need that was covered by the same lords who waged

---

20 On the different Jutlandic feuds of the period and their connection to the political rivalries of the period, see Netterstrøm, *Fejde og magt*, 2007.

the feuds. This led to a continual reproduction of lord-peasant relations at a time when the peasant class was otherwise growing more confident and well-organised. As Bjørn Poulsen points out, Gadi Algazi's model applies in the case Denmark.[21] In the Late Middle Ages, lordship over peasants was based on protection, and evidence can be found that noblemen protected their peasants in times of feud by defending them in the law court or by force.[22]

One problem of applying Gadi Algazi's theory on late medieval Denmark is that it does not consider the feud practices of the peasants.[23] In Algazi's narrative, peasants only appear as helpless victims of noble feuds. But in Denmark, the peasants had the right to wage bloodfeuds until 1537, and in the fifteenth century they even seem to have had the right to declare honourable feuds similar to the German Ritterfehde. As mentioned before, Fenger knew about peasant feud practices in the Early Modern Period. In addition, there is a surprisingly large amount of evidence from the scanty source material of the Late Middle Ages of peasants actually waging feuds. It has been speculated that these feuding peasants belonged to an elite of land-owning peasants. It can be shown, however, that also ordinary tenants and serfs waged feuds. This can for instance be seen in so-called letters of *orfejde* (non feud, cf. German *Urfehde*). Such peace acts were made between peasants to stop bloodfeuds and other types of feud, and in some of them one comes across peasants that turn out to be tenants or serfs possessing average holdings. And there is enough evidence apart from these letters of *orfejde* to suggest that feud practices were widespread among all peasants, not just allodial peasants. For instance, in 1492 an ordinance for the island of Funen was issued, which allowed the estate owner to demand bail from the tenant when evicting him from his household. This was supposed to serve as a guarantee that the evicted tenant would not wage a feud (*feyde*) against the tenant who replaced him. The ordinance implies that the background of peasant feuds were often conflicts over tenancies.[24]

---

21 Bjørn Poulsen, "Med harnisk og hest. Om adel, krig og vold i dansk senmiddelalder", Per Ingesman and Jens Villiam Jensen (eds.), *Riget, magten og æren. Den danske adel 1350-1660*, Århus 2001, pp. 44-77. Cf. Gadi Algazi, *Herrengewalt und Gewalt der Herren im späten Mittelalter. Herrschaft, Gegenseitigkeit und Sprachgebrauch*, Frankfurt a.M. 1996. See also Bjørn Poulsen, "Adel og fejde i dansk senmiddelalder", Erik Opsahl (ed.), *Feider og fred i nordisk middelalder*, Oslo 2007, pp. 85-105.

22 On the protection system, see Jeppe Büchert Netterstrøm, *At forsvare til rette. Værnsforholdet og bøndernes retslige stilling i Danmarks senmiddelalder 1400-1513*, Kerteminde 2003.

23 This, of course, is also a problem within the German context; see Reinle's contribution to the present volume.

24 On peasant feuds in Denmark, see Jeppe B. Netterstrøm, "Bondefejder i Danmark 1450-1650", Erik Opsahl (ed.), *Feider og fred i nordisk middelalder*, Oslo 2007, pp. 35-72.

Generally, feud practices were socially levelled. Noblemen feuded with noblemen, and peasants feuded with peasants. If a peasant came into conflict with a person of superior social status he turned to his lord for protection. If a peasant was killed by a superior person, the lord would prosecute the killer in order to prevent future assaults on his peasants.[25]

The lords not only protected their peasants against superior opponents, they also intervened in peasant feuds and gave support to their own peasants against peasants subject to other lords. An example of this can be seen in 1468 when the nobleman Åge Sandbæk declared a feud on one of Åge Axelsen Thott's peasants who was engaged in a feud with one of Åge Sandbæk's peasants.[26] As Åge Axelsen entered the feud, the conflict threatened to escalate, but unfortunately we do not know how this feud ended. Of course, peasant feuds could not lead to major noble feuds. But they could add to the tension between rival lords, or they could serve as excuses for rival lords to take actions they could not have legitimised in other ways. One final aspect worth mentioning is that just as the lords gave support to their peasants in feuds, the peasants in some cases assisted their protectors in feuds against other lords. In 1459, Philip Axelsen Thott, the noble royal officer of Langeland who was involved in an inheritance dispute with the nobleman Erik Eriksen had to prove that he had not mobilised his peasants to feud against the servants of Erik Eriksen. One suspects that the allegations made against Philip Axelsen were not entirely unfounded – under all circumstances the case shows that it was not impossible for contemporaries to imagine public servants of the nobility using peasants in their entirely private feuds against other noblemen.[27] A consequence of this dynamic relationship between noble and peasant feuding was that the noble protectors sustained feud practices among the peasants instead of exterminating peasant feuds within their lordships.[28]

In the course of the sixteenth century the feud system lost most of its importance both among the aristocracy and among the peasants. Why did this happen? The most obvious answer to this question would be that the expanding royal power gradually gained a monopoly of violence and in the end became the single source of justice and protection in the kingdom. According

---

25 For examples, see Netterstrøm 2003, pp. 102-103.
26 William Christensen (ed.), *Repertorium diplomaticum regni Danici mediævalis. Fortegnelse over Danmarks Breve fra Middelalderen med Udtog af de hidtil utrykte*, 2, 1-9, Copenhagen 1928-1939, no. 2370.
27 Vilhelm Lütken, *Bidrag til Langelands Historie*, Rudkjøbing 1909, no. 3. See Netterstrøm, *Fejde og magt*, 2007.
28 Netterstrøm, "Øvrighederne", 2007.

to a recent work by early modern historian Gunner Lind this development was a consequence of the so-called 'military revolution' of the sixteenth and seventeenth centuries. The breakthrough of new military technology and organisation placed the control of the military performance of the Danish state in the hands of the king to the detriment of the nobility's role as the traditional warrior class. According to Gunner Lind this process culminated around the year 1600. Around the same time, the royal power intensified the punishment of violent criminals of noble status. The monarchy gained control of the use of violence against external foes and in the same process it gained control of the legitimate use of violence internally, within the kingdom.[29]

This explanation probably holds true, particularly with regard to the final stages of the elimination of the feud system. But it does not fully explain that large-scale noble feuding vanished already during the first two decades of the fifteenth century. At that time, the military revolution could not yet have caused such a fundamental change, and the nobility seems to have been in firm control of the king. It seems plausible that the process of feud abolishment in its opening stage around 1500 was based on support and initiative among the nobility.

This change in the nobility's attitude towards noble as well as peasant feuds was caused by a change in economic and demographic conditions. During the crisis of the fifteenth century, the noble feuds in many ways represented a competition over the reduced outcome of agrarian production, both in the case of noblemen feuding with noblemen and in the case of noblemen supporting their peasants in feuds. As the rural economy improved towards 1500, the risk of conflict between the lords was reduced and so was the need of giving support to feuding peasants. The noblemen now gradually refrained from economically devastating feuding and instead cooperated with the king to prosecute feuds among the peasants.[30]

This united royal and aristocratic peace policy was reinforced after the great revolts leading up to the reformation in 1536. King and nobility joined forces to suppress the unruly peasants – whose revolts may have been perceived

---

29 Gunner Lind, "Våbnenes tale. Våben, drab og krig i viser og virkelighed i Danmark 1536-1660", Flemming Lundgreen-Nielsen and Hanne Ruus (eds.), *Svøbt i mår. Dansk Folkevisekultur 1550-1700*, 1, Copenhagen 1999, pp. 251-280.

30 Netterstrøm, "Øvrighederne", 2007, and idem, "Feud, Protection, and Serfdom in Late Medieval and Early Modern Denmark (*c.* 1400-1600)", Paul Freedman and Monique Bourin (eds.), *Forms of Servitude in Northern and Central Europe: Decline, Resistance, and Expansion*, Turnhout 2005, pp. 369-384.

by the peasants themselves as collective manifestations of their traditional right of waging feuds.[31]

The feud elimination process was rather drawn out, however, and there were significant regional differences; Zealand seems to have been easier to 'domesticate' than Jutland and the eastern and northern parts of Scania. There was a big difference between the official peace policy and the realities of everyday life in the countryside. The feudal organisation of production still encouraged lords to protect their peasants even when they committed feud-like crimes of violence. For instance, court records and royal ordinances from the second half of the sixteenth century show that lords continued to defend their peasants in murder cases instead of prosecuting them.[32] It seems realistic that the process of feud elimination could not have been completed without the total centralisation of legal protection by the early modern monarchy.

---

31   The importance of the reformation is stressed in Netterstrøm, "Bondefejder", 2007. The same publication discusses peasant feuds in relation to peasant risings.
32   Netterstrøm, "Øvrighederne", 2007.

The Natural History of Blood Revenge

CHRISTOPHER BOEHM

Characterising Feuding in Terms of Human Nature

A characteristic feature of extant nomadic hunting groups is their reaction to a homicide within the band, and it was anthropologist Bruce Knauft who first discerned this widespread pattern. Once one man has killed another, he has to 'get out of town' as it were; he, and often his family, as well, will immediately leave and find a distant band to join. The move may be forever, or he may be able to return after a period of many years, but the reason is simple. The relatives of the man who is slain will want revenge – in kind.[1]

The taking of blood revenge may not be universal to all human cultures, but in the recent natural history of our species it has been very widespread indeed. If we begin with today's nomadic hunting bands, we may reasonably assume that what is being done now was also done by bands of Anatomically and Culturally Modern Humans in the African Late Stone Age and the European Upper Palaeolithic.[2] This means that a strong pattern of lethal vindictiveness between families goes back for at least 50,000 years.

Today, this practice of actively killing in response to an earlier killing manifests itself in a variety of ways.[3] If we consider the world's tribesmen – people who have acquired the practice of domestication of plants or animals but remain politically egalitarian just as hunting nomads do – the majority practice some type of retaliatory killing including, not infrequently, protracted bloodfeuds. Of this majority, a large number have patrilocal family units, and

---

1   Bruce M. Knauft, "Violence and Sociality in Human Evolution", *Current Anthropology*, 32, 1991, pp. 391-428.
2   Christopher Boehm, "Variance Reduction and the Evolution of Social Control", *Santa Fe Institute on-line publications*, Santa Fe, New Mexico 2002.
3   Edward Adamson Hoebel, *The Law of Primitive Man: A Study in Comparative Legal Dynamics*, Cambridge 1954.

Van Velzen and Van Wetering brilliantly identified a pair of social-structural features that make serious feuding likely. When you have a large number of males who are bound together by a patrilineal ideology and marry close to home, very predictably such localised kin groups become socially very solid, and they readily involve themselves in lethal vengeance over homicide. Injure or kill one of these closely bonded males and they will all want to retaliate.[4]

Feuding is mainly a preoccupation of males. In matrilineal societies that also are matrilocal we have a mirror image of these 'fraternal interest groups', but the clusters of closely-related women do not form political units that are extremely prone to feuding. Lethal retaliation is mainly a male activity, and so is homicide in general.[5]

Otterbein and Otterbein have put the original "fraternal interest group" concept to further use in surveying world feuding. However, such groups are not a necessary element for feuding to develop among tribal peoples; their presence merely intensifies a general tendency of people who live in groups to bond strongly, and also a predictable human tendency to retaliate over a homicidal loss of life.[6] In this context grief, anger, and aggressiveness seem to have some deep connections within human nature.

It is tempting to automatically associate any and every human universal with 'human nature', and also to wonder if patterns of behaviour that are widespread but fall short of being universal have some significant basis there as well. However, the ways that genes prepare readily learned human behaviours remain mysterious, and surely even when someday we begin to discover specific behaviour genes, they will prove to be complex, with different behavioural tendencies working against others. All we can assume, at present, is that very complicated interrelations of genes make us naturally ambivalent about many things,[7] including, often, killing another human being even when the revenge motive is strong.

Fortunately, there are other ways of looking at human nature which we will meet with presently. Bringing this nature into the explanation of feuding helps one to understand not only why this practice has been so widespread in

4   Thoden H.U.E. Van Velzen and Wilhemina Van Wetering, "Residence, Power Groups, and Intra-Societal Aggression", *International Archives of Ethnography*, 49, 1960, pp. 169-200.
5   See Martin Daly and Margo Wilson, *Homicide*, New York 1988.
6   Keith F. Otterbein and Charlotte S. Otterbein, "An Eye for an Eye, a Tooth for a Tooth: A Cross-Cultural Study of Feuding", *American Anthropologist*, 67, 1965, pp. 1470-1482.
7   See Christopher Boehm, "Ambivalence and Compromise in Human Nature", *American Anthropologist*, 91, 1989, pp. 921-939, and Christopher Boehm, *Hierarchy in the Forest*, Cambridge 1999.

egalitarian or lightly centralised societies, but how feuding systems actually work psychologically and politically. I am not speaking here of starkly oversimplified, 'either-or' notions of human nature, of the types that perennially preoccupy Hobbesians and Rousseauians. Rather, I have in mind a human nature that is richly complex and involves opposing forces.[8]

One lethal-retaliation situation that seems to trigger strong innate ambivalence is the feeling that situationally one is socially obliged to kill a known member of another family or clan in the same tribe. Driving such retaliation is a deeply-felt, aggressive need to avenge the death of a loved one, which is culturally reinforced by a need to publicly satisfy honour. Yet if your target is someone other than the original killer, which is not infrequently the case when larger feuding units are active, there can be both moral and social inhibitions. If the avenger and his target have previously been bonded by friendship, the social inhibitions can be quite strong.[9] Northern Albanians actually have special charms, which keep the avenger from fainting on the spot when he satisfies his obligations to honour and kills a blood enemy from a targeted clan.[10]

A similar but far stronger ambivalence emerges *within* the kin group. There is the natural impulse to retaliate against a close relative who has killed within the clan,[11] but also there is a very strong inhibition against killing a kinsman. This is compounded by a practical sense of inter-clan competition that is endemic to a tribal society. Politically, feuding is often about the relative clout of groups of related males that compete with one another, and in small-scale societies clan size is always vitally important; from a practical standpoint it makes no sense, when this in-group has just lost a warrior, to double the loss.[12]

Thus, revenge killing involves both deep emotions that stem from human nature, and practical calculations of group political advantage. The latter is not just a matter of size; a group that retaliates swiftly and decisively is less likely to be victimised in the future. So, one reason to kill is for emotional satisfaction; but another is to strengthen the local group's political potency as it competes with similar groups. The latter is accomplished not only by refraining from retaliation within the group, but by taking vengeance vigorously when a group member is killed by an outsider.

---

8   Boehm 1999.
9   Boehm 1989.
10 Margaret M. Hasluck, *The Unwritten Law in Albania*, Cambridge 1954.
11 Christopher Boehm, *Blood Revenge: The Enactment and Management of Conflict in Montenegro and Other Tribal Societies*, Philadelphia 1986.
12 Boehm 1986.

These practical calculations are widespread, and especially in tribal societies their ramifications are fascinating. For instance, if a clan member is recklessly aggressive and his behaviour is likely to get his group into 'unwanted' feuds that are not necessary to its honour, the group may cut its losses and get rid of the troublemaker even though this will reduce its manpower.[13] So, in spite of the strong personal emotions involved in the vendetta, feuding groups operate by a rational political calculus that is quite sophisticated – and highly patterned.

Capital Punishment without Vengeance

One area in which tendencies to lethal retaliation must be 'managed' is social control. In egalitarian societies like bands and tribes, the custom of lethal retaliation presents special problems when groups need to exert such control against really serious deviants. When groups identify dangerous miscreants who, it is commonly agreed, must be eliminated, a dilemma arises. If the group's leader is delegated to kill the deviant, even if he has solid backing from his group the man's close relatives may kill him in retaliation.

Nonliterate people have arrived at two different solutions to this problem. The rarer solution is for the entire group to collectively execute the deviant by throwing stones,[14] or by 'porcupining' him with arrows;[15] this makes lethal retaliation impossible because as a practical matter the actual killer cannot be targeted. More often, the group manages to enlist one of the deviant's close kinsmen to 'do him in'.[16] In this case, retaliation by close relatives is foregone for reasons I have just explained: the family suffering the homicide does not wish to further weaken itself.

Not too long after September 11th, 2001, when the American news media turned its attention to a long-neglected Afghanistan, I watched coverage of one of the public executions in Kabul. The commentator mentioned that a kinsman was chosen to do the deed, and then a man proceeded to kill his own

---

13   Sally Falk Moore, "Legal Liability and Evolutionary Interpretation: Some Aspects of Strict Liability, Self-help and Collective Responsibility", Max Gluckman (ed.), *The Allocation of Responsibility*, Manchester 1972, pp. 51-107.

14   E.g. Boehm 1986.

15   Richard B. Lee, *The!Kung San: Men, Women and Work in a Foraging Society*, New York 1979. See also Raymond C. Kelly, *Warless Societies and the Evolution of War*, Ann Arbor 2000.

16   Christopher Boehm, "Egalitarian Society and Reverse Dominance Hierarchy", *Current Anthropology*, 34, 1993, pp. 227-254.

brother for having killed several of their 'cousins'. The public reaction in the West was likely to have been outrage over the Taliban's brutal and immoral approach to legal discipline, but in fact this practice was quite in keeping with traditional modes of feuding, which still prevail in Afghanistan at large. The clan cannot retaliate against its own member when he acts as executioner.

This Afghani strategy was probably a wise one. In historical Montenegro, as a small Balkan state was forming, there were instances of a Serbian clan's killing the judge who sentenced their clan member to death. Eventually, government firing squads made a practice of issuing only one rifle loaded with real bullets while the others had blanks; furthermore the firing squads were composed of men from different clans, so that neither a specific executioner nor a specific clan could be targeted for revenge.[17] The Taliban's policy achieved the same purpose.

I have used a variety of examples here, to show that egalitarian human beings, while innately disposed to retaliate for a homicide, can create highly practical rules of thumb which channel their vengeful acts in ways that are culturally patterned. Revenge killing is often highly rule bound. For instance: 'Kill only one person at a time to fulfil the need for revenge'.[18] But sometimes it is relatively unstructured, as with the Yanomamo Indians whose general-purpose revenge expeditions can involve killing of women[19] or even wholesale killing of infants,[20] along with as many males as possible. So, even though taking vengeance tends to become associated in people's minds with 'manly honour', what constitutes honourable revenge killing is culturally quite variable.

What we have, here, is a highly emotional raw human response, upon which local cultural edifices are built. The more widespread patterns I have discussed are partly practical rules of thumb having to do with political strategies, and partly moral rules by which groups, recognising that socially disruptive lethal retaliation is inevitable, at least set up covenants to govern and restrict the taking of vengeance.[21]

17 Boehm 1986.
18 E.g. Boehm 1986.
19 Napoleon Chagnon, *Yanomamo: The Fierce People*, New York 1983.
20 Ettore Biocca, *Yanoama: The Narrative of a White Girl Kidnapped by Amazonian Indians*, [Autobiographical account of Helen Valera; translated by Dennis Rhodes], New York 1970.
21 See Boehm 1986.

The Question of 'Instincts'

The emotions involved in feuding are far more complicated than simply feeling a hostile impulse to take revenge over a loss. Although we may start with the social bonding that makes the sense of agony over loss very intense, and connects anger with grief, there are also what might be called political emotions. These stem from the deep human tendencies that lead all people, everywhere, in the direction of forming social hierarchies, setting limits in their expression, and competing as groups.

When animals live in social groups, individual competition over resources is regulated by impulses to dominate and submit. Once all the individuals in a group have sorted these relationships out, the group can function efficiently with minimal disruption by fights. However, in higher primates domination and submission are not controlled by the biological equivalent of 'all or nothing' on-off switches; rather, those who submit would still prefer to dominate – or at least increase their freedom of action.[22]

It is for this reason that small-scale human societies are so predictably politically egalitarian, in the sense that the rank and file combine forces as a moral community to see that the alpha-males in the group do not dominate others too much, and that their chosen leaders will not try to increase the very limited authority they are allowed. The result is very weak political centralisation,[23] which is willed and enforced by the group.

This is directly relevant to feuding because homicidal 'self-help'[24] flourishes in situations of weak political centralisation. Families must retaliate lethally to keep their heads above water politically, as it were, for there is no centralised authority to back them up if they are victimised. Once really strong chiefdoms or primitive kingdoms arise, there is sufficient authority at the political centre to punish homicide, and eventually, if such societies progress in the direction of city-states or nations, feuding tends to be definitively outlawed because of its disruptive social effects. In simpler, 'acephalous' societies, however, feuding is considered to be an inevitable – but honourable, and at least understandable – disturbance.

In egalitarian societies the practice of taking blood revenge is sufficiently widespread that the *propensity* to do so can be called universal; I say this because

---

22 Boehm 1999.
23 See John Middleton and David Tait (eds.), *Tribes Without Rulers: Studies in African Segmentary Systems*, London 1958.
24 Middleton and Tait 1958. See also Donald Black, *Toward a General Theory of Social Control*, Orlando 1984.

if exceptions can be found,[25] this is because the societies in question have unusually strong values that favour social harmony. This, too, is a human universal; all people, everywhere, preach in favour of harmony and take steps to promote it. But statistically, it is usually the custom of taking revenge that wins out – in spite of its obvious disadvantages in creating tragic grief, disrupting cooperation, reducing group size or causing premature fissioning, creating psychological stress for all group members, and so on.

This cultural edifice is built upon universal political tendencies in human beings, and these dispositions stem directly from a human nature that is at the same time disposed to competitive aggression and fighting but also to peace-making within the group. In this broad context it will be of interest to consider what our more distant, pre-human ancestors were likely to have been doing, for they provided us with many of our most basic political behaviours, including ones which help to shape the pattern of lethal retaliation.

Ancestral Political Behaviours

Once primatologist Richard Wrangham's pioneering work was published on what he called our Common Ancestor,[26] we gained a reliable method for reconstructing certain general behaviours of our direct ancestors. All that is needed is to find a pattern of behaviour that is shared by all of that ancestor's descendants, and that pattern can be assumed to be ancestral because of natural selection's conservative properties. For instance, humans, gorillas, bonobos, and chimpanzees all have obvious 'hierarchical' tendencies that involve dominance and submission, and in turn these dispositions generate resentment of dominance in subordinates.[27] Given this unanimity, we can assert that an African great ape, one that lived 7 million years ago and was also our Common Ancestor,[28] had those same dispositions. We also can say that this Common Ancestor lived in groups and formed coalitions of subordinates to limit the power of alphas, for all four of its descendents do these things.

25   E.g. Douglas p. Fry, "Conflict Management in Cross-Cultural Perspective", Filippo Aureli and Frans B.M. de Waal (eds.), *Natural Conflict Resolution*, Berkeley 2000, pp. 334-351.
26   Richard Wrangham, "African Apes: The Significance of African Apes for Reconstructing Social Evolution", Warren G. Kinzey (ed.), *The Evolution of Human Behavior: Primate Models*, Albany 1987, pp. 51-71.
27   See Boehm 1999.
28   See Wrangham 1987.

This means that our Common Ancestor had fights, because in hierarchies there are always differences of opinion as to which member of a dyadic pair is dominant. In addition, all four extant species also actively intervene triadically in fights with peacemaking as an objective, which makes peacemaking equally ancient. These complementary patterns are ancestral, predating humans and even hominids, and they apply to all of our *direct* ancestors, without exception. They apply to culturally modern hunters 50,000 years ago, to today's foragers, and to all human beings, everywhere.

Peacemaking is complex. After a fight two ape disputants will spontaneously tend to reconcile and re-activate previous bonds of friendship.[29] This is highly relevant to many feuding patterns of humans—especially the practice of paying blood money, which is intended to foster reconciliation. In addition, there are power-interventions by third parties[30] in all four species today, so conflict management, too, was ancestral. Again, when tribal people try to resolve a vendetta, this is a form of conflict management, for others try to assist the feuding parties.

Ancestral *Pan*

I could tell you more about this Common Ancestor, but there is a more recent direct ancestor who is of still greater interest. From DNA evidence we know that gorillas split off on their own at 7 MYA, so at 5 MYA we can identify a more recent ancestor that founded both the human and *Pan* lineages as a closely related clade. The same methodology can be used to reconstruct the behaviours of this more recent direct ancestor, who was the immediate forbear of the earliest hominids and can be called Ancestral *Pan*.

To start with, all the Common Ancestral features we have discussed would obviously have carried over to this more recent ancestor. With gorillas out of the picture, however, we can add some significant new patterns. Let us begin with territoriality. Humans and both *Pan* species (chimpanzees and bonobos) live in groups that are quasi-territorial and xenophobic, insofar as there is a natural tendency to bond with other members of the permanent male in-group but to fear and dislike socially unknown members of other groups. The

---

29 Filippo Aureli and Frans B.M. de Waal (eds.), *Natural conflict resolution*, Berkeley 2000.
30 Christopher Boehm, "Pacifying Interventions at Arnhem Zoo and Gombe", Richard W. Wrangham, William C. McGrew, Frans B. M. de Waal, and Paul G. Heltne (eds.), *Chimpanzee Cultures*, Cambridge 1994, pp. 211-226.

relevance of this basic in-group/out-group tendency to competition between fraternal-interest groups or other types of human local groups is apparent enough.

An obvious question to ask, about such a potentially bellicose ancestor, is whether it was disposed to retaliate if its close kin or allies were killed. Killing within the group takes place rather frequently in chimpanzees and humans[31] but is not reported so far for the less well-studied bonobo. Thus, the question is moot with respect to Ancestral *Pan*. This lack of uniformity means that we can say nothing about ancestral lethal retaliation within the group, because bonobos do not engage in killing. However, even if the ancestor was just like a chimpanzee, there would be no evidence for retaliation following the death of a relative or ally.

All three living species are capable of political 'payback' in one way or another, nonetheless. One type of 'retaliation' that is engendered by receiving aggression is 'redirection of aggression'.[32] This usually involves an individual being attacked by a superior and then, fearing to directly confront that superior, taking it out on a vulnerable inferior who happens to be handy. This does not apply directly to human feuding, obviously, but there is in fact a 'retaliation' element in this pattern of vicariously redirected aggression, which appears widely in the more aggressive primates including African great apes.

When two animals of equal rank are involved in a conflict, there may also be rapid back-and-forth hitting behaviour that definitely has a 'tit-for-tat' aspect. Furthermore, major quarrels may be re-initiated later by one party or the other. And retaliations may take place whereby subordinate victims later enlist help from a stronger ally, or wait until their adversary is attacked by some other individual and then join in.[33] Bonobos are not well enough studied to say that most of these patterns are strongly operative, but there would seem to be some payback tendencies for Ancestral *Pan*. On the other hand, a prominent, overall pattern of serious vengeance-seeking among political equals – based on long-term grudges being repaid – is not identifiable there, the way it is with egalitarian humans.

Ancestral *Pan's* hunting pattern also bears mentioning. Chimpanzees and bonobos not only hunt, but they rather grudgingly share meat. This pattern was ancestral, but humans carried it much further. Living human hunter-gatherers

31   Michael L. Wilson and Richard W. Wrangham, "Intergroup Relations in Chimpanzees", *Annual Review of Anthropology*, 32, 2003, pp. 363-392.
32   E.g. Jane Goodall, *The Chimpanzees of Gombe*, Cambridge 1986.
33   Goodall 1986.

prize large game because of its fatty content, and they have rigidly-enforced rules that basically dispossess the successful hunter and make the meat he has killed the property of the entire band so it can be shared even-handedly.

This cultural practice took early humans to a much more significant level of sharing, and this was accomplished through moral rules[34] – something obviously absent in chimpanzees and bonobos, and therefore absent in Ancestral *Pan*. This new development was relevant to feuding, in that moral rules regulate the expression of lethal retaliation.

Human Conflict and Peacemaking

Whenever it arrived, this early dependence on moralistic cooperation made it easier for our human forbears to control or resolve conflict within the group. It was the arrival of moral communities that not only gossip, but consensually sanction deviants and work for group harmony, that led to humans controlling their own conflicts in ways that are unprecedented in the animal kingdom.[35]

Although intervening in conflicts within groups is ancestral and obviously has a strong innate basis, in fact today's hunter-gatherers tend to be rather ineffectual when it comes to actively and forcefully stopping intensive conflicts that are verging on homicide. On the other hand, they are true experts at heading off incipient conflicts which threaten to escalate to the homicidal level. They use a variety of techniques, ranging from distraction and getting the parties to talk to each other,[36] to setting up nonlethal duels to discharge the tensions,[37] to bring about resolution before a conflict becomes homicidal and the group must split. Ethnographically, this capacity to turn enemies into friends has remained in the shadow of blood revenge, which as a violent activity somehow captures the human imagination. However, we know now that both are very deeply rooted in our basic emotions, because both of these basic patterns go back for millions of years.

---

34 Christopher Boehm, "Conflict and the evolution of social control", *Journal of Consciousness Studies*, 7, 2000, pp. 79-183.
35 See Boehm 2000.
36 See Fry 2000.
37 See Hoebel 1954.

Feuding and the Social Self

A final ancestral element that paved the way for feuding was the social self. All four African great apes are capable of self-recognition in experimental settings,[38] and as home-raised captives they like to play games of 'making up' their faces with lipstick and powder. The sociologist George Herbert Mead saw a 'social self' as being at the core of human social and moral behaviour, and this evolved capacity placed humans far above apes in the sense that we have social and moral self-concepts. In this context, we have developed a sense of shame that is so well-evolved that it has a physiological component in the form of blushing in situations of serious social malaise.[39]

One general result of this sense of 'self' and 'other' is that humans come to understand complex social rules or 'mores', and they understand that the approval of others is important to their social well-being – whereas social disapproval can result in not only lowered public esteem but in punitive sanctioning. Apes, too, are capable of understanding the authority of individuals and, at times, groups. They also understand 'rules', even though there is no moral element to this understanding. For them, it is a simple matter of power, not of right and wrong, whereas for humans it is both.

A culturally elaborated concomitant of this sense of shame, which is universal, is the notion of 'honour'.[40] It is difficult to gage the degree to which a sense of honour is operative in a small hunting band that has no elaborate rules of feuding the way tribes often do, but in which people as individuals are just naturally prone to retaliate for homicide against a close family member. However, some bands behave more like tribes, in which the fear of shame over behaving submissively constitutes a further and major reason for lethal retaliation. It was probably in tribes that revenge killing first became highly involved with the honour concept – as a widespread phenomenon.

Worries about losing honour can help to culturally activate a principle that Kelly calls 'social substitutability'. Kelly is referring to the fact that where large kin groups are present, lethal retaliation often becomes a matter of *groups* on both sides, rather than individuals.[41] This is easily explained. Among the

---

38 See Gordon G. Gallup, Jr., "Self-awareness", Gary Mitchell and Joseph Erwin (eds.), *Comparative Primate Biology, Behavior, Cognition, and Motivation*, 2, New York 1987, pp. 3-16.

39 George Herbert Mead, *Mind, Self and Society*, Chicago 1934.

40 E.g. Boehm 1986.

41 Kelly 2001.

Montenegrins I studied ethno-historically,[42] let us say that someone in my clan is killed. Honour demands that any member of my clan kill one male of the other clan. If I lost my brother, I would prefer it to be myself who killed the actual killer; but if he is inaccessible I will go for his brother, or his paternal cousin, or even, if my honour is becoming seriously jeopardized because too much time has passed, a male child – even one in its cradle. Likewise, clan honour would at least be reasonably well satisfied if, say, my cousin were to kill the original killer's cousin. Rare among hunter-gatherers, such a cultural blueprint for 'generic' or group-wide retaliation is widespread among agricultural or pastoral tribesmen. Social substitutability transforms individual vengeance against a killer into a very controlled kind of 'clan warfare',[43] which is driven as much by fear of shame as by deep needs to retaliate after a painful loss.

This transforms not only the emotional but also the cognitive nature of feuding, for, as discussed earlier, someone who by kinship is only moderately close to the victim may find himself in the position of killing someone who had nothing at all to do with the original homicide. It is thus that heartfelt lethal retaliation becomes culturally abstracted into a matter of clan honour, and it is in such societies that feuds are likely to involve a long series of lethal exchanges, rather than ending with a single, emotionally-satisfying instance of lethal retaliation as they may among hunter-gatherers.

The 'Peaceful' Side of Feuding

By itself, the emotive need to retaliate can explain why feuds can persist over some years, on a reciprocating basis. This takes place with Bushmen hunters,[44] and a small number of other nomadic hunting societies. Add a major focus on clan honour to the equation, however, and a feud can go on forever. Fortunately, our ancestral tendencies to intervene in and manage conflicts have led many tribal humans who feud in this way to create countervailing pacification institutions. At one end are people like Montenegrin Serbs,[45] who have elaborate rules not only for feuding, but for making peace between clans – and even between entire large tribes – through payment of blood money. At

---

42   Christopher Boehm, *Montenegrin Social Organization and Values: Political Ethnography of a Refuge Area Tribal Adaptation*, New York 1983. Boehm 1986.
43   See Boehm 1986.
44   E.g. Lee 1979.
45   Boehm 1986.

the other lie people like the Yanomomo tribesmen of Venezuela and Ecuador,[46] who have virtually no codified rules for how to take vengeance. The Yanomamo make peace between feuding villages only for special reasons – as when a pair of them see the need to form an alliance against a common enemy.

With respect to homicide within a multi-clan tribe or village, people like the tribal Montenegrins can resolve or temporarily stop an intratribal feud that threatens to strongly weaken the tribe, whereas once a homicide takes place within a Yanomamo village, the village has no alternative except to fission into two different villages in order to keep the hostile clans separated. The Montenegrins became experts at peacemaking because the Ottoman Empire threatened them from the outside, and because land was scarce and a tribe could not split. The Yanomamo lacked such an external predator and had plenty of land, so they developed clumsy and uncertain institutions for managing or repairing rifts between their clans.

A feud can be incredibly costly, not only in weakening the larger political unit, but in economic losses due to the effort put into defence and offence, in psychological stress, and in damage to everyday cooperation. When political cooperation within the group is essential – as in tribal societies where political units are in serious competition for natural resources, or are trying to defend themselves against centralised external political predators who would dominate them – the divisiveness that results from feuding can be catastrophic.

To avoid this, formal institutions of peacemaking become culturally institutionalised, with the payment of 'blood money' being a very prominent peacemaking mechanism that has been invented over and over again, all over the world. Where the only evidence of a feuding pattern is historical, as in medieval epics and myths, often the payment of blood money becomes diagnostic of the entire honour-based feuding pattern I have delineated here for tribes.

A Naturalistic Explanation of Feuding Today

Human nature makes us rational as problem solvers, even though we are seldom rational enough to entirely avoid feuding and its much less socially-restricted big brother, warfare. Let us summarise some of the ways in which this nature sets us up not only so that patterns of lethal retaliation become likely in our species, but so that we develop institutions to either reduce the costs of feuding or else actively terminate vendettas.

---

46 Chagnon 1983.

The tendencies already present in our ancestors included a capacity for retaliating after being victimised by aggression and a fighting capacity that made homicide possible, along with a sense of self that enabled individuals politically to understand rules imposed by other individuals or by the entire group acting as a moralistically aggressive coalition.

Also present, ancestrally, was an innate aversion to conflict. In recent hunting bands and surely in those of 50,000 years ago, this capacity was expressed pre-emptively because there were no alpha males to step in as peacemakers. However, if a homicide did actually take place, then third parties became irrelevant and the killer would simply leave the group. Usually, the resulting spatial and social distance ended the potential feud, and among today's nomadic foragers payment of blood money is very rare.

It was after the domestication of animals and plants that our human groups – as tribes rather than bands – became larger and more attached to specific pieces of territory, and an avoidance pattern simply became too costly. Back and forth retaliatory killing was unavoidable, particularly where local cultures became imbued with the notion of male honour. Such tribal cultures developed various local rules for feuding, widespread ones being that you do not kill women, only men, and that, again, normally you only kill one person at a time; both keep feuds from escalating to all out warfare.[47] If these rules seem rational, it is because they were invented and maintained by egalitarian people who realised that revenge killing was inevitable, but wanted to minimise the adverse societal and demographic consequences.

These rules, along with institutionalised means of ending feuds through compensation payment, created a social, political, and cultural matrix in which very basic (and sometimes inexorable) human emotional needs for retaliation could be enacted without a total destruction of the social fabric.[48] This solution to the problem of deep needs for vengeance was very widespread among tribesmen, and also in weaker chiefdoms – ones that did not develop very strong authority at the political centre. However, with the coming of primitive kingdoms and states the dysfunctions associated with feuding were not only recognised, but were dealt with quite summarily in many cases.[49]

The end of 'self-help' was possible because states develop sufficient coercive power at the political centre that feuds can be coercively suppressed by the

---

47   See Boehm 1986.
48   See Boehm 1986.
49   See Elman R. Service, *Origin of the State and Civilization: The Process of Cultural Evolution*, New York 1975.

leader, rather than merely being arbitrated if the two parties are willing. Thus, for historians, ethno-historians, and students of the epic, the payment of blood money becomes diagnostic of a type of egalitarian political society that rather strictly limits centralised authority, and in which honour is of high importance culturally.

Feuding is predicated on a political order that is so egalitarian and devoid of centralised control that self-help is the answer to homicide. Violent self-help and these egalitarian approaches to political life generally go together. However, if demographic and ecological exigencies are just right, and if local political history has not involved feuding, and if child-rearing practices do not promote male retaliation too much, small-scale societies can exist without a salient pattern of lethal retaliation.[50] This is the case even though in all nomadic bands, over time, male competition over females is likely to lead to at least a few intragroup homicides.

What I have tried to do here is to show that humans are a species innately prone to compete and fight, and because of our large-game hunting background our males are expert at killing. Both homicide and homicidal retaliation are disruptive to group life and jarring to individual personalities, and it is fortunate that our ancestors had already evolved to be adverse to conflict. With this excellent head-start, we have evolved a variety of peacemaking institutions which range from trying to manipulate conflicts before they become serious, to payment of blood money to achieve a hopefully permanent truce.

I believe that blood revenge and protracted feuding are far from being *determined* by human nature, yet they are very well *prepared* by it. All that is required is a situation in which authority is not allowed to develop, and predictably self-help will become the order of the day. At the same time, members of our species are innately well-prepared to manage the conflicts that arise between local or kin groups. The widespread antidote they have developed is the custom of paying blood money, but people in feuding societies are also very good at nipping potentially lethal conflicts in the bud.

Feuding is an institution of egalitarians, and it is mainly an institution of tribesmen who have domesticated plants or animals. It may continue in weak chiefdoms, but as kingdoms or states emerge, with their coercive power, feuding tendencies are managed mainly from the top down, rather than by societies of equals.

---

50 See Fry 2000.

Authors and Editors of this Volume

CHRISTOPHER BOEHM

Professor of Anthropology and Biological Sciences at University of Southern California, USA. Has conducted field-work on feud and blood revenge among Montenegrins, resulting in the book *Blood Revenge. The Anthropology of Feuding in Montenegro and Other Tribal Societies* (1984). Now researches into social behaviour, conflict resolution and altruism among primates and early humans.

JESSE BYOCK

Professor of history and archaeology, Old Norse and Medieval Scandinavian Studies and Cotsen Institute of Archaeology, University of California, Los Angeles, USA. Has published *Feud in the Icelandic Saga* (1982), *Medieval Iceland. Society, Sagas and Power* (1988), and numerous articles on medieval Iceland. Participates in the excavation of Mosfell, Iceland.

TREVOR DEAN

Professor of history, University of Roehampton, London, England. The author of many books and articles on late medieval and renaissance Italy focusing on crime, violence, and gender, among them: "Marriage and Mutilation: Vendetta in Late Medieval Italy" (1997).

JEPPE BÜCHERT NETTERSTRØM

PhD scholar, Institute of History and Area Studies, University of Aarhus, Denmark. His PhD thesis deals with feud, especially in Late Medieval Denmark. Has written "Feud, Protection, and Serfdom in Late Medieval and Early Modern Denmark (c. 1400-1600)" (2005).

BJØRN POULSEN

Professor of history, Institute of History and Area Studies, University of Aarhus, Denmark. A specialist in the social and economic history of medieval Denmark, Bjørn Poulsen has published on feuds: "Med harnisk og hest. Om adel, krig og vold i dansk senmiddelalder" (2001) and "Adel og fejde i dansk senmiddelalder" (2007).

CHRISTINE REINLE

Professor of history, Institute of History, University of Giessen, Germany. Has published extensively both on noble and non-noble feud in late medieval Germany:

Bauernfehden. Studien zur Fehdeführung Nichtadliger im spätmittelalterlichen römisch-deutschen Reich, besonders in den bayerischen Herzogtümern (2003) as well as numerous articles.

DANIEL LORD SMAIL

Professor of History, Harvard University, USA. Specialises in social and legal history of Marseille, France. Publications include: *The Consumption of Justice: Emotions, Publicity, and Legal Culture in Marseille, 1264-1423* (2003), "Common Violence: Vengeance and Inquisition in Fourteenth-Century Marseille" (1996), and "Hatred as a Social Institution in Late-Medieval Society" (2001).

HELGI ÞORLÁKSSON

Professor of history, Department of History, University of Iceland. A prominent scholar of medieval and early modern Iceland, Helgi Þorláksson has dealt with feud and blood revenge in "Hvað er blóðhefnd?" (1994), and "Feider, Begrep, betydning, Komparasjon" (2007).

HILLAY ZMORA

Senior Lecturer, Department of History, Ben-Gurion University of the Negev, Israel. Has concentrated on state-making, aristocracy, and feud in late medieval Germany: *State and nobility in early modern Germany. The knightly feud in Franconia, 1440-1567* (1997), "Adelige Ehre und ritterliche Fehde: Franken im Spätmittelalter" (1995), and "Princely State-Making and the 'Crisis of the Aristocracy' in Late Medieval Germany" (1996). Currently writing a book on the reign of Margrave Albrecht Archilles of Brandenburg.